LIKE FINE WINE

Other Lotus Titles

Anil Dharker	*Icons: Men & Women Who Shaped Today's India*
Aitzaz Ahsan	*The Indus Saga: The Making of Pakistan*
Ajay Mansingh	*Firaq Gorakhpuri: The Poet of Pain & Ecstasy*
Alam Srinivas	*Women of Vision: Nine Business Leaders in Conversation*
Amarinder Singh	*The Last Sunset: The Rise & Fall of the Lahore Durbar*
Aruna Roy	*The RTI Story: Power to the People*
Ashis Ray	*Laid to Rest: The Controversy of Subhas Chandra Bose's Death*
Bertil Falk	*Feroze: The Forgotten Gandhi*
Harinder Baweja (Ed.)	*26/11 Mumbai Attacked*
Harinder Baweja	*A Soldier's Diary: Kargil – The Inside Story*
Ian H. Magedera	*Indian Videshinis: European Women in India*
Jenny Housego	*A Woven Life*
Kunal Purandare	*Ramakant Achrekar: A Biography*
Maj. Gen. Ian Cardozo	*Param Vir: Our Heroes in Battle*
Maj. Gen. Ian Cardozo	*The Sinking of INS Khukri: What Happened in 1971*
Madhu Trehan	*Tehelka as Metaphor*
Moin Mir	*Surat: Fall of a Port, Rise of a Prince, Defeat of the East India Company in the House of Commons*
Monisha Rajesh	*Around India in 80 Trains*
Noorul Hasan	*Meena Kumari: The Poet*
Prateep K. Lahiri	*A Tide in the Affairs of Men: A Public Servant Remembers*
Rajika Bhandari	*The Raj on the Move: Story of the Dak Bungalow*
Ralph Russell	*The Famous Ghalib: The Sound of My Moving Pen*
Rahul Bedi	*The Last Word: Obituaries of 100 Indians Who Led Unusual Lives*
R.V. Smith	*Delhi: Unknown Tales of a City*
Salman Akthar	*The Book of Emotions*
Sharmishta Gooptu	*Bengali Cinema: An Other Nation*
Shrabani Basu	*Spy Princess: The Life of Noor Inayat Khan*
Shahrayar Khan	*Bhopal Connections: Vignettes of Royal Rule*
Shantanu Guha Ray	*Mahi: The Story of India's Most Successful Captain*
S. Hussain Zaidi	*Dongri to Dubai*
Thomas Weber	*Going Native: Gandhi's Relationship with Western Women*
Thomas Weber	*Gandhi at First Sight*
Vaibhav Purandare	*Sachin Tendulkar: A Definitive Biography*
Vappala Balachandran	*A Life in Shadow: The Secret Story of ACN Nambiar – A Forgotten Anti-Colonial Warrior*
Vir Sanghvi	*Men of Steel: India's Business Leaders in Candid Conversation*
Narinder Singh Kapany	*The Man Who Bent Light*

FORTHCOMING TITLE

Vandana Shiva, Shreya Jani	*Slow Living: What You can do about Climate Change*

LIKE FINE WINE

Nine Real, Rare Love Stories

Syeda Imam

LOTUS COLLECTION
ROLI BOOKS

Lotus Collection

First published in 2023

The Lotus Collection
An imprint of
Roli Books Pvt. Ltd
M-75, Greater Kailash II Market, New Delhi 110 048
Phone: +91 (011) 40682000
E-mail: info@rolibooks.com
Website: www.rolibooks.com
Also at Bengaluru, Chennai & Mumbai

Cover design: Nitin Srivastava
Layout design: Mohammed Firoz
Production: Lavinia Rao
Photo credits:
Page 63: Personal archives of Yuvraj Vikramaditya Singh
Page 119: Alamy
Page 149: Karam Puri, Roli Books

ISBN: 9789392130076

Typeset in Didot and Bembo Std. by Roli Books Pvt. Ltd
Printed at Saurabh Printers Pvt. Ltd., Greater Noida, India

Strange, how love does not
leave you alone

CONTENTS

PREFACE

Words wear different garbs very often, almost playfully, as they go along. As time and use and events overtake, they cannot stay pristine. In each phase, a particular sense, an aura asserts itself.

Take the word 'encounter', for instance. What did encounter mean to people in the first place, unlayered, unladen? Quite simply, two persons or things coming up face to face with each other. A meeting, with a suddenness to it ... when did it come to mean more?

Did it stretch to acquire this redolent flavour when David Lean in his very first film *Brief Encounter* had Celia Johnson and Trevor Howard making sure it does? The British film director, so wooed by Hollywood, presents an unusual romance that tugs at you almost hauntingly. Two people who chance upon each other in the waiting room of a railway station, giving encounter a meaning beyond a 'hello, how do you do' or just the discovery of a bond beyond a common train route. What unfolds is that rare spark when two stones strike, steady to a flame, refuse to recede or flicker or sputter out. They remain insistent. The audience wants to see it more than once. Producers feel they should repeat the formula, back a winning horse, renew a legend. Two more versions of the film want to thrive on its success, but no, the mystique is missing.

The century turns – and along with it the meaning of the word. The blaring headlines across newspapers, television, radio, and internet, have now grabbed the word, altered it, given it another meaning altogether, shedding the delicacy, the draw it long possessed. 'Encounter' has now entered the portals of danger, deceit, violence, and dishonour and has very little, if anything at all, to do with a relationship. It now warrants easy attention, becomes pet property of the news hack – rife with the possibility of that intricate horror story that guarantees eyeballs and avid readership.

The attempt in this book is to restore to the term 'encounter' that earlier rare potential – of entering lives curiously, significantly, often entirely unbidden. And then staying, uniquely: deepening, rising, becoming stronger.

The nervousness that daunts the prospect of 'till death do us part' or its equivalent in every language, is more daunting today than it has ever been. And it invites one to wonder at anointed romances over which wonder and speculation remains.

It must be acknowledged that our history brims over with feeling: whether in the patience of Ram and Sita in their separation, the valour of Samyukta and Prithviraj against Jaichand's cruel opposition, the unsung devotion of Chhatrapati Shivaji as he dies crying out 'Sai! Sai!' to his favourite queen. The instances abound.

How did the Moghul Prince Salim, later Jehangir, graduate from his reckless pursuit of Anarkali, his father Akbar's youngest harem favourite, to his resolute courtship of a startlingly beautiful young widow who then ruled his life, his court, his empire? What was Noor Jahan's particular draw? Was it the fire in her eyes, her unabashed gaze, unusual in a gentlewoman? Was it the mystery of what lay behind the veils and layers of modesty? For Noor Jahan was a woman as gifted at polo as at chess. Was it recompense on Prince Salim's part to enthrone as his consort this widow of Sher Afghan, the gallant man who had saved his life while gravely endangering his own in astounded public view? It could be any or all of these – along with a shrewd sense that she would best partner him in overseeing the troubled affairs of his extended empire. Given Jehangir's love for the pleasures of wine, the latter may have been the reason foremost.

The Taj Mahal stands testimony to the love his son Shah Jahan bore Mumtaz. To the legend that this Emperor, still handsomely gracing many a miniature, had eyes for no other woman than his queen.

The West is equally fraught and engaged in this arena. No one escapes unscathed. What was so compelling about Mrs Wallace Simpson, that England's heir apparent spurn for her an empire at its very zenith? Was he choosing the privilege of royalty without its pain or burden by rejecting the entire Commonwealth as his domain? Not deeming this a noble sacrifice, legend has spurned him.

And the following irony is in sharp contrast. Born with a speech defect yet forced into kingship, his brother George VI lives out with his queen every vow they had pledged under the pealing church bells. Too good to be true, even a shade boring ... and hence not legend.

And what if Winston Churchill claimed he poured out everything to his darling Clementine, 'telling her each detail, talking to her about everything' through all his years of war and peace, storm and calm, victory and defeat. Whether she may have been yawning and he too drunk to notice, there is no knowing. Their fifty-six years of married devotion insists on mention but perhaps does not qualify as legend.

More seriously, does Camilla's romance with Prince Charles, now King, overshadow every other for endurance, restraint, the stiff upper lip? Love that stayed despite being disallowed. Love that survived years of a hectic schedule in a celebrated marriage with another woman, the darling of the British people. Not undone by the staunch and justified disapproval of his people, his Church, his parents, his children. A couple undeterred. How vindicated Charles and Camilla must have eventually felt in leading the congregation as the world watched – declaring the act of penitence from the 1662 Book of Common Prayer:

> *We acknowledge and bewail our manifold sins and wickedness, Which we, from time to time, most grievously have committed by thought, word and deed, Against thy Divine Majesty, Provoking most justly thy wrath and indignation against us.*

Consider Camilla's panic right before the event, after all those years of assiduous waiting. When the wedding suddenly stood postponed – at the very last minute to 9 April! Even though it was fleeting, just for a day and for the good reason of Charles having to rush to be present at the Pope's funeral. Then again the wrench for Charles, that Queen Elizabeth, his mother holding the rank of Supreme Governor of the Church of England, must absent herself on his big day.

Charles and Camilla's first 'encounter' could never have had any of these premonitions. And now with much to do as King and Queen Consort, these may well have receded.

A generation later the barriers lift, dramatically. Prince Harry and Meghan Markle of America manage their ceremony like a cakewalk. They even chance his country, renounce its claims on them, doing their very own thing, uncaring.

Turning to poets, one wonders if they fared differently altogether. Would their poetry move and affect as much if their loves were less frustrated, lives more complete? Would Ghalib have embroidered Persian and Urdu into verse of undying beauty, if blissfully joined to the woman he most desired? In our century, a long-standing marriage to Shabana has neither deterred nor numbed expression in the man she calls Jadoo. Javed Akhtar's poetic sparks continue to fly. On the other hand, Gulzar may have not been so eloquent in his consistent stream of couplets if his romance with Rakhi had flourished long and steadily. There is no knowing.

How did the Stratfordian Anne Hathaway become Mrs William Shakespeare? When did John Donne set eyes on his Anne before she had him undone, by his own confession? You will remember his quip in verse:

John Donne
Anne Donne
Undone!

Would T.S. Eliot have written these lines to his wife and helpmeet Valerie had he not weathered years of an earlier, tortured marriage? Would he have given the English-speaking world the poignancy of his *Dedication to My Wife*:

To whom I owe the leaping delight
That quickens my senses in our waking time
And the rhythms that governs the rhythm of our sleeping time,
The breathing in unison.
Of lovers whose bodies smell of each other
Who think the same thoughts without need of speech,
And babble the same speech without need of meaning...

And then, this anglicized American long domiciled in London, shares with you his song while denying you his haven:

No peevish winter wind shall chill
No sullen tropic sun shall wither
The roses in *the rose garden which is ours and ours only*
But this dedication is for others to read:
These are private words addressed to you in public.

Lines the poet may be gifting me as a fitting frontispiece to this book!

Back home, poet Dom Moraes set it down pat with a kind of adolescent charm, well before he wed actress Leela Naidu:

All true love I know is
Patience and care.
Such grain as I grow is
Hued like your hair.

He underscores here that love is no infatuation. That discovery may be sudden or headlong, the journey fraught, the formula elusive. But the magic in the end is in the giving. He turns encounter into a state of interesting and interested permanence. But drink probably came in the way of all his good intentions.

Finally, a word on what the reader and I have a right to be curious about. What trigger is it that takes hold, escapes logic, is there to stay. Is it sheer instinct? Or an all-defying chemistry which insists that *this is it.* Or is it an Achilles heel type vulnerability, a moment of weakness, a sense of incompleteness without the other?

Would Indira Nehru become Indira Gandhi quite so readily had Feroze Gandhi not caught her off-guard at a strangely vulnerable moment? When at a vast Congress Party congregation milling with crowds, the young man had rushed to her mother – to carry to safety the frail lady in his arms as she collapsed. Mrs Kamla Nehru had fainted suddenly, unstrung perhaps by the strain, the heat, the claustrophobic crowd. And he was there. There was no premeditation here, no formal introduction; no meeting of stars or unusual phases of the moon. There was only the vulnerability of that moment: Indira's alarmed helplessness was rescued. Who was this young, attractive stranger, who had sped out of the blue to save the shrinking violet her mother was?

'What would I have done without you' could be the irrational impetus that seized the adolescent Indira fearing for her mother's life, wellbeing. It may have been just that unexpected nudge to make an otherwise strong and independent young woman feel powerlessly, unduly attracted. But what starts accidentally, needs the will to coincide, concede, not get distanced by pressures of duty, of circumstance.

Nargis and Sunil Dutt reigning over Bombay films had a story not dissimilar: a startling fire, an emergency, during the shoot of *Mother India* is meant to have precipitated their lifelong and celebrated marriage. When he risked all, diving fearlessly to save her from the fire blazing on the sets. And she tended to him night and day till he recovered from the raging fever that had punished his heroism. Love was realized, as it were.

What heartens especially is when the partnering in life extends to partnering in work, in life's chief mission. After singularly privileged childhoods and education, Bunker and Aruna Roy chose to head for remote Tilonia in Rajasthan. To give India its first and only Barefoot College, readying rural women to flourish through solar energy support as much as giving local farmers a recognized, cogent platform, a voice. Their being in tandem was surely their secret – to every one of their forays.

Another Roy couple, Radhika and Prannoy Roy of NDTV, India's pioneering and stalwart news channel, have shone in their own arena – through thick and thin, long inspiring confidence in what we believe is news. Patience and care more than drama and flourish have profiled all four Roys.

And Bengalis known to be stubbornly romantic have more Rays (another anglicized version of the same name) who blazed uniquely on this horizon. Growing up in love as first cousins may have been forgiven, but marriage between first cousins was arduous. But nothing would stop Satyajit Ray and Bijoya, his beautiful, nightingale-like first cousin. They went ahead and became man and wife – a move that uniquely supported his life's ambitions. Whether it be the all-time greats of *Pather Panchali* or *Charulata*, or the Oscar or much else after and in between. A young genius unwilling to have his love thwarted had a lot to do with India earning its place in world cinema.

PREFACE

What gave rise to this book actually was an insistent request from a publisher friend for a monograph on Sir Ali and Lady Imam and their fateful discovery of each other in the year 1918. A passing reference to this event had appeared in the *Sunday Times* which had a series on eminent Indians of the twentieth century, week after week. The reference to Sir Ali being 'extraordinary' in every conceivable respect was detailed and repeated across his hectic, studded career: his legal caveats for the division of Bihar and Bengal, his saving many princely states from accession to the Empire even while being Law Member of the Viceroy's Executive Council. How he formed an Executive Council for the Nizam's rich-beyond-the-dreams-of-avarice State of Hyderabad of which he was Prime Minister; how he enabled the function of Lord Hardinge's Viceroy's Council during his six-month hospitalization in India; indeed down to locating the premises for the Viceregal Lodge in Simla, now an academic haven. In the midst of all this welter came a throwaway sentence, saying that his marriage at the peak of his career to Anise Karim was as extraordinary as the man himself. And left it at that.

'Isn't she the lady who brought up your husband – and spoilt him rotten? You just have to share this rare story!' was the repeated clamour. The almost absurd quaintness of the facts, as well as my familiarity with them, made me agree to the request. The grand old lady had been a compelling 'been there, done that' figure in times when women were not expected to have been places or done things. What helped greatly is the fact that her memory was a storehouse most remarkable.

Pramod Kapoor (whose rare and established finesse had earlier published for me *The Positive Side* – a much-awarded volume) read the less-than-8000-word story. He was now clear, indeed adamant, as Pramod alone can be, that this should decidedly be a book, a collection of monographs, not one. Telling of such lives and relationships – notable, intriguing, in ways all their own. Most of all, extraordinary.

The recklessness of agreeing hit me later. And it took a while, a long while – life had already crowded me with many work commitments. And very crucially the fact that what is private is also sacred, needs to be handled with the wisest of care, certainly not in a cavalier or business-like rush. That it is a delicate matter, not an easy or flippant one.

What may come as a surprise to the reader is that the monographs do not follow a set pattern – they are all cast differently in the telling. I am hoping the reader will welcome these variations, since each treatment is organic to the story.

Happily, the 'protagonist' couples were pleased indeed and graciously wishful of being part of the book. With almost all, I was able to clear their monographs for any inaccuracies. For any errant detail or inaccuracy that may have escaped attention in any one of them, I submit a fervent apology right here. I have the publisher's assurance that an error pointed out will be duly corrected in the very first reprint.

More and more, a symbiosis in pledged unions seems rare, elusive, too seldom real or lasting. Catching glimpses of a few unusually dovetailed ones, whether designed by accident or otherwise, may well spur more to occur.

———

This story was the source of it all. But it was not content
to remain solo – it sparked off a curiosity to explore
this mystique. How rare are these uncanny instances?
Are they designed by accident? So why not give the cynic
in ourselves a start, go out, discover more? Regardless
of decade, century, age – person, region, profession, ideology.

For this extraordinary quality of connection
could happen anywhere.

In the case of 'Life in a Question', it is a confided
recollection of matters considered very personal,
sharedonly with those deemed one's very own.
The world had these 'extraordinary' persons on show,
they were public persons. Anything personal was not
anyone's affair but their own, it was not to be shown off,
not to be trivialized either. What follows seemed the most
regardful way to set down as grand daughter-in-law.
Her untold affection I did not deserve, nor does she deserve
whatever lapses committed in my recounting
her rare, wondrous, and unforgivably generous ways.

LIFE IN A QUESTION

Sir Ali & Lady Imam

LIFE IN A QUESTION

His account

Tomorrow is not a particularly early start. But that is not why I am drawn to setting this down. This I must do, if only to clear my thoughts. And so I head for the alcove in which nestles my desk. Yes, I must set this down before I give up the day, though it is already close to a hushed, sultry midnight. The dinner was unexceptional but could not be faulted. The Governor had a couple of fine, even riveting stories that went down really well, had everyone rapt for a good hour or so. A number of the gents present will dine out on these all week, no question about that. The DPI (our Director of Public Instruction), a man of education, was someone the Englishman enjoyed, which gladdened me. It sort of corroborated my own response to his approach. At every meeting with him, the man would make a couple of points, which would have me thinking that he was not just a bright conversationalist. He would be the right sort to take things forward, go beyond just the animated discussion. One has this trust in a square-cut jaw, which has so far not been misplaced! The rest of our contingent were too avid, almost zealous, to impress.

Old Gov on the other hand, loves to linger over his many cognacs, which in this weather of ours is inexplicable. Yet, at work tomorrow, he will be razor-sharp in his grasp, clipped in his wit, all there, as they say. He may even quiz me on details which would miss the attention of most.

I played the good host tonight, nothing remarkable occurred, nor anything untoward. I am probably not elaborating on the dinner reception because earlier in the evening, the Annual Function at the Bethiah Girls' School had me quite taken aback. Yes, it did. It is not often that one surprises oneself now. And today, I certainly did that. To start with, I just barely got there on time. It is so impossible to exit a Council meeting at anything like the right moment. To our rather exalted members, a school appointment is of value, of course, but it *had* to recede, it could surely wait, when matters of the state were being pondered over, debated, ironed out. Especially when it actually involves two or even three provinces, the appetite for argument thrives. The dialectic we have been brought up on relishes debate, no matter how infructuous. Leaving well alone is seen as not being thorough enough, you see!

The last thing I wanted was to be tardy arriving at a school where I hoped for more seriousness to be engendered, both in the curricula and the young persons. Why consider yourself the finest education portal for girls unless something distinguishes you beyond a very fine British faculty taking a regular interest? I was intrigued that they had chosen someone other than an eminent lady like let's say, the Governor's wife, as Chief Guest.

I was going to hold them to a challenge. Would they, both faculty and alumni, consider their institution as one which prepared the young ladies for life, if not for office; one which developed in them a habit of assertion, making them persons ready to influence others as much as to be influenced *by* them. This has been of concern to me, the place we give our women. The elegance that comes with education is basic to our womankind; assertion is not. The girls may have found my speech unexpected and a little exacting – not hectoring, but certainly demanding. Our women will be significant in making the difference in our country, and this needs to be recognized, sooner rather than later. One had to engage in this process with resolve – and with some impatience. The present confines of *purdah* and *zenana* were stifling, reducing the potential of both, the men as much as the women. Yes, the men need to be primed too!

The Principal and her retinue led me through a gallery of exhibits to a hall of impressive proportions. The rows of girls were orderly but far larger in number than I had expected. A hymn, a *dua*, a *bhajan* greeted me, one after the other. The instruments accompanying the singing were also handled by the students, which was impressive. The piano adopted the low notes, almost acquiring the timbre of an organ. The *dua* was a chorus of bell-like voices stirring up a *qaseeda*, which was uncommon but not too long. The *bhajan* singers were as ringing and mellifluous in their tones except that the sitar and harmonium resounded, not letting their voices flourish.

Collecting their prayer books and leading them aside was a girl, not a teacher. She then moved right across the stage to a lectern and began her opening address, to and about the school she had passed out from the year before as head girl. Her opening remarks ensured I listened attentively.

'You certainly value your school a great deal more once you leave it. And today as I walk in here after a year, a sense of belonging seizes me – and elates me. It will happen to each one of you I feel sure and it will make you feel you are readier for what you want from life ...'

I looked again. Her grace was striking, it was a kind of to-the-manor-born grace. Her eyes had a spirit in them and the accent – well, it was very educated, civilized, if you know what I mean. Unusual, I thought. Outside the court, my attention tends often to relax just a little, yes, even in the corridors of the government. Here, I had expected the usual string of formalities, sending me into that indulgent glaze which envelopes a man going through the motions of duty well performed. I found myself more than a little agog instead, not wanting to miss anything. Who may this girl be? What is this air she has about her? I even remember, near verbatim, a couple of things she said. Not sentimentally or affectedly or formally but gravely, and with an intriguing, quiet confidence.

Here, an interruption in my account is imperative. As I turned to sip water while I was waiting at my desk, I noticed it. That particular gleaming salver with five sealed envelopes claimed my attention. It was always placed in my line of vision when seated at my desk. Telegrams have a way of summoning attention, and holding it till you have dealt with them, staring reproachfully all the while that you do not. I found the paper knife. The five folded and sealed bits of paper carried no bad news, but yes, some pressing requests. One from Benaras, one from Hyderabad, two from Delhi, one from Harrow, England. The Maharaja of Benaras was fulsomely grateful that I had saved some of his prized land from being acquired by no less than the British Indian Government and that I was now needed there for some 'new developments'. He also, typically, named for me a prize of his own land as fees. The Nizam's message from Hyderabad was a very graciously extended invitation, bordering on a gentle summons by a liege, a liege who sought to be a future employer. He wanted dates named, I expect, seemingly in no mood for delay or postponements – he had enclosed the British Resident's request to me along the same lines as his own. One of the Delhi telegrams touched on the same subject, suggesting strongly that I heed the Nizam's request and proceed to the Deccan. As his prime minister, I could make a difference in a State that the British eyed with acute interest. The Nizam happened to hold in his coffers more wealth than any other man in the world. That decidedly interests the British, as indeed it would any occupying power. The second message from Delhi was as urging, but to do with a dire family dispute in court, the hearings for which were imminent.

I opened the Harrow envelope with some trepidation. At their various ages, my sons were well within their rights to cause concern of one kind or another. It was almost fitting, even justified. But, there was relief here. Young Naqi's injured foot was a severe sprain, not a fracture. This was good news. Worse could have happened in a tennis championship. Since the sprained foot had mended, could he be granted permission to visit Cambridge over the weekend to watch his brother's tournament in the boxing ring? They seemed in favour of it. The boy had won and then succumbed to the injury, he could surely step out of school, even hobble with the sprain, to watch his big brother who was a Blue already. I agreed. Any sense of home could only help the young fellow, I thought. I appreciated these gestures from his teachers – it was, after all, a race not given to sentiment. Sometimes, I did worry that the boys may lose all sense of family, of their own tradition, but there is little I can do about it sitting here. I must remember to ask whether my youngest son's weight was the cause of his fall – or was it his sudden ambition to end a closely fought rally with triumph!

In relief, I resume here to say that there were even shades of wit, mild wit, in the young lady's speech at the school. There was a confidence in her tone, as she said, 'I feel happy to say about my school that we make here a difference between turning out little ladies from a finishing school and developing each one of us as individuals. Persons who may not be important to the world yet, but who learn and listen, so that one day they too are listened to by others. Not just by retinues of their staff but by outsiders, by others in the world outside themselves, their families.'

Well said, I thought, and well spoken too. It always bothered me severely, if privately, when a language was not treated right – whether in Britain or in India; whether English, Urdu, Bhojpuri or French. Whatever you choose to speak in, I'd say, do it the favour of some civilized, even discriminating attention – or keep your peace in silence. She had a fine, unaffected way with words. Where from? I had not got the girl's name. Her tall frame moved off the stage, and I noticed that the height was all hers – she wore no heels, which they now tend to do, not to school perhaps but on special occasions.

Next came the results of the school and the awards. I made a quick mental note and alerted my secretary, Burhanuddin, that I would stay for tea in the school grounds. It would only set me back by less than forty minutes or so. I got a sense from the school and the quiet dignity of the proceedings that

I had done well to decide on making my speech much wider in its scope, covering many aspects of what is afoot in the country, the Empire and the world. How I felt that the present company of several young women, absorbing knowledge that will serve them well in their lives, must constantly see how those learnings actually applied in their life ahead. That they should let this world touch them at every opportunity that their homes afforded them. That they should then walk beside and not behind their chosen men, looking for their own significance in that world, whatever it might be. A woman standing beside an administrator, a person of science, law or medicine; beside an agriculturist, an academic, an architect; beside a musician, a poet, an artist, a sportsman or a philosopher had a right to say, 'I think –' and be duly heard. If they were to persist in the spirit of enquiry wherever they were (which I was happy to note from an alumnus' speech today), they would go beyond 'I think' to 'I will now do'. And so, one day soon, they would walk with their men readily, not behind them, not waiting to be invited – with shyness maybe, but not coyness; with confidence, not arrogance. I had noted from their short recitals of Shakespeare, Shelley and Arnold that they would well be able to make all the nuanced distinctions in the terms I used.

I had spoken for longer than I had intended. Standing on the stage now was the former head girl holding the scroll that she handed to the current incumbent, the new head girl, who presented it to me and walked away from the stage. When the senior student began to lead me off the stage, she was directing me to a high table laid out for tea. While she guided me, I commented on my exceeding the time allotted to my speech. To this she very quietly but firmly pointed out that there had been total silence while I spoke and very lasting applause when I finished, so it may have been right for me to say all I had to rather than hold back. As she proceeded, rather formally, to pour the tea, I turned to her willowy, erect, curiously collected presence and before she could question me on the quantity of milk and sugar I preferred, I gently intervened, 'You may know who I am, but we have yet to meet. Be properly introduced!' I ventured a smile. As I extended my hand to shake hers, she gave me her name – Anise Kareem. At this point, I looked at her and – without fuss or plea or preamble – I found myself saying what I did not expect myself to say, '*Anise, will you marry me?*'

That was indeed what I said, what I asked her, and I meant it in complete seriousness, as would a man of forty-eight years and much behind him. She did not flinch. There was no flurry of any kind. This girl, Anise, let a moment, just a little more than a moment pass and then she said in a low, even voice: 'This is a question you should not be asking me. It is my guardians … they should be the ones you ask.'

I am not sure what I had expected her to say. 'Your guardians?' I asked, a little puzzled. I also wanted no vagueness attached to my next move. I had to know who I would have to approach. 'I consider my parents my guardians,' she smiled quietly, but quite seriously. Her high forehead gleamed in the light of the setting sun.

Anise Kareem. I will remember that – her name – more staunchly than any point of law, I thought. The principal of the school and her entourage of teachers were now with us to escort me away. I did not have the presence of mind to hand over to the young woman even one of the many resplendent bouquets that had been presented to me. It did not occur to me. As I drove away amid a profusion of fuss, flowers and applause, I had no idea what was stirring within her. This young woman draped in a dupatta of the palest blue. I had not missed that. Nor that head, held just a little high, through the evening. How did she know that I was the more vulnerable one in all this, not she? How else was she so unnervingly self-possessed? Should I be grateful for that, or less flattered? Should I have bided my time?

No, I for my part, have no regrets.

Sir Ali Imam
Patna, 1918

Her account

Of all the days, why did Khatija have to run a temperature today? Actually it was 100.8 degrees which is branded a fever, not 'temperature' that is more like 99 degrees or thereabouts. This had irked me through the day as I was readying my Annual Day speech for the school. This burden was because I had passed out as head girl amid many farewells and honours, I suppose. I missed it a little, but I still had regular news of my alma mater.

Khatija was still there with three more years to go. A favourite sibling, only a bit younger than me, she was now the link I enjoyed with the school, reporting vividly every little hum of the place: who was now which teacher's pet, who was leaving mid-term to be married off, who was caught giggling over Mrs Prasad's latest spoonerisms; how the gym mistress doesn't spare the new head girl her fits of rage, how fingers bleed when the Piano Miss runs amok, rapping little knuckles with her wooden ruler. Right now, I could barely sound her out on my speech, she felt so warm.

The Principal had called my parents with a request that I address the school at the Annual Day for a very eminent chief guest. Who could say, this celebrity could choose to help the school get important international affiliations or a teacher or two. 'Sketch for us a cameo of what you believe your school stands for,' said the Principal, 'we need to make an impression.'

Khatija was more excited than I was. But eventually, what with her being down with this wildcat 'flu', she had to opt out of her tableaux and the hymn singing with the orchestra for the Big Day and just stay home. Both my mother and the family doctor were quite firm in this regard. All she could manage now was a fuss over what I should wear as an 'old girl' and 'not just an ordinary one'. 'Remember, they all know you're my sister. Don't let me down, Apajan, please. I will fall more ill, I am sure of it.'

She insisted I dress in the palest of blue, her favourite colour not mine, that I should wear *her* blue and silver bangles, not mine. 'Mine are much prettier, they have more silver in them, use a little soap to slip them on, it will take a second. And remember to wear the sapphire studs, Apajan. Of course, you have the time. Ammee does not even lock them. They are on her dressing table …' I had to silence her, worrying that the excitement would raise her temperature all over again.

When I got back that evening from the school celebrations, Khatija was up. '*Tell me everything*' was her plea, though her forehead was still warm. So, off I launched into little vignettes of the performances that would amuse her, the excitement over some missed lines, Mr Roy's coughing fit as he began his pompous vote of thanks and Miss Sutton's fancy blouse that outshone the stage lights. I was not bad at telling a story.

'*Aapki* speech, Apajan! Tell me how you fared. Who clapped? I heard you telling Abba something about the Principal holding both your hands, tell me everything Apa.' So I told her how Miss Gardener, Mrs Hasnain and even Miss Ahmed had taken turns to grip me by the shoulders in turn; how some of the girls came rushing for autographs in their notebooks which they had actually brought for the chief guest's signature – wouldn't it irritate him to have his famous flourish in the same pages as that of a mere ex-head girl?!

Making sure she was tucked in, I said, '*Khuda hafiz, shabakhair*' and went in and sat down to this. Even to Khatija, I will talk only after I have put it down here. Actually, I was in need of writing this out in order to believe that it really *did* happen.

He is *the* Sir Ali Imam, isn't he! Is life going to be so wildly unexpected for me? Supposedly, he was not just an eminent man, but a great man. Is this how they decided on crucial questions … intuitively? Are all important men as striking and straightforward as him? I don't think so. Not even in the formal, flattering portraits, lining the walls, they are not. This man you couldn't miss. I noticed his wide forehead over his steady gaze, his finely shaped hands, not paws; his shoes shining as though he were a man of the military. I didn't have a chance to notice more for after his question, he was gone.

The next afternoon, when Abba appeared for lunch, he had news for Ammee – Sir Ali, yes Sir Ali Imam, was desirous of calling on them after six days, on returning from his trip to Benaras and Delhi. I said nothing. He had tracked down 'my guardians'. I was not in the least sure of what he planned to say or do. He did not seem to me to be the type who would be worried about '*Log kya kahengey* (what will people say),' although given his eminence, he should be worrying more than most! Ammee and Abba were trying to guess what this could be all about.

'Maybe there's some work in Neora, his zamindari, land matters which he wants to consult me about, maybe he wants me to provide managers for his famed orchards in Ranchi. Or is it that his daughter is returning from England and should meet our Anise?'

Abba was still listing the many reasons he could think of. Ammee added hers, quite undecided as to what it could be, and then they began to plan. 'We must invite him for lunch. If he can't manage the time, it will have to be a sumptuous *naashta*. He is a small but fussy eater, one hears. Bring out the best cutlery, the family silver, he is used to calling on royalty,' my father laughed, 'Working and mixing with the Viceroy, no less, you understand! The man most consulted by the Viceroy, it is said.' Though he was smiling, Abba was serious.

I was going to tell them nothing. They would not believe me, most likely. Also, now it seemed to me that his asking for my hand in marriage was a confidence placed in me by him to be kept, not given away, to be guarded even from my 'guardians'. I did feel a twinge of doubt, though. Having asked him to address his question to them, I probably owed it to them to tell them. But I didn't. There would be time for confidences, I thought. But not yet. I would rather watch him approach the subject, conduct his meeting with them as he planned. My curiosity on this subject was now acute, if not agonizing. I wanted them to have that first shock, far less than mine, but nevertheless. Enough for now.

Thank God for the comforting softness of this large, leather-bound friend, this journal of mine with an embossed Lewis Carroll's Alice on the cover. It came on my twelfth birthday, but only served me after I turned fifteen and had my first argument; not just with my mother but also my father. That's when it started filling up. Later, I started reading *War and Peace* and *Madame Bovary* – and the poets, one by one, and jotting away for myself the lines that struck me. I would talk to no one about any of that, nobody was interested either.

To most, this is a self-indulgence, certainly no help in running a home! And then came the intense preparation for the Cambridge exam, the nail-biting wait for the results, the excited celebrations after they did. All that while this confidante of mine languished in the old oak cupboard along with my bangles, my *baali*s and *thinka*s (trivial jewellery), my Parker and Schaeffer pens. After all, my university years were yet to come. Would they come at all unless I insisted, I wondered.

Even Khatija was not privy to my plump little journal, then or later.

When his car crunched into our drive that morning, six days later, I hadn't heard it. I had wondered how accurate his pocket watch would be. He had a way of clearing his throat with a decisive sort of sound – it was unmistakable, I had noticed. I heard that sound in our *daalaan* (courtyard) as he entered our drawing room. I had moved to place myself away, so I could not be seen at all, but I was not going to miss the exchange. Not one word of it.

Accepting the tea, exchanging the *aadaab*s and the

formalities, he talked of Bihar's newfound identity as a separate state. Abba congratulated him for the prestige and recognition he had brought his region and his people, which he brushed aside gently. Almost ruefully, he said that he must at the outset tell them that this was not what he had come to discuss. I thanked God for the elaborate screens that separated our drawing room from the equally large dining area where I was seated, forgetting to sip the tea that my hands were clasping. What followed had me riveted, and strangely, much more moved, than his one question to me on the school dais.

'I would like to prepare you for the fact that the subject is a very serious one, and I come to you without warning you of it.' He paused a little.

'This you must both forgive. I have come to ask for your daughter Anise Kareem's hand in marriage – yes, with abject humility. What I do offer her is my complete devotion, my world and all I possess. But yes, I do realize that with it comes a burden that is immense and unfair for her young shoulders. May God forgive my presumption but I feel a confidence that she is capable of carrying this weight – and with a rare grace. I assure you one thing though. I will spare her what she does not have a taste for but share completely my public and private life with her. And move her gently into the new life, at a pace she chooses.'

My parents were silent, and he continued speaking, probably also gesturing to them that he had not finished yet.

'You must know that I have lost two wives in the past. My first, who gave me all our children and left the world, and my second wife, who died within a year of our marriage, a victim of the Asian Flu, which took many. These facts are common knowledge. Since my work with the Government and my practice as a lawyer causes me to grossly neglect my family, I have arranged in England all the care and education that I cannot provide my children here. Yes, even the girls, my daughters. And this I will continue to do. They are my responsibility, not hers – and will remain so. Anise will have no obligation to them except exactly what she chooses, entirely of her own volition. I do know this. I know that each one of my dependents, and most of all I, myself, will gain a new life from having a person such as her in our midst. You will see this happen, I assure you. And yes, each one will cherish her as you would wish your daughter to be cherished.'

The silence from my parents took a while to end.

'So flattering this is, really and truly, Sir Ali. But an honour not easy for us to accept! The age difference, Sir … impossible!' said my father eventually. My mother more emphatically, 'Anise is just eighteen this year, still a child. Yes, she has finished school with honours but knows nothing of the world. You will understand, you will forgive! It's such an amazing compliment, but please …'

Sir Ali laughed gently but continued seriously. 'I have to apologize for my age. You have a right to spurn my request on both counts. First, my age, not hers. And second, the cross I bring her of my life thus far, a considerable burden. This proposal is daring of me, I realize that. Yes, the prospect I suggest would daunt an older woman, a more seasoned woman, an ordinary woman. I am hoping desperately, yet with conviction, that it will not daunt a person like Anise. With her beside me, we will both be immeasurably strong. Forgive me for the presumption that I will, despite my liabilities, give your daughter a life she will be proud of and content to lead.'

'She's much too young, please that is the only reason,' my mother continued, plaintive and insistent.

'I understand Begum Sahiba, and I cannot change that. But I urge you to seriously consider my request, my proposal … my plea. I am not known to give up easily.'

He must have then risen from his chair. I saw him emerging into the verandah that led up to the porch, his hand raised to his forehead as he bid them goodbye.

At the portico, he held out an assurance that embarrassed and comforted my parents yet again. I heard every word clearly, though his voice did not boom. 'You may know of my public life, but whatever you may wish to know about me and about each one of my family, you have a right to ask. Please feel free to do so. Suffice it to say that my family will welcome my bride and I will welcome any question at all from you before you promise your daughter to me. For this, my time will be yours.' He paused, hesitating. 'For my part, I will want to know Anise's mind on this subject. Her considered view to me is all-important. This you must let me know.' And he left.

I had remained out of view all through the exchange. Only when he entered his car, he could see me standing beside my parents. It was a polite nicety which I felt was owed to him. He could not have made me a more ardent proposal. Would I ever accept a man with eyes less piercing and honesty not so outright, so unafraid?

My mind was strangely clear, and it was made up. It found no room for my parents' nagging, mounting anxieties. I prayed that my instinct be right in trusting myself to this straight-backed, straight-jawed person, with eyes that looked no way but straight at you. I also prayed this instinct would see me through all my years, my entire life. His age never occurred to me as a subject to consider. How was it, I wondered, that I was so certain? I barely knew the man! It was Khatija who was more the falling-in-love type, not I.

Anise Kareem
Patna, 1918

The great grandson recounts

I never got to see Bare Dada Abba but she, Bari Dadda, would make me feel as though he was right there. She made me curious about him actually – insisting that I was his spitting image ... and about this one thing, she was unstoppable.

'How can you not see this likeness?' she would demand of her entire entourage, all too young to remember her long-gone husband. 'Which one of you here would remember Sahab? Everyone seems to have disappeared, gone, even the servants, the neighbours. Take my word for it, bring all the photographs. He has the features, the complexion, the nose, the jawline, the forehead, the defiance of Sahab, there is no one else so like him, no one!'

The only way to stop her was to agree with her. I could neither agree or disagree but knew that this conviction of hers made me an unrivalled favourite. 'This one is mine,' she would say, her eyes glistening with pride. 'This uncanny resemblance is surely a decree. He will be the centre of my life, which he cannot be of yours, you both work.' But my parents were quite firm, they did not part with their child – so they had to visit at every opportunity without protest. Her affection was compelling.

Bari Dadda thought it her right and privilege that I was kept entirely to herself, holiday after holiday for the nearly twelve years she was in the world for me. I had to sleep in her four-poster bed when I visited, with herself exiled but blissful in a mere cot attached right to the side of the four-poster! What I wished for had to be produced, those were my first memories – whether cricket bat or kite, chocolate bar or *Maner ka laddoo* or two huge plates of potato chips, one after the other, at the Bankipore Club. All else could wait.

I had grown up looking at their portraits in the study, in the corridor, in the family albums – a fairytale splendour cloaking both of them. They are there on the internet, if you want to find them. In quaint poses reminiscent of the time – one with him standing and her in a chair and one more, the other way around.

As a child, I found all these pictures of the past very vivid, of flesh and blood somehow, because the stories about them abounded, as did the phrases, the *bon mots*, the lore. These great grandparents of mine, bursting with uprightness, cussedness, eccentricities, absurd generosities. Yes, also with a strong streak of unspoken, unlauded, unspoilt romance. Told to me by perfect strangers, in different places, often most unexpectedly. Each one bettered the story, produced a more cherished anecdote.

Close to home, there was more authenticity and immediacy to the anecdotes. How else could I be kept amused for hours indoors when the sun was blazing outside over what seemed like endless vacations? The stories had spice to them, even twists and turns. Of how Bari Dadda brought up my father most assiduously, yet spoiling him anew each day. Not having any children of their own they had adopted her sister's daughter as their own, giving her all their attention. And when Sir Ali's youngest son returned from England, they thought it best to have him marry their adopted daughter! There seemed nothing amiss with that – they were not related to each other in any way. And the difference of twenty-two years between them was brushed aside!

When their first born arrived, the old lady took over, appropriated him entirely, dismissing his mother as a mere child. Any child would be envious, hearing those accounts of my father getting away with every whim and prank – and getting his way the rest of the time. Her pampering was ruinous, no protests were heeded from either parent. She would completely brush aside the frantic protests of Naqi, his father, who wished for his son what he had – the distinctly rule-bound growing-up in Harrow and Cambridge and Middle Temple – and thereafter by courts of law in London and Bihar. He was firmly of the view that the world had no place or patience with the pampered. Harrow was unthinkable, said Lady Imam. 'I am too old and it is too far,' she pronounced, and that was that.

But remembering her husband's long reliance on boarding schools for all his sons, she did ultimately relent. But within our shores it had to be. So off he was to Dehra Dun, to Arthur Foote's Doon School where her youngest brother and nephews had grown up. And she proceeded to Dehra Dun with her full and embarrassingly fussy entourage, heedless of all protest. 'Every possession of his, his milk jug, his brush and comb, shoe horn, his writing case, his fountain pen has to be monogrammed with his initials before the first term starts,' she declared and went ahead. My father had seven years in Doon School but even the mention of this got him flushed with embarrassment for years thereafter. 'Go with him all this simply must. I am breaking no rules, these are necessities. Meant to be used only by him. We will drive down from Patna to Dehra Dun with it all.' There was little you could do.

My mother was saved a tough time at the hands of the grand dowager because possessiveness was not her way. One more person to indulge she considered a bonus. Particularly because she was a Bilgrami from Hyderabad, the granddaughter of a man who too shone in the Nizam's government, years after her own husband had moved on. This coincidence delighted Bari Dadda. 'Your grandfather Sir Akeel's sister was an intellectual, apart from being the first Muslim lady graduate in India, and would spend many an evening with Sahab, your Dada Abba. Neither she nor I observed purdah, you see, *dulhin*. It is not that we were anglicized, we were cultured,' she insisted.

In my mother, Bari Dadda had an apt, even rapt audience. As she recounted, re-living her youth, her prime, her discoveries of how the world demanded, even needed, her husband across India and in England. The Hyderabad connection was a bonanza. It amused my mother that the grand dame would not hear a word against the many famed eccentricities of the Nizam, even in jest. Lady Imam would get infuriated even if it was mildly suggested that the seventh Nizam had a widespread reputation for being miserly despite the untold wealth he was famous for throughout the world.

'Bring before me any rascal who has a story that he was niggardly, and I will silence him. His wealth rescued his country, his State, the poorest of the poor in Hyderabad's villages – and his State was then as large as the country of France in Europe.'

Then she would go on to emphatically recount how, when she lost her husband, the Nizam had sped two ministers from Hyderabad to call on her in Patna with the most insistent request that she spend the rest of her years in a special mansion set aside for her and her retinue in the city in which her husband had served outstandingly as prime minister. 'You call that mean-hearted … when he owed me nothing? A bereaved widow in a faraway city who could be of no use to him in any way at all. Why? Amazing humility *beti,* which no one today has the grace to admire. The richest man in the world he was declared. Not by courtiers – but by international reckoning, for heaven's sake. The sheikhs had not discovered oil, no one rivalled him. What need did he have of me, or any like me?' Evidently she would break into Urdu for emphasis – or in sheer exasperation! 'You should have read his *daavatnama* (invitation) to me. It is still lying among old papers, I have kept it. He actually wrote saying:

"It is such a shame that I can only plead and request, I cannot order you Begum Sahiba." These were his words – and these are not easily forgotten.'

My mother remembers feeling cheered, listening to all these vivid accounts of a man who had quietly stepped down from Nizam to Raj Pramukh in 1948. She was intrigued by the quaintness of Bari Dadda recounting her trips for the Round Table Conferences in London. Here, the young Lady Imam was relieved that matching her youth was another young woman, newly married to her royal husband, Prince George, also contending with protocol and ceremony – the Princess who had adopted her as a ward, showing her the ropes and rites of the many functions and receptions that they had to cheerfully suffer. Years later, from among her letters, Bari Dadda fished out the one in which the erstwhile Elizabeth, later the Queen Mother, writes to her saying that she may now be far less regular in her communication with her since fate had seized her for a role she did not expect. Her husband was now to be the King of England, yes, George the Sixth.

Maybe all this explains our old lady's impeccable accent, my mother would laugh, before launching into the story of her own consternation at their very first meeting, when the feisty lady had flown down to Calcutta to give a once-over to the girl her adored grandson had chosen to marry.

'As I entered the doorway I could hear an exclamation in the crispest accent, "Oh, that's a violent demonstration of affection!" as she sat watching her toddler grandchildren falling upon each other in greeting across the room. Then turning to greet me, she reassured me, "*Aao, aao bitia, sab Bihari itne aape se baahar nahin hotey*. (Come, come, dear girl, not all Biharis are quite so uninhibited)."' She had broken the ice.

Despite all the mellowness and fullness of affection, Bari Dadda had a will that could not be swerved. When my aunt's wedding was being organized with the usual fervour, mother reports that Bari Dadda was firm. 'You may plan it to the last detail and with all the splendour we can afford. But before the day of the formal wedding dinner, the entire *ryayaa* (the many families living on all her farms and all servants) have to be handsomely fed, a menu I will personally supervise. And no less than the wedding dinner it would be,' she warned.

Yes, yes, but Dadda please, let us do it the day after the wedding, not the day before, we plead with you. We know your rule, they'll partake of the wedding banquet, the same food will be readied all afresh, the very next day, but please let all the formal ceremonies get done, let the "baraat" and other guests dine!

But no, despite the chorus of pleas, the old girl was adamant. Your parliamentarians and VIPs will not be neglected, but these people will celebrate first,' she firmly held. 'They have served you, they care about you – this is the least you owe them. That's the first thing God tells you – much before I do. Feeding the poor is your first priority. Yes, yes we will look after the *baraatis-saraatis*, the President of India and every other entourage, all your wonderful friends, God willing, in the best possible way. All retainers will work tirelessly, but make sure their *dastarkhaan* (dining spread) is laid out first with a proper wedding menu.

I heard the story of how my great grandparents had met and married, way back in the early twentieth century, a period which I would read of as history otherwise. It fell into place somehow. I thought to myself that her unerring instinct at eighteen in choosing her man had served her well, very well all through the twenty-three years she had with him and the thirty-five years after he was gone, her prime adult years. For she did continue to live as though he was living through her. And also it was so like her to share it with none, prizing her privacy with the one man she knew and she regarded as peerless. I thought that underlined the romance uniquely.

I can't help feeling that a lot of that pioneering gent rubbed off on her. My great grandmother was strangely imposing. A large person and yet not unfeminine. Her completely crisp, white sari of the finest muslin draped faultlessly over her entire form and her head of silver, not-entirely-white hair, covered with the *pallav* of the white sari, which always made that slight concession to colour: the narrowest strip of blue. And blue it nearly always was by all accounts, a colour she most favoured. Her arms were the whitest alabaster, rested always on the arms of her chair, but not resigned to lassitude. Her gestures when making a point or taking your *aadaab* would be firm, especially the approving nod of her head.

But for all her attempts to make those around her feel comfortable, Bari Dadda did cast this overawing effect when she stepped into a room. There would be a hush, a restraint in all present, despite her trying to ease and lighten the air, or ask a casual question. Then losing patience with the fuss, she would snap, 'What's going on, why the *sannaata* (stillness/silence)? I hear no voices, I want your news, your stories, your laughter – *haai, ham koi havva thhori hayn?* (heavens, I am not an ogre, you know!)'

With me, there was an indulgent eagerness to please, always. Seeing me amused by their tales, the retinue would warm up to more. All my holidays were peppered with charming snippets and an attempt to paint a picture for me about who I was and what I had missed. Stories not allowed to fade.

To this day, a castle stands there in Ranchi, Anise Castle as he wanted it named, where her husband wished them both to rest. In brown-at-the-edges photographs, I would be shown what was a near replica of Windsor Castle in total, ruinous shambles in Ranchi, named after her and home to his imposing grave – the man never had the time to spend in confabs and architectural drawings and so, the team of experts just chose the model they could most easily and reliably imitate! Locals would ooh and aah over it in its heyday – the rare visits, the marble statuary, the avenues and lawns. Then came the years of abandonment with the family busier everywhere else but Ranchi, unfortunately. They would recount the most absurd stories of wavering flames in the windows, now blazing, now flickering; of benign ghosts and nocturnal ambling. Vagrants thought nothing of vandalizing the marble statuettes and whatever else could be dislodged. Every year it looked more shorn I was told and I could believe it. Sir Ali's grave rests as a modest mausoleum in its own arbour, cared for now as a heritage site, its simplicity moving. It has fought time well.

I often wondered if my brother studying film at Columbia would bring himself to tell this story, dare to chance it, to elaborate, to contemporize the quaintness of it. Or would he continue to dismiss it as ancestor worship? He certainly would be in a spot casting for their roles. Liberties would be tough to take … certainly with those two people.

Perhaps a quiet account suggesting their aura would be where they would draw the line. And forgive it being shared thus, with that indulgence they had in abundance for those they chose to love.

A marriage is hoped to be a lifelong commitment.
It is seldom expected to last 'till death do us part' for two
individuals who fly highest in two professions most
in the public eye, most under attack.

Tiger Pataudi and Sharmila Tagore defied these conventions.
They surprised. Their magic still does. In surviving him,
she keeps proving it, glowing in testimony.

STARS COLLIDE, COINCIDE

Sharmila Tagore & Tiger Pataudi

STARS COLLIDE, COINCIDE

Let us start at a time when he is going to be eleven years old and she is nearly eight. She is elsewhere, completely outside his ken, a different sky to look up to, a different language to speak, a different set of dos and don'ts. Two childhoods that have their own stories to tell and no possibilities of overlapping.

Pataudi and Bhopal – young Mansur was prince in two places, as it were. This happened regularly in this echelon – it was expected that you grew up and married someone of a similar background. In *rajwadas* (Indian royalty), it would continue to this day, if grandmas had their way.

Bhopal's Nawab Hamidullah Khan had no male heir. His eldest daughter married the Nawab of Kurvai and in 1950 left for Pakistan. His second daughter, Princess Sajida, now heir to the Bhopal throne, had a suitor in Iftikhar Ali Khan Pataudi, prince of a smaller state, but quite the cynosure of all eyes, an international figure, a more than distinguished student at Balliol College, Oxford – a Billiard Blue and hockey champ to boot, with many unusual firsts on the cricket field.

Begum Sajida Pataudi looked as striking on a *masnad*

The prestige of being a Tagore was manifold. The name meant you were a Thakur, a landowner, which then was redolent with aura. Family lands aside, a gift for art seemed inherent in the genes of the Tagores. There was Rabindranath Tagore himself whose talents were multiple and whose stature as a national leader was decidedly unusual. Besides being a poet, an artist, a musician, he had spawned the whole genre of Rabindra Sangeet which captured the Bengali imagination. No Bengali girl was considered marriageable unless she had mastered singing these compositions. He was not called Gurudev for nothing. Sharmila was a great grandniece of this Nobel Laureate from both sides, hence also a descendant of the famed artist, Gaganendranath Tagore. Sufficient to say then that her talent in the arts came as a shock to none.

Since Bengal revels in *daaknaam* (nicknames) alongside the formal names, Sharmila became Rinku soon after she came into the world and her two siblings also gave up lilting names like Oindrilla and Romilla for Tinku and Chinky.

Sharmila's father often said that no son could have managed exceeding expectations, as each one of his daughters did. His transferable job did mean moving from school to school, managing with local tutors. So it came to be that at thirteen, Sharmila moved back to her parents' in Asansol. Now Satyajit Ray, having seen her sister Tinku aged six in Tapan Sinha's *Kabuliwaala,* tested her sister Rinku for the part of Apu's child bride in *Apur Sansar.*

'Bapi (my father) was called by Manikda (Ray), much revered after the worldwide acclaim for *Pather Panchali,*' says Sharmila. And so came *Apur Sansar*, the third film in Satyajit Ray's trilogy. As a filmmaker, Ray had earned a place and a devoted viewership abroad after his *Pather Panchali* caught the eye of cinema connoisseurs in Europe, America and elsewhere. The Apu story to young Sharmila was a mystery, and the experience of shooting it a self-discovery.

But the Principal of St. John's Diocesan Convent was not amused. Tight-lipped, she summoned Sharmila's parents and requested they choose between film shoots and the highly esteemed haven of instruction to which she belonged. The Tagores, with their innate commitment to the arts, were swift to move Sharmila away and into Loreto Convent, Asansol.

Her rite of passage in cinema smoothly passed, the young teenager was led into a career by a wand, not a hand. Equally, whiz-kid Tiger Pataudi was swinging his bat and proving unexpected things at Winchester in Sussex, and soon, Oxford. Neither knew of the other then.

Next, in his *Devi,* Ray had for Sharmila a complex role of a young girl becoming invested with divinity, unbeknownst to her. It was a finely balanced full-length feature, requiring innocence and restraint as much as histrionic skills. She did not fall short.

With her father posted in Madras, Rinku finished her schooling at Lawrence School, Lovedale, looking forward to reading history at Loreto College, Calcutta. Now came the rub. Mother Ancilla suggested that Sharmila, given her distractions as an actress, opt for the Pass course not the Honours degree. The young woman paused now to make up her mind. She would pursue her education her own way, she decided – her chosen profession would be her focus.

Directors now flocked to find roles for her. All of 1963 suddenly became chock-a-block. Tapan Sinha's *Nirjan Saikate* was quickly followed by Partha Pratim Chowdhry's *Chhaya Shurjo*. She was not squeamish about popular Bombay cinema, was rather happy to experiment, even daring to be different with Bombay director Shakti Samantha, another Bengali.

And so came *Junglee,* the energy of Shammi Kapoor in his heyday of the '*Koi mujhe junglee kahey*' bravado – and her own brand of unusual prettiness. The very first 'Bombay film' *Kashmir Ki Kali* was a slightly coy, blushing start – but it was to stardom. Shy, dimpled, head and hair covered in local Kashmiri style, she set about losing all her shyness on celluloid to a film hero who blatantly hogged the screen, leaping about wildly in scene after scene as only Shammi Kapoor could or would. Sharmila's debut in glitzy Bombay cinema was accomplished.

Yash Chopra and Hrishikesh Mukherjee sought her out – the latter a stalwart, favouring a slightly genteel, thoughtful, wholesome genre of Hindi cinema. Next, she was back in Calcutta with *Nayak* – Satyajit Ray presenting a contemporary dilemma with Bengal's matinee idol, Uttam Kumar, playing a beleaguered political leader. Seven years had seen Sharmila mature. As she completed Brijbhushan's *Yeh Raat Phir Na Aayegi* and *Sawan Ki Ghata,* she happened to meet Tiger.

The actress has a disarming way of happily confessing to her teenage obsessions, 'I was completely cricket-mad much before I met Tiger, actually.' Curiously, she was not starstruck by celluloid men, world film premieres, festivals and glitzy parties. The sport and scene of cricket, the clubs, pavilions, stadia seemed more her home ground. Calcuttawallahs were crazed by cricket after all – whether urchin, butler or *burra sahib* or his mother-in-law.

Some players clearly caught the imagination, outshone the rest. Jaisimha, Jai to friends, had been around wowing every teenager who fancied cricket. With him as friend, Sharmila's running into the elusive champ called Pat was inevitable. He was friends with Jaisimha, but his aura was different. He hardly spoke, yet you could not miss the man. There was something irkingly interesting about this cool, slightly aloof character. With no airs at all actually, but yes, enigma.

Tiger Pataudi had returned to play for India. They had met cursorily a couple of times in Bombay and Calcutta. The third time they spent time talking almost over the entire evening at a restaurant in Kolkata, then Calcutta. And there that evening, Rinku and Tiger exchanged telephone numbers.

'I was heading then for a song sequence in Nainital with Shashi Kapoor and Raj Kumar. You had to stop over in Delhi on the way. And staying over at the Imperial Hotel in Delhi, I called Tiger. Not finding him home, I left a message of congratulations for the double century he had scored that week against England in Delhi. Just like that!' she recalls. That, for a while, was that.

A couple of months later, Dheera, Sharmila's Bombay host, announced that Pataudi had called to note down her address fully and accurately, announcing that he had bought Sharmila five refrigerators, and the Bombay dealer was now impatient for the local address to start deliveries. '*What!* I was in a panic – how was I to handle this?' Sharmila called him in a flurry. Tiger Pataudi knew that returning the refrigerators was hardly a problem ... he had disarmed her quite. The rest you may say is history.

The attraction grew and perhaps the fact that both had fan followings, admirers close and distant, gave them common ground. They were both under pressure to keep work dates, abide by schedules, perform at peak – and then on their own time, attempt getting away from it all. Sharmila had friends among cricketers and greatly enjoyed meeting his university friends ... this helped. Because Pataudi felt no rapport with the *filmy* world and it was amply obvious that he was not about to start now. And that did remain that.

The game would take Pataudi away to different parts of the world – over dates and venues he could not control. Sharmila herself could not fob off shooting dates tying her down and away from him. One film hit followed by another grander success did matter to her, as much as to her co-star, even more to her producer, her director, whether it was Yash Chopra or Hrishikesh Mukherjee or later, Gulzar. She knew the nature of the game she was playing.

The courtship ensued – amusingly stormy if not tempestuous. She once travelled with him to Britain, during his country match series in Sussex – getting away with being introduced everywhere as his sister! They just could not afford to be discovered. And in Bombay, she slipped out quietly from her friend Dheera's house to stay at the Taj so that he, staying at the Cricket Club of India, could see her without friends cackling, spoiling the specialness of it all. 'I did slip out bag and baggage to the Taj without even telling Dheera. There was a prankster in me too, I think. Or was I learning from him?' she laughs. Getaways often demanded some deception which they both quite enjoyed.

As is often said, the root and short form of the word fanatic, is 'fan', and both of them had more than their fair share. The stories of the fans for Tiger Pataudi were legion, cricket being a serious preoccupation in quite a few countries. Perhaps Sharmila remained cool about his many admirers because he too had to contend with that. Their confidence had to be mutual. The hoo-haa that a sweeping stroke created on the spot, on the field, in the stadium, was abetted at the parties, exaggerated by the news, the sports journals and the books! The world of cinema was equally abuzz. The fan club was various, ebullient, everywhere. The gargantuan appetite of the country's cinemagoers for gossip, an asset the promoters hoped for and encouraged, was something to contend with in the world of celluloid. And it all started in the early days when they began meaning a lot to one another.

After *Saavan ki Ghata,* Shakti Samantha had ambitious plans. The location would be European and Sharmila would be making a splash. She would surprise with oomph and sophistication in *An Evening in Paris*, a title that announced the film's location and cashed in on the name of a French perfume – one that managed to trickle into India at a time when few things foreign got past Indian shores. The title, the star line-up, the location – nothing short of a coup.

As it happened, Sharmila sported a bikini during the swimming pool sequences in Beirut, in keeping with depicting a with-it Indian girl abroad, not daring so much as distinguished in showing leg and a perfectly elegant figure, minus all self-consciousness. And yes, with a distinct, if understated oomph.

Daring it did turn out to be. Sharmila's picture sporting this slinky bikini appeared large as life on the *Filmfare* cover. This, in 1967, took India aback – an unexpected blow-up in more senses than one. Headlines soon blared shock and disapproval, right across India's film media. Since it guaranteed eyeballs and footfalls, hype and gossip, the upside was obvious. But anxieties rode high: banning, censorship, anything could happen. Promoters, financiers, director, producer, bit their nails while they welcomed the full houses in the movie halls. *An Evening in Paris* could very well be withdrawn. This was India of the 1960s – not Hollywood post the shock of Hedy

Lamarr's *Extasie*. Movies at that time were not given the PG or parental guidance tag, there were hardly any declared 'For Adults Only'. India disapproved.

'Sharmila shocks India in scantiest bikini', 'First Indian Film Star Dares to Bare', 'Cover Girl or Uncover Girl', publications were cashing in on the sensation. No one dared to appreciate.

As news reached Sharmila she was startled, puzzled. While shooting in Europe, this came to her unexpectedly. 'I was furious – so upsetting, this unnecessary fuss, unforgivable!' It seemed unfair, and it rattled her.

Tiger was not around. Yet he, playing tournaments for Hove at Sussex, had only to send off an eight-word telegram, setting the whole matter to rest for her. It said. 'Relax! You could only be looking very nice.' Sharmila relaxed and kept her peace. She let the moment pass.

The young actress noticed with relief that Pataudi's cool was not easily undone. This sureness was typical of him, of his outright confidence in her and in himself. Unfamiliar with this response in herself, Sharmila particularly welcomed it in him and from him – time after time. In fact, she began to expect it from him, feeling inwardly very secure on its account.

'He felt so okay about himself – and me – and us – in all circumstances! I'd never had this chance before to be myself … impetuous, even adventurous.'

The man was irrepressible himself, regularly thinking up a zany prank and pulling it off. He would rope in his teammates to happily play ball in joke after practical joke – unflappably.

As *The Hindu* reported on 22 May 1961, 'Pick me a target,' said the young Nawab of Pataudi to a fieldsman in Britain after hitting two spectacular sixes. The opponent pointed out a very swish convertible parked beyond the farthest boundary. The next ball the Nawab hit landed on the car roof. The motorist, the owner of the car, delighted at the honour, pleaded for the twenty-year-old Oxford captain's autograph on the dent. Tiger happily obliged. Carefree times those were, and this adulation was a spur.

Tiger would keep pushing his luck, his tricks becoming more elaborate when least expected. Being married to him would be a life that would not entertain a dull moment. Nor would it be entirely easy. It would be peppered, she mused, with expectations and demands, demanding much patience, elegance, even formality. He was more than just a world-famous cricketer. *That* prospect was daunting. It also seemed a moment to pause, change pace.

The furore on both sides had already started. It was typical and to be expected. 'Marrying a Nawab?' 'A Muslim?' There were enough among the well-wishers of the Tagores and Baruahs to raise an alarm.

The din around her parents was getting louder. 'And he is a star cricketer to boot. You seriously expect this marriage to last? Will he let her act, are you sacrificing her talent, her career, her future? She's much too young – and so is he. D'you know a Nawab to be married just once? Or care what anyone says? For them it's a norm to stray, to officially stray! It's expected of them!' The 'friendly' warnings came often, directly and blatantly. Family well-wishers do want to show they care. The expressions were frenzied and no one was embarrassed to repeat them!

The girl's brow furrowed often, but not for long. There was no getting away from this barrage of concern. In the end, young Rinku listened quietly only to herself and her dimpled smile returned. She was going to be all right.

For she also listened to that unshakable confidence Tiger Pataudi had in himself, orphaned of his father and mentor when exactly eleven years of age. And then deprived within the decade, of his most crucial ally as batsman, bowler, fielder – his right eye. Set back in a faculty entirely crucial for the brilliance of performance he expected from himself. This was no debauched playboy or cosseted cricket champ. This was no wayward princeling. What emboldened her even more was his delightfully unexpected confidence in her. 'You're pretty now,' he would say to her, 'but you have no idea what you will be like twenty years from now. I do.'

Unflappable, his trust seemed to be in her and in all she did. She could sense it without it being said. And that really was the crunch. Time after time in their lives, she found this the anchor nothing else had been for her. It also seemed the indulgence her temperament needed, to be herself, to take chances.

The Paris shoot of *An Evening in Paris* brought with it a bonus. Tiger had fractured a finger while playing in England, which turned out to be a blessing in disguise. Unable to play, he could fly out for the weekend, snatch time with her between shooting dates. She, no less adventurous, would move into his hotel for the time, causing in the unit much distress, expressed in silently seething disapproval.

After a shoot one evening, the couple decided on a quiet dinner in Paris followed by a drive around the hot spots of the city, ordering a cab to fetch them post dinner. Now, they relished the wine, the hors d'eouvre, the entrees, rather like young locals. As they ordered their dessert, they noticed a noisy flurry across the room and the loud, overpowering presence of co-star Shammi Kapoor with a bunch of hangers-on, keeping the waiters busy. As they stepped out of the restaurant, Sharmila was aghast to see Shammi Kapoor sailing off with his gang in the very cab that they had bespoken for their city-by-night drive.

Turning flaming red at this horrendous 'unchivalry', she insisted the hotel staff should whistle to stop their cab and empty it of its passengers. In a rage, she turned to confront her flamboyant co-star ... then began giggling softly. Tiger had in a flash picked up the largest bouquet of flowers in the restaurant and was kneeling before her with a promise of nabbing the next cab to show her all of gay Paris! Everyone around held their sides laughing. No scene, no friction with the superstar who would face her next morning. Pat, as much as Tiger to many, had tricks up his sleeve at all times, rare ways of making her feel grounded.

The same sureness in Mansur Ali Khan saw him manage his family and their ample reservations against their match. The Tagores will resist, his family felt. Will Tiger's girlfriend ever be ready for this new life role, of a wife, a *bahu,* a family luminary in the states of Pataudi and Bhopal? Will she not hanker after tinsel town – after all, the cricket glamour will belong to him, not her. From actress to princess would be no easy transition. From guaranteed glamour to being a demure, dignified begum and a flamboyant sportsman's bride in the pavilion while his admires flocked. It would not be her autograph being sought, she would resist taking second place. Bombay movie directors could feel discouraged to cast her as romantic lead in film after film with a husband like Pataudi standing guard. All the *adab* (culture protocol) and *lehaaz* (formality and restraint) of Bhopal and Pataudi will pall.

The heroine knew she had to be guarded while trusting her instinct. She had to ponder, think it through, not just take the plunge. Fortunately, Sharmila was not a stranger to the game which was his life. She had always found cricket exciting, had more than a passing knowledge of the game, found the players attentive in the pavilion and admirable on the field. She was happy to accept an invitation after a match and listen avidly to talk of the day's game between tournaments.

But Tiger being different won her. He did not say very much. He looked unmistakably stylish. And unusual. You could barely hear what he said. His accent was not a familiar one, his humour even less so; not affected or formal, but all his own. He had you figuring him out most of the time; you could not take him for granted. He had this habit of startling you. He has enough to be arrogant about, she thought, but is not. She liked that.

'His sense of humour was what floored me. There was a cool, rock-like ease and – and yes, dependability. That was it, I think.'

Let us not forget that by the time they met and courted, young Pataudi had put a lot away. Without fuss or fanfare, he had been a batting prodigy at Winchester in England where he went to school. He had captained the school team, scoring 1,068 runs in 1959, beating the school record set by none less than Douglas Jardine way back in 1919, a fact that became more significant because Jardine as cricketer had been his father's arch rival. In the cricket arena, this is myth and cause for great pride for the Indian side. Particularly since the BBC series *Bodyline* had so captivated audiences worldwide. The 'noob' had made his first-class cricket debut playing for Sussex at sixteen years of age, playing thereafter for Oxford while studying French and Arabic. The young man was quietly versatile too. He had won the school Rackets Championship with partner Christopher Snell!

Sharmila's suitor had also established something else. At the start of his cricketing prime, he had met with an accident driving back after dinner with a friend, Robin Waters, in Sussex where they were playing a match. A car had hit Robin's Morris Minor even before he could start his vehicle or Tiger could fasten his safety belt. This threw Tiger right out, through the windscreen! His injured right wrist caused the players much concern. He was expected to save his side the next day on the field by notching up runs. It was only in the early morning at Brighton Hospital that he discovered a glass shard off the windscreen of their car had caused an irreparable injury. And that no surgery could save for him the sight of his right eye.

The rest is cricket history – of how he bore up as only Tiger would. 'A bit of bad luck' was what he called it then and right through. Knowing well that it affected his game with a finality that little else would. Within six months of his eye injury, reconciled to the use of just his left eye, he made his first Test debut in 1961 when he was not yet twenty-one.

Back home in his country and hers, M.A.K. Pataudi earned quick seniority. Credited for India's first win against England in Madras, scoring 103 in the first Test, he was quickly appointed vice captain for the West Indies Test. He found himself elevated to captaincy since skipper Nari Contractor was laid low by an injury caused by the demonic bowler Charlie Griffith. At twenty-one years and seventy-seven days, Mansur remained the youngest country captain until 2004 when he was overtaken by Taiku Twinba.

At age twenty-three in 1964, came the Arjuna Award, the Wisden Cricketer of the Year in 1967. Pataudi's career amazes one more particularly as he was refused to be undone by the loss of an eye at its very beginning. Leaving all his rivals behind, Sharmila's suitor more than kept pace with her own triumphs; Pataudi had scored a Test century against England, six months after losing the sight of one eye and an unbeaten double century. In 1967, while dating her, he top-scored with 64, despite the distraction of her gracing the pavilion, maybe because of it.

The genius of Pataudi shone in a crisis. In the embarrassed, shamefaced follow-on when the Indian team was all out for 64, Tiger Pataudi amassed 148 runs in the second innings, saving face if not match or tournament. England's team had already amassed 950 runs! Rare spirit when least expected was his trademark. In 1967-68 Pat came to bat in Melbourne when his side was 75 for the loss of 5 wickets. Despite pulling a hamstring before this match, he hit a glorious 75 runs, batting with much flourish. In the second innings, his brilliant stroke play rustled up 85 runs – not the least undone by the limp or the pain. 'One eye and one leg!' exclaimed the elated Bishan Singh Bedi. It had become Tiger's habit to amaze.

It is rarely a list of reasons or reassurances that compel the 'forever' plunge, a commitment for life. Instinct does its own thing, even urges you to break rules you would not for any other. Sharmila recalls darting off to the airport right in the middle of a shoot to see off the man she wished to marry.

'I was shooting in Panvel, a couple of hours away from Mumbai for *Milan ki Raat.* There was an issue with the camera, and we had to pack up. Tiger and Raj Singh Dungarpur were leaving for the latter's cousin's home in Gujarat for a couple of days. I thought if I hurried, I could surprise them at the airport. I made my driver drive super-fast; those days the traffic was not what it is today.

'I got to the airport as Tiger and Raj Singh were getting out of their car! They were *certainly* surprised to see me. Then Tiger said, "Why don't you come along, it's only two days." I thought it will be so much fun. I called my secy to figure out how I could get out of two days' work and boarded the plane. *Still* in my work make-up, with *no luggage whatsoever!* This was do-able, those days. The welcome when I reached the destination was a joy. Toothbrush, clothes, toiletries, all were provided. Best time I have ever had. How impulsive we were!'

'True,' says Tiger, 'but it was far, far from a walk-over,' he adds ruefully. 'She batted on for four long years.'

It was time to bring it out in the open. To seek permissions, settle dates, conquer all opposition. She remembers Begum Pataudi receiving her on the sprawling lawns of 1, Dupleix Road in Central Delhi, her residence in the capital. 'I want you to know, my dear, that we do not have money,' she said to the young actress her son presented to her as the girl he had chosen to marry. 'But he is a fine young man you may have discovered. And *should* give you a life you wish for, since he has made up his mind that you're the one he will marry.' She had that twinkle in her eye she was famous for, and Sharmila, shy and a little formal, duly melted. She could see that Tiger's mother would be indulgent when she had a mind to be and stand her ground if she did not. Her strong will had served her well all those years she had been alone and in her prime.

Now Tiger was not going to let this very precious moment pass without approaching the spectacular, the unforgettable. The proposal had to have an unexpected flourish: of chasing her with flowers, kneeling by Paris' Eiffel Tower to propose. And not just on any day, but 14th July, Bastille Day. Yes, 14th July when the city was berserk with wild flurries of fireworks and celebratory rowdyism. This sportsman suitor knew well that back home, form and propriety would insist on taking over.

The welcome by the family and the two states was graceful, not conciliatory. There was Sharmila Tagore, choosing readily and happily to be their Begum Ayesha Sultana – adopting his faith and his family. Rinku was welcomed now as their princess, amid rituals elaborate and pleasing. Her faith in her man strengthened her, did not allow her to dither. Given the two rather glamorous worlds each inhabited, the furore was natural. The news travelled around the country and among his many friends across the world.

But the simplicity of the ritual fascinated her quite. The traditional detail of the ensemble she wore, how she looked beside him in his formal *achkan*, made her feel very chosen, very cherished by a smilingly, unchangingly loyal audience, rare for an actress who gets varying responses after a hit or a flop. And curiously endearing she found this fealty in her *sasural:* the family both close and extended, the retinues both in Pataudi and Bhopal. It was touching to find herself so valued, so important to those for whom she had not done anything yet. Except fall in love with their prince.

When Sharmila now recounts different times and phases with her husband, she has the look of both pride and disbelief. 'Always cool he was, often irritatingly quiet. Asked questions on techniques and strokes that he could answer eloquently, he would in just a phrase. "You sound *so* unforthcoming," I'd say to him. But it wouldn't work!'

There is a very unspoilt spirit in Sharmila, which reminisces readily. 'For God's sake, once I held forth on how movingly he wrote and sang his early outpourings to me, proudly rattling off the couplets of "*Dil e naadan tujhe huwa kya hai, aakhir is dard ki dava kya hai* (Child-like heart, what has come over you, what may the cure be for this, your heartache?)." Loud guffaws greeted me on how he merrily assumed my not knowing what everyone did – that it was Ghalib, not him at all.'

Life had to be a sport one way or another. The intentness to prove to himself what a great aim and shot he could muster, despite the loss of an eye, never left him. Almost childishly, he would play truant when he should clearly have desisted.

Their move from Bombay to Delhi meant living in 1, Dupleix Road where Begum Pataudi presided over a lovely, sprawling home. Sharmila found nothing oppressive about the rules of the house, which were very benign. They could return from a party any time of night or morning. Indeed, they often found company because the Begum was up. Amma was a nightbird, happy to read, have her hair brushed, in no hurry to sleep. And though Rinku was much indulged as the strenuously busy young *Begum sahiba,* she could not fiddle around with what was close to Amma's heart. Not a leaf could be moved or the tall all-white flower arrangements tweaked in the slightest. Each member of the retinue was aware, wary.

'Often, we would come back laden with bouquets, but no. There were enough rooms in the colonial Dupleix Road home for liberties to be taken elsewhere. But in the public rooms, no.

'And then suddenly one day you'd find she had decided to clean the priceless chandeliers herself, re-assembling them piece by crystal piece, flawlessly, the servants standing around her as she would climb the ladder, knowing exactly which bit fitted where. They made them different those days,' the actor adds, smiling ruefully.

Yet certain unspoken taboos were also real. Tiger had no taste for cuss words, which given all his various exposure here and worldwide, was an oddity.

'He would raise his eyebrows if I used words like "crap", which I did in the early days and thought nothing of it. But then I began to see how graceless it actually was. And very quickly dropped using it. And yes, the rule of the house, for all without any exception was – a firm ban on the use of the 'f' word. Yes, despite being a boarder and a cricketer, and a man's man, these were surprising quirks. But I liked them, especially after the kids came. "No marriages are made in heaven, they need very down-to-earth adjustments and yes, you make them," he would say. And we did.'

There was a sureness they had developed about each other. Of being equal to whatever befell them. After all, the man was known to always play deft and unperturbed, picking up any bat he fancied just as he walked out onto the field. This left other batsmen foxed, often aghast. Especially since most times his scoring and style amazed just as much.

Knitting her own values with the newness and unfamiliarity of Pataudi and Bhopal, Sharmila's role as Ayesha Sultana came seamlessly. It was not borne down on her formally or frequently. The ceremony of it all was intriguing, often attractive. Tiger was not regular in prayer or ceremony of any kind, the values of his religion were imbued in him. Aside from the family motto of *Nasr Minallah fatehun qareeb* (with God willing, victory is near), he kept a framed Arabic calligraphy of a favourite Islamic precept, which he believed applied age after age: *Allah kisi bhi qaum ki haalat jab tak nahin badalta jab tak ke voh apni haalat badalne ka iraada na farmaayen* (God does not change the condition of any people until they themselves resolve to embark on that change). Fortunately, for her and for the three children, living with independence and a natural dignity remained a rule of the Pataudi household.

The closeness to the older generation too, Sharmila welcomed for herself and her children – it was gentling, mellowing. Both their routines meant travel, so in Delhi, catching up with each other and with friends was natural, given the snugness of coming back to a generous, well-run home. Her own daughters married and involved in lives of their own, Begum Sajida Pataudi relished the slightly formal but delightfully affectionate *bahu*, who smiled over most requests, whether domestic or public. And got things done dimpling away in both cheeks and did it all a shade better than was expected.

The Begum herself was busy and mostly in Delhi. Visiting Bhopal and Pataudi, dropping into hill stations over summer, during the polo season. Begum Sajida had that dashing, independent streak, which did not go unnoticed. In Mussoorie over the racing season, you could see her zipping by in her Jaguar from the Sunday races, often driving herself. Knowing too that she could fix the engine, if need be! State matters were fewer as time went by. She would spare her son the irk of ceremony and protocol and smiled over the irony of his cousin Shahryar becoming the mover and shaker for cricket in Pakistan. It delighted her that their childhood bond could flourish, thanks to the game and its pride of place in both countries. His mother also knew that to Tiger, the game came first. And to Rinku her own work – and her husband. This Begum Sajida approved of, especially since they did not delay giving her their bright-eyed first-born, a baby son.

Tiger and Rinku thought up a double whammy, especially for her. They would call the son and heir Sajid, the male equivalent of her name. Begum Sajida was not impressed. *She* would choose, she said, it was her prerogative. And she chose Saif. Simple, strong, easy to spell, tough to mispronounce. Quite a cinch. So Saif he was, and Saif he has remained, retaining it even as he hit Indian cinema, big time. The preference for the sibilant 'S' and for a simple monosyllabic impact settled on Saba and Soha, as names for the two daughters who followed.

When it came to the family, the sharing of responsibilities between the couple adapted naturally to their lives and routines. From the time of their birth when he would read the short ceremonial prayer in each ear of the infant as Rinku watched ... and through the years of their varied routines as they grew up and moved on.

In the early days his commitments were as hectic as hers. Pataudi's game and his spirit continued to sparkle while the kids romped around as infants – she simply had to be there.

It was the December of '74 – Pataudi was playing against the daunting West Indies. Tension was soaring. With Eden Gardens' heart set on India's victory against West Indies, Andy Roberts' bouncer went straight for batsman Pataudi's jaw – and broke it. (Rinku bit her nails, sitting in Bombay, listening to the commentary. 'Our cricket fiends are known to burn the entire stadium down, don't I know it, I'm a Bengali!'). But the next innings saw Tiger back in the field, his jaw all wired up, giving India a clear 85-run victory, hitting four boundaries in one, yes, in one single over. Exciting it was to watch, to listen to, hearing their children run around the house and garden in Bombay, clapping for Abba.

Of course, between Tests and games, he would be home – and as the years went by, more regularly. But still, Sharmila was the one who would worry about school, parent-teacher meetings, managing to attend them very nearly each time, on time. Listening and participating as Mrs Khan, as the student's mother, not the star actress, nor the ace cricketer's wife, nor Begum Ayesha Sultana, Begum of Pataudi and Bhopal. Sharmila Tagore she chooses to use consistently, believing it identifies her best.

Tiger could not muster the patience and interest that would keep him in the school auditorium to see overly long theatre performances. That was more her commitment. He would be off after the scenes in which his kids performed with: 'School shows tend to be endless, don't they? He could be droll too, unstoppably scoring 250 runs 'not out' in Saif's school when invited to play a match! They must have wished they had asked him to merely give away the prizes.

Yet he, Abba, was the anchor at home for them when his wife was away on outdoor or location shoots – solid, unfussed and often unexpectedly amusing. It both reassured and amused Sharmila that he would not indulge them unduly. For instance, the phone could not be used extravagantly, it was often kept locked! And wasteful use of petrol was frowned upon too. Given Delhi distances, the kids' yen for zipping around could get out of hand, he declared.

Never pedantic when using his authority, he would not waste words – or sentiments. And yet, unexpectedly rock-like and life-saving on crucial occasions he would be. As indeed he was at his daughter Soha's graduation ceremony from his own alma mater, Balliol College, Oxford. All set for this very formal ceremony, the girl stood transfixed right at the last minute without the crucial black stockings – these were an absolute essential. Her spanking new formal black high heels with her ceremonial black gown were no good without this particular formality. She had forgotten to order them. This meant she was disallowed walking onto the dais to receive her degree! Dad Pataudi sat himself down that very minute, divested his feet of the formal black socks he had put on for the occasion and pronto, handed them over to his daughter. Crisis averted. Triumph afoot. He had his tearful little girl smiling, then stepping up solemnly to catch the moment that he had flown out from Delhi for, the moment that was to be his proudest. At Balliol, the college where he had studied, and his father before him, and where Soha had just acquitted herself well in Modern History.

With each one of the kids, growing up, Pat's protective presence was comforting, not restraining. Nothing was compulsory except the pursuit of what you chose – and yes, to a certain standard, a certain distinction.

Saif's stature as an actor and a star has been outstanding as a result – though he does not seem to be avaricious for either. It seems to come as naturally as cricket records came to his Dad and, even more, as screen presence and charisma comes to his mother.

The parents had not meddled in the least to narrow his choices, no tyranny of expectation was exercised. He was coached in cricket and did play. He certainly had to learn the tabla! The house had music living in it, as it were. Tiger himself was such a natural with music, sang readily, played the harmonium, the tabla, even dabbled in coaxing melodies out of the flute and never travelled without a couple of musical instruments.

Sharmila and Tiger smiled seeing Saif experiment at playing that carefree, roguish hero superstar in the beginning of his career and equally enjoyed watching him later depicting the villain in Vishal Bharadwaj's *Omkara,* the Bollywood rendition of Othello and then as the incurable romantic in Pradeep Sarkar's *Parineeta.* Quizzed about this romantic hit, Saif very spontaneously countered: 'Oh, I just played Dad in *Parineeta* ... simple!'

Deeply admiring of Tiger's steadfast qualities, he says, 'I think of him as Al Pacino,' sizing up his father's understated charm. The young Pataudi must surely cherish how understanding and supportive Amma (his appellation for Sharmila) has always been.

Saba too found her niche. Each sibling discovered quietly and confidently the particular skill they considered their own. She started playing about with the camera, turned family photographer readily, adeptly. But then her fascination with aesthetics led her to the Delhi School of Art, cultivating an eye for gems, for cuts, carats and facets. She then set off to the Gemological Institute of America in Carlsbad, California, to train at the distinguished institution. The shy and serious girl had to know more, get it right, before setting to work with craftsmen back home. Happier being the home bird, closer as a result to the larger family, Saba now is the *Muthawalli* for the *Auqaf-Shahi,* the Royal Trust of Bhopal. Although Sharmila blesses each familial gesture or formality in Bhopal, she knows Saba is looking into every detail and is more familiar with nuances, whatever they may be.

As a couple, Pat and Rinku believed in letting the kids discover their focus rather than be directed to it. Soha had set her heart on Balliol, the family college, from where she graduated. She opted then to work in a bank, which she enjoyed. The temptation of having a go at cinema before deciding on finance as a career, seemed necessary to her. Having shone in Sudhir Mishra's *Khoya Khoya Chand*, she was snapped up readily and with a splash in the much acclaimed *Rang de Basanti,* making her mark. As new and differently demanding roles entered Soha's arena, so did the man she found she wanted at the centre of her life. Her elation over her marriage with Kunal Khemu and now their daughter Inaaya continues as the couple mastermind Renegade Films, a production house which seems to be in a continuous buzz.

Retirement eluded both Rinku and Tiger. Aside from a series of films and awards, Sharmila headed up the Film Censor Board, became the Indian UNICEF representative – would on and off accept modelling assignments. Tiger Pataudi played his roles as editor of *Sportsworld*, umpire and commentator frequently at cricket stadia and yes, also as a model. Gwalior Suitings, Asian Paints and Lays chips would show him off, using some throwaway lines of nonchalance, specially written for him.

Crises do have a way of intermingling with triumphs, and the Pataudis certainly had their share of these: politics within the arena of cricket influenced selections for crucial matches – and this irked Tiger. There was little he could do to eliminate it, he noticed. Equally, he shrugged his shoulders too at his own failure in actual politics when he stood for elections from Bhopal and Haryana. He had no wish for it as a career. It was only his form of protest against the abolition of the privy purse, which he considered an outright breach of a pact – a protest he wished to register in no uncertain terms.

Aside from being a most unusual man and cricketer, he was the prince who gave his state the finely equipped Venu Eye Institute in Pataudi – an institution Sharmila connects with at every turn, updating facilities for the less privileged – and one to which Tiger donated the one eye that had served him so well.

Shunning all airs and ostentation through his life, Pataudi remained a legend. Though he never flashed it around, the slinkiest two-seater white Jaguar PAT 3 graced his garage and drove him to Pataudi now and then. An evening playing bridge became regular for him once a week. Even more keenly were the menus masterminded for the intimate dinner parties every now and then, which amazed and refreshed the guests each time.

Just as they would remember his many quips, which caught them unawares over the evening, remembered best for being subtle, unexpected, often a little daring. Few knew that the host was very much the remote control chef, making his man Friday Ghiyasuddin liaise with the kitchen honchos. That he had his way of throwing in a bit of music or mimicry, egging on one guest or another to perform. That after years of knocking back his brandy, he had moderated himself to a glass or two of wine.

His wife has been no less in her field of operation. From being the highest-paid actress of her time, she has, quite uniquely, remained a much-sought-after actress over the half century that followed, and to this day. Unstoppable, she continues to be throughout. Winning the National Film Award for Best Actress in Gulzar's *Mausam* and the French Legion d'Honneur for the Arts as well.

She is still the actress that Satyajit Ray sparked off in her sixty years ago. The thespian sought after for roles, and being a woman of varied experience, for views and opinions and participation – whether for a memorial of Rabindranath

Tagore or a retrospective of Satyajit Ray or the Annual Day at Doon School. It was often said in the film world decades ago that greats such as Hrishikesh Mukherji, Ashok Kumar and Sharmila Tagore may talk often of leaving the world of cinema – but never will. And she has not.

Each year, come December or even earlier, Sharmila would be found making plans. An unusual celebration centred around music. 'Indian classical music is very much Tiger's thing. Let's surprise him with a singer, or an instrumentalist, or even a qawwali, this birthday.'

The celebration was never on his actual birthday. Always a couple of days earlier or later. 'Why have it on Sarkar's *barsi* (death anniversary), makes no sense,' she'd say.

An exception was made for his milestone 70th birthday, waiving the rule about Sarkar's *barsi*. Fifth of January 2011 would be a day at Pataudi Palace – then a quiet and elegant hotel. A whole bracing winter day of celebration with about fifty friends and family, close and special, rolling in well before lunch, catching up with the couple: the two film star kids from Mumbai, close family from Bhopal, Hyderabad, from other parts of the world. The hall filled comfortably, watching *Dastangoi* by Danish Husain and Mahmud Faruqui, the star duo of this theatre mode known to roll out tales amusingly, trippingly off the tongue, improvised wittily around the host's life, his career, his persona. It had the audience agog.

Then came '70 Years & Still Game', a film picking out the prime moments in the life of the man she loved and had married. Sharmila had commissioned Vani Sundaram to cull this out, reminding us all of the kind of ace Pataudi is. The drinks were various, keeping everyone in mind. The lunch lived up to the reputation of Mansur Ali Khan Pataudi as a gourmet and Sharmila Tagore as hostess. There was something magical about the day – everyone felt it. They said it in different ways as they said their goodbyes, leaving at sundown, unusually replete. It was magical for the family to stay back and bask in the togetherness. Saif had brought Kareena and Soha from Mumbai; Saba was radiant, as were her parents, to be *en famille*.

Yes, the day had gone as splendidly as it possibly could. But the year did not. A few weeks later, Tiger had a chest infection. Every known lung specialist was tracked down, the finest in the country contacted. A trip was made to London, checking for expert international opinions without any specific or heartening result. The renowned Delhi doctor seemed best qualified, most familiar with the patient's constitution – and Tiger was hospitalized at Sir Gangaram Hospital in Delhi. Everything was attempted to check and reverse the disease but idiopathic pulmonary fibrosis has not relented yet to the salvoes and solutions of modern medicine. And it did not.

The weeks in hospital turned out to be quiet and almost undisturbed for those who held Tiger close and dear, his immediate family. Almost a sort of unplanned boon, a blessing. They had a strangely peaceful and private sense of being able to talk about things they never had the chance or time to share over the years. Quip at each other, recount anecdotes, one leading to another, even sing a little. It was not easy to unnerve Pataudi. Even the news that a cure for what had seized him was not in sight. He was made of not just sterner stuff, but saner, sanguine stuff. 'I quite enjoy the very mundane view from my window, the regularity of the cars coming in each morning, getting parked below, the doctors, the visitors arriving, leaving. The sameness of it all is not monotonous, I actually find appealing, even soothing.'

'Grace under pressure,' long held as the pithiest description of a gentleman, applied best to the man who displayed it for all his seventy years, unfailingly. Tiger Pataudi's sense of wit was not about to die. One day, like on every other day, the nurse got him bathed and changed for the day and served up breakfast. She then came to clear the tray when he finished and announced cheerily as she drew the curtains aside: 'See how wonderfully you did everything this morning?' His prompt retort came, eyebrow raised: 'You call that *everything*?' That had both Sharmila and the sister burst out laughing. Which is exactly what he wanted.

22 September 2011 came. And Tiger Pataudi went. But for his wife of nearly forty-two years and his love of four years even before that, for Sharmila, he is there.

'Very often, whenever I need to actually ... I check things out with him. Yes, I do, every now and then. He makes sure somehow, that I'm never at a loss.'

'Being in love' tends to upstage every other relationship, without so much as a 'by your leave'. Who has decided when and where to enshrine it so? Most talked about, written about, sung about, it inspires every kind of art as it simmers to a height... Or torments with absence or neglect. Surging at the outset, it is expected to steady or mute, even dwindle, as time goes by.

And yet, when led by an urge for learning, shared learning, the opposite may well happen.

TO LOVE IS TO LEARN

Dr Karan Singh & Yasho Karan Singh

TO LOVE IS TO LEARN

I tell you now of two people I got to know when they were half a century into their marriage. Yes, fifty whole years. And it was young, their marriage. It had an unobtrusive glow about it. He has lost her now, only recently, in the sixtieth year of their marriage – and it was still young. Which is why it had to be here, in this book.

The first time I saw and heard Dr Karan Singh was when he addressed a vast gathering of communication honchos – to declare India's television open for commerce. It was the birth of a whole new medium for the country, now taken to a whole other level of hectic development of itself and of the country. The event was celebrated with an all-India gathering of representatives of media, communication, industry, and of course government, at Vigyan Bhavan. No celebrity had declined the invitation.

I was in my twenties then, an age when I was quite firm about not being easily impressed – with formality or grand ceremony – or with anything else for that matter! The Bombay advertising, marketing and creative community was well represented in the vast auditorium. A whole new exciting medium was now granted for communication. Both vivid and powerful – against which both print and radio paled. This was live – a boon and a big deal for making brands reach out and move the viewer. The schedules and shows over the days in Delhi promised to be various, but the inaugural speeches would be entirely predictable. The expectation from the Minister of Tourism and Civil Aviation and his inaugural address was, to put it mildly, on the lowish side.

He did not move or look or speak like anyone in the government – or politics or media or academia, for that matter. There was something utterly natural about the man. Despite the formal, almost 'venerating' way in which he was being treated and addressed, he carried it all lightly. And we, the tough-to-please younger bunch in the audience, were a whit taken aback.

My first response was a private exclamation: I didn't know they made ministers like that. His verve, his directness, his lack of airs and affectation and officious form, the sense of humour he used liberally through the entirety of his inaugural speech – how could one explain that? I remember my own reaction well. Childishly, I attributed this to the man's stint in Doon School, which whatever else it did or did not do, certainly brought princes down to earth and made them grow to be men with minds and wills of their own. There was also something disarming in this man's honest plea to communicators and corporate honchos that they use well the fact that television was developing in an earning capacity. He looked as though he would do the same hands-on if he were in charge – not just preach or delegate. He clearly was a prince with none of the affectations of one. A politician with none of their typical prevarications.

Years later, I saw and met and heard the same man in totally new avatars. It was affecting, deeply so, to meet and hear the sage in him come through, without fuss or ado, as much as the litterateur, the raconteur, the statesman.

I noticed that his headgear was custom-designed, a kind of fixture, he wore it then and now and at all times. It was not any royal or feudal headgear, more a nationalist one. What they had seen prime ministers of independent India like Nehru wear, and later Shastri, and what the world called a Gandhi cap.

I realized that he was an irrepressible self-educator, undeterred by his schedule over the years as regent, as Sadr-i-Riyasat of his State of Kashmir (at the ripe age of twenty-one!) and as holder of many important positions in his own state and Delhi. He would go back to education relentlessly, time after time. To do his BA, learn Sanskrit, study Philosophy, then do his MA, meet *swamis* and seers like Sri Aurobindo and Sri Parmananda – reading, reflecting with a boyish enthusiasm that never left him.

When I was getting to know him, I discovered the fact that while he insisted on teaching himself and seeking new gurus, he was himself an avid teacher. That he had done this all the way through since age nineteen when he met Yashodhara Rajya Lakshmi of Nepal.

Yasho's freshness was palpable at thirteen. As was her natural confidence, being the eldest of five siblings – protective, calling the shots, always there for them, in their sprawling Lakshmi Nivas Palace in Nepal. Their schooling was at home but the discipline considerable, her father being an Army General, her grandfather, Prime Minister Maharajah Sir

Mohan Shamsher Rana of Nepal. Like Karan Singh's father, he too had to surrender his royal status in 1951.

Young Karan sensed a natural flow in his feelings while sharing, explaining, musing over subjects dear to him with a person who grew dearer to him each day. Young Yasho was Asha to him, promising both freshness and depth of beauty as she flowered, starting avidly to master English and Hindi and refining her painting skills. She said she most enjoyed two things – being with him and being unusually good at what she was learning.

Despite the vortex of Kashmir politics, Karan Singh grew as a thinker, a statesman, a humanist – and he shared happily. He was a sought-after speaker across the board at conferences – at academic, cultural and environmental fora. Yasho was familiar with what he planned on saying. She was often there with him. And many times, she was busy herself, her independent streak remaining graceful and intact.

There was clearly a collaboration and an understanding. Her painting and his music were their personal pursuits but they were shared and encouraged charmingly by the other. He pursued classical vocal music, sang well, was regular with his weekly *riyaaz*. Often she would say, listening to him from an adjacent room, '*Kya kamaal thha aaj aap ke gaane mein!* (How well you sang today!)' There was spontaneous appreciation and a fondness too, in that comment. But she did not sit facing him or intruding – it was always in the adjacent room, where she could be having her *chhọti haazri* or sipping her cup of tea. He would recount to her his early, boyish excitement over the music of the *vedas* being recited, the chants, and then the Dogri devotional songs they sang around the basil plant in Kashmir, swaying to the music of their own singing. She could picture him learning from the village folk, from his mother's ringing voice, from the swamis at the temples, from his teacher Balram Singh Rawat and from Vilayat Husain Khan of the Agra gharana.

Quaintly, the language between them was Hindi, not Dogri which was his mother tongue, nor Nepali which was hers. And throughout, they used '*aap*' or the respectful 'you' between them, as the genteel often do.

More years went by, and I began to meet Dr Karan Singh regularly because he was the Chairman of the Rumi Foundation of which I was a founder member. At each meeting of the Foundation, and they happened very frequently and always at his home, Yashoji was extraordinary. For matters close to his heart, he would not name a formal meeting room, but his informal study, where her dropping by to say hello was an expected bonus.

She greeted and talked and smilingly ensured that you were served and well fed each time, making certain that her menu was never repeated (how did she remember?), exquisitely served and re-served because all too often, you could not resist that second helping anyway. The warmth was hers, the tea as each one liked it. And then the floor was his. As you got into the thick of debate for those two or three hours, you hoped she would reappear. Because you did want to comment, question, compliment her on her panoply of new temptations that wooed you so unobtrusively each time there was cause for a meeting.

Another striking thing she had about her, which was her very own, were her looks. In her fifties, when I first met her she bade your eyes to stay on her. Very often there is an expectation that a royal daughter would have an air about her, features that are striking, a mien that is distinct, a grace that is natural rather than practised. And yet, we know too well that many escape these natural endowments.

In Yasho Rajya Lakshmi of Nepal and later Kashmir, this was unmistakable – without obtruding or trying. You noticed it afresh each time. It became clear that in some unspoken way, it was the way of the house, that this man had made up his mind on this subject through the years and years of being Yuvraj: that he was and is used to pulchritude and causes it to surround him.

What follows is a story relating to this aspect of Yashoji and one which has an ironic twist. When I was looking for a successor to Maharani Gayatri Devi of Jaipur for her long-standing endorsement of the rather splendid solitaire line of diamonds that the De Beers Diamond Company presented to the world as their flagship offer, no one else in the array of erstwhile royalty seemed right.

Between travel every week to Mumbai and a city-hopping schedule, I managed to bring up the request of the De Beers endorsement with Mrs Karan Singh at a dinner party in Delhi. The idea amused her at some level, while making her a little tentative. She seemed curious, willing and maybe even flattered as she said, 'If you think so, it must be a good idea. Let's talk, you must tell me more!' I knew that the reference of Maharani Gayatri Devi having done the first campaign helped give it a cache, supported its legitimacy.

'I'll ensure the half-hour film is suitably elegant! But please do check with Dr Karan Singh before I commit you in any way to De Beers or to a solitaire!' At this, her eyes twinkled. 'I'm quite sure you wouldn't suggest anything he'll disapprove of! Please come home, we'll ask him together.'

Oddly enough, I was the one who desisted. I dropped the subject for a very cogent reason that developed within weeks of our conversation. It was just then that Dr Karan Singh was being considered and mooted as the next President of India.

Dr Kalam's stint in the Rashtrapati Bhavan was over. The reasons to back the veteran parliamentarian from Kashmir were legion. The public and the cognoscenti concurred heartily on this choice. The man can think – more, he can reflect. He had held office as ruler and servant of the State. As scholar and politician, he can speak rivetingly. He has shone as our US ambassador representing India, its history, explicating the *shlokas*, reciting from Milton, Saadi, Iqbal. He knows India's ancients deeply – he is modern without being young. A living example of a religious Hindu, he is broadened by his religiosity, not narrowed by it. He remains a philosopher and a man of the world. He would add just the gravitas and the grandeur the post deserved.

I certainly wanted no disqualifier, however remote. It seemed entirely inappropriate, almost tactless, to arrange for Yasho Rajya Lakshmi to patronize solitaires for an international diamond merchant, as she readied to be the First Lady of the country. This speculation and buzz went on for weeks but didn't go through. I still felt relieved, I hadn't chanced anything.

When I interviewed the man who had not become President for the very first issue of the journal *HU The Sufi Way*, I was pleasantly surprised by his easeful familiarity with poetry of all kinds – lyrical, romantic, epic, religious: in English, Urdu, Hindi, Sanskrit. I could not explain the total and prompt recall, his readiness with the right quote, the instant cross-reference. I could only envy it. No student of elocution could compete with his flow of Shelley, Ghalib, Milton, Kabir, of the

Upanishads – not just a line or two but an entire poem. Once, at a book launch, I suggested, almost lightheartedly, while he was still speaking, how aptly Sri Aurobindo's poem *Who* would fit the moment. He actually recited it. Right there and then, with no recourse to book or paper. The entire poem of two and a half pages. In quoting anything, you and I stop triumphantly after our two favourite lines, desperately searching our heads for the third. Watching Karan Singh's memory take off and never stop or miss a word leaves you plain awestruck, envious.

It made me wonder too whether he courted his Asha this way. For he certainly always had the presence of mind to stir and strew a conversation with lines and stanzas from this language and that. With her he would have the presence of heart too. Do not forget that he found her at age thirteen, when his own nineteen-year-old adolescence would have been even more irrepressible. He certainly had the urge and the ability to share what she was yet unexposed to in the world – and indeed as much in the world of books.

As he grew older, with education in worldly affairs, in intricate matters of state, in the quandary and the torment of watching his father being deposed, in replacing his father unwillingly when he was appointed regent, young Yasho must have been there by his side and listening, commiserating. For challenges did not seem to desert Karan Singh, nor did they come to him in ones and twos.

Though she avoided all limelight, her days seemed always full. Setting up and supervising a fine Institute for the Mentally Handicapped in Okhla which she then re-christened 'School for Special Children'. Here, she had an active board taking the facility steadily forward, expanding their skills, arranging a steady sale of handcrafted items they could produce, adding to these, holding fetes at festivals, keeping in regular and caring touch with their families. Letters of spontaneous gratitude from parents for changing their lives as much as those of their children enabled her to keep each one involved, highly motivated. Keeping up a personal equation with each one of the staff and students, artisans and facilitators seemed to come to her effortlessly. As indeed her graciousness as hostess. Her husband so enjoyed watching her flourish among her own friends, organizing weekly games of bridge, making their home a place where family and friends felt welcome, remembering birthdays and anniversaries, choosing presents with care – and laughing every now and then over a lore of anecdotes. Yashodhara was an anchor whose aura he cherished – just as others who reached out to her did.

Let us begin at the beginning. The beginning that shaped the man who shaped her.

A baby boy is born to the Maharaja of Kashmir and his Maharani Tara Devi at the Hotel Martinez at Cannes in the South of France on 9 March 1931. He is their only child, a very prized baby. His father had tried through three earlier marriages for a child – and not succeeded. For his father, being an only child, the only way of not losing Kashmir to the British through the Doctrine of Lapse, was to keep, protect and nurture his heir.

Maharaja Hari Singh, by sailing with his consort all the way to another continent had ensured a safe, unencumbered birth in a haven where neither local nor British intrigue could interfere with it. So it had to be in the seclusion and comfort of three contiguous suites of the Hotel Martinez, overlooking the glistening Mediterranean. Attending to delayed labour pain complications were Dr J.H. Hugo, the Maharaja's personal physician and the sought-after obstetrician Sir Henry Simson, who proclaimed on the 9th of March 1931 that the anxiously awaited male heir – a vigorous nine-pounder – had arrived into the world. When the news reached home, a three-day public holiday was declared as celebration while shooting and fishing was also called to a halt for those three days. Every child near and far received sweets, and prayers were offered for the prince's long and healthy life.

Shree Yuvaraj Karan Singhji Bahadur was the name declared for the newborn as a plethora of familial and formal post-birth ceremonies were conducted. With all the care, prayers and good wishes, the routine was severe, almost unkind. From age three the prince's establishment was his own. And it was a palace. He was assigned precisely one hour a day as time to be spent with his mother in a different mansion altogether; his father he could see but thrice a week, and in yet another palace. Would this make him a cold and aloof man growing up, enveloped in his own life and ego? Would it make him react and seek company, warmth and recompense, making up for lost time? Was the psychological strain of this solitary schedule even considered? What seemed to rescue this young boy was a gifted imagination – it was his succour, being curious and inquiring and thoughtful, never bitter.

His first recalled visual memory is of a black eagle vanishing from sight as he watched it fly from a window in Srinagar's Amar Mahal. A grand swoosh of nature as it were, right before his eyes for which most things as yet were new. Thereafter, what dwelt in his mind as another very early memory was the image of his own face looking back at him, in the bathroom mirror in the same palace. He was coming to recognize himself, as it were.

Snippets of his childhood that remained with him may have left a subliminal residue. Like he says, 'I was standing in a room when Mahatma Gandhi came in. He walked up to me and put his left hand on my shoulder and took my right palm in his other hand for a moment and said quietly, "You are going to be a very wise man".'

He remembers a series of guardians and private tutors, ones that were around for many years. Also, his two companions, sons of the Maharaja's Rajput officers, Digbi and Bilti, who even accompanied him to Cathedral John Connon's School in Bombay for a year or so. His father had made Bombay his second home. Then came Doon School, where the food, the schedules, the sheer monotony of discipline were a shock to begin with and plain tiresome as terms and years went on. The dorms too were decidedly uncomfortable. But the school inculcated a clarity of thought, common sense and a spirit of self-reliance, with no resort to class or creed, which stood young Karan in good stead. This prince too had to have his bout of toughening, like every other Dosco.

A nagging trial surfaced around this time. A pain in the hip which was acute and mild in turns, a puzzling problem that mystified doctors. It resulted in solitude, which made time for reading and reflection, but none for the camaraderie on the sports grounds, the regular Himalayan treks or the rougher field games. Very often the swimming, tennis and riding too came and went. This could not continue. For long periods, the boy in him feared and the man in him overcame.

Despite much attendance, there was no family beside him through hospitals, tests, procedures and surgeries, to say it was all going to be all right. Repeated operations, excruciating pain, and perhaps worst of all, uncertainty. Uncertainty of every kind in terms of recovery, fitness and the ability to live without a crippling handicap in one or both legs. International consultations were advised.

In the meanwhile, Kashmir had been ravaged relentlessly post-Independence and the Maharaja had to be rushed away to Jammu, only to say upon reaching safely, 'We have lost Kashmir.'

But his heir Karan Singh's treatment could not be delayed. On New Year's Eve of 1947, he arrived in New York, bound to his wheelchair, attended on by his friend Ranjit. To greet a freezing 1948 in a New York hospital, with the American hospital staff tucking him swiftly into the room and bed assigned to him, readying to break into Auld Lang Syne.

The repeated procedures, the attendant pain and anxiety eventually achieved a bone graft and the insertion of a several-inch pin which would save his hip and get him back on his feet. Slowly and quite miraculously, it all came right in the end. The doctors in New York and Bombay could not avoid the procrastinated suspense for the young man, but they were eventually able to make him an 'upright, ready-witted swimmer and tennis player'. After nearly fourteen months, Karan Singh returned home only to face other curious challenges. His father received him in the car and not at the airport on account of an assassination threat.

The Yuvraj discovered that his engagement to Princess Shanti of Ratlam had been mysteriously called off. Indeed, he is soon to meet in Delhi, en route to Jammu, a Nepali princess, granddaughter of the Rana Prime Minister of Nepal.

Karan Singh now found himself torn between an imperialist father and a burgeoning democrat, Jawaharlal Nehru, whose books and persona he had grown up admiring immensely.

With the political climate getting distinctly murkier, he hoped the personal front would provide a touch of brightness.

Not yet a teenager, Yasho was most unusually pretty as she sat between her parents and was introduced to him over the lunch in Faridkot House. She seemed composed and happy to be there in the little she spoke. When the meal and conversation (mostly between the two mothers) was over, the answer from Karan Singh was in the affirmative. He would marry her. Yasho may not have been asked for her assent at all. Which probably made the groom eager to prove to them both that she had made the right choice. He considered himself very lucky in her quiet affirmation which made his task a lot easier.

But the course was not going to be that smooth or simple. On a casual *chakor* shoot in Khrew near Srinagar at a time when bird was legitimate game, something else overtook the prospective groom. Unexpected rain caused a truck to skid right into the car trying to avoid it, leaving the Prince's left leg fractured and the hip out of joint. And after weeks of being in plaster and in pain with blisters, surgery with a metal strip with six screws came to the rescue to restore both the left leg and the hip. But that too passed.

The wedding *mahurat* of 15 January was moved to 5 March. Since he may not have been able to stand the strain of the ceremonies and celebrations in Kathmandu or Jammu or Kashmir, Bombay it just had to be: between his father's home on 19 Nepean Road and the Kutch House, on the adjacent Nepean Sea Road where the royal Nepal contingent was housed. Each detail was prepared for meticulously by his father in Bombay, with the full intricacy and ceremony of Rajput tradition. Both the Dogra prince and the Nepali royalty had antecedents they could trace back to Rajputana beginnings, after all.

A few weeks before the wedding, thanks to the *chakor* mishap, Karan Singh was on a wheelchair and resting a little between meals. But at the *mandap* he was elegance itself in the regalia that a Yuvraj of Kashmir marrying a beauteous princess of Nepal would be expected to have. Mercifully, his royal sword served well as his walking stick, perhaps adding to his dash as bridegroom.

Typical of his sense of fun, he reports in his biography that during their *phera*s, his shy but elated Asha was racing ahead and he could hardly keep up, swinging his sword to the floor at every step to keep her pace. Eventually Maharaja Hari Singh, his father, arose to whisper into the bride's ear that it would be better if she slowed down to a coyer pace.

Dr Karan Singh can, to this day, describe vividly all that happened: the Packard in which they drove with his father to Kutch Castle, the clothes he wore and the ones his bride was snowed under, the palanquins and the bedecked maidens, the rows of attendants and the *milni* ceremony between the two fathers … a picturesque and lifelike account, with wit thrown in to embellish the details. On reaching their appointed bridal room at two in the morning, they pledged as near strangers to make a life together – he a much rewarded and punished man, she a babe in the woods.

Also typical of his regard, one of the first calls he made when he took his new bride to Delhi was on the severely ailing Sardar Vallabh Bhai Patel. During those years, Hari Singh of Kashmir had often turned to Patel in despair over the brusque nexus that Sheikh Abdullah and Nehru presented to him. Indeed, it was Patel who had suggested the Princess Yasho of

Nepal for his son, Yuvraj Karan of Kashmir. Patel would lend more than a sympathetic ear to the Maharaja, and Karan Singh thought it only right, even imperative, to thank him and ask after his welfare.

Without respite or honeymoon, the pair was then thrown into the thick of intrigue where Sheikh Abdullah was all set to democratize Kashmir with the help of Pandit Jawaharlal Nehru. In their conviction and their zest, these two men were bent on leaving the Maharaja estranged, with fewer ways to relate to his people, even less to exercise his rights as ruler or express his concern for the Dogra community, which was receding to the margins in the new scheme of things.

In the midst of all this, the Yuvraj held the promise of being the new young leader of the region, inspired by Nehru's vision of a modern, democratic, unfettered, young India. As a convalescent, this young man had read Nehru's autobiography and was already smitten. The next bout of enforced rest, and he had consumed *Discovery of India* by the same inspired author – his admiration would not be, could not be smothered by anything. It was a sure-fire beacon: Karan Singh believed this man was going to show the way, and India would listen. Very likely, the world would listen too.

So, when the time came, at the crossroads of giving up the *gaddi,* the throne, the court, the state and girding his loins for the job in hand, the path to the Yuvraj seemed limpidly clear. But not easy, far from easy.

Karan Singh must have been gnawed by what he needed to do and what he was expected to do. In the end, he had to scan all choices conscientiously without being able to exercise any except one – and that was not the filial one.

The choice was of outgrowing his feudal beginnings,

responding to the nationalist surge in the air. Jawaharlal Nehru or Panditji, as he was known, made sure that this young admirer was at hand, sending notes from time to time addressed to 'Tiger' (Karan Singh's early pet name favoured by his father and by Nehru – conferred on him as an infant by Raja Umaid Singh seeing him toddle on all fours while they confabulated!) Notes urging the vibrant young Tiger to be that new Indian that India needed. Nehru was in no mood for niceties with old-timers wishful of stagnating in the past. In young Karan, he sensed a ready answer. He also felt confident that the eager gent will manage his family prestige and his father's feelings with the panache that his upbringing would have given him.

Thus estranged from his imposing parent, never allowed enough time with his robustly emotional mother, Karan Singh was ready for a fullness of love he had not ever known or had. Something and someone he could call his very own, no questions asked. It was a natural, unequivocal turn to his Asha, Yasho to everyone else. He recalls in some detail several highly tense political situations coping with Sheikh Abdullah on the one hand, the Jammu phalanx of politicians on the other and the growing impatience of the Indian leaders in Delhi on the third. He remembers to this day returning home post a crisis, rushing up the steps to reach her at 4 o'clock in the morning in sheer relief. She would be up and waiting.

One has the ear or the shoulder of a good friend, but of a partner such as this, one has the whole being. She had become an untold comfort to a young husband who had grown up in the beleaguered world he had. She had grown up too.

The nuggets of this intensity at crucial moments in their lives are best said in his own words: Of his wedding night, he talks of how celebrities of Bombay gathered and champagne flowed, remarking that it was just as well that Morarji Desai was unable to come, which may have been, for his own sobriety, a blessing in disguise. 'When we finally got into our room it was past 2 o'clock in the morning. After we had taken all of our jewels and our brocades off we realized that we were in fact very young strangers. And thus it is that we became man and wife.'

Appointed Sadr-i-Riyasat on 15 November 1951, he realized that signing the acceptance of being Head of State was fraught with much more than joy or celebration. 'On the night of the 16th, Asha and I sat up into the small hours of the morning. I knew I had irrevocably severed my links with the feudal system; also that however cordial our relations would be on the surface, my father would not forgive me for accepting this offer. The die was cast and I would move on to a fresh stage of my life and destiny.'

His fifteen-year-old wife in their marriage of two years realized that this was quite a juncture for them. They would cope together, no other way. As indeed again, just two years later, on 8 August 1953, when mounting pressure and disarray forced him to a dramatic but necessary decision: to dismiss the formidable Sheikh Abdullah and his entire cabinet and very surely risk inviting his shock as much as his ferocity: 'I knew what I had done was for the national good, that all the danger, the risks were worth taking if it served the country. Asha too sat up all night. Slowly I climbed up the steps. "It is over," I said and we both smiled. She sixteen, going on seventeen. I twenty-two going on twenty-three. I was asleep almost before I hit the bed.'

They would always turn to each other and to music, they both said. Making one wonder what he sang to her when their hearts were light – and when they were not? Because singing came and comes all too naturally to him – and poetry undeterred and effortlessly. After all, he does not miss or forget a single word, whether reciting or singing.

Apart from enjoying this privately, Asha glowed when at parties this flair in him came to the fore, citing the appropriate phrase, the stanza, the *dhun*. Whether he looked across at her or not, he knew that she was 'glistening with pride', as he puts it. He grew to sense what she felt most times because she was not one to make her feelings obvious. This was not shyness. The upbringing in Nepal asked its daughters to display immense restraint. 'Girls were not to show emotion, they were not to ever cry,' she told him once. He held these glimpses into her life dear over their fifty years together. This may have been a relief ... men do find tears their curious undoing.

He certainly relished the appreciation, even applause that his partner triggered spontaneously, everywhere they went, through all their years together – often, he is only too happy to quote it. Very fondly, he retains a letter of Indira Gandhi's which aptly says: 'I enjoyed my tea with you and your very beautiful wife. The word beauty is used often and far too casually but she really has a quality for which there is no other word.'

The six years they had to themselves had also stirred the hope and expectation of an heir. Their first-born being a healthful baby girl delighted the parents, having had six years entirely unto themselves. Indeed, since a girl child came to this family almost after a century, the feminist in him came to the fore; he celebrated very especially indeed, particularly on noticing that his parents were a shade disappointed. Six years after the romping Jyoti came Vikramaditya to much hurrahs and wide celebrations – and then reassuringly the youngest,

Ajatshatru. Both parents and the Dogra line could not ask for more.

Inevitably, all of their years shared together meant that Yasho was different things to him at different times. They were teased that he was the sage Yagnavalkya to his eager consort Maitreyi sharing his mind and thoughts, his knowledge and its riches. He would instantly protest: 'But she, with her name itself, gave me everything: Yashya, Rajya, Lakshmi, no other husband can claim that!'

Life gave the Singhs a very belated but cherished honeymoon, which they extended, taking in Turkey and Egypt alongside Europe and which they often talked of with quiet glee.

Then in 1954 came a quiet voyage of learning and being uplifted when he took her to his discovery of India and all its sacred places. His Asha was wide-eyed and receptive as he found new shrines, new sages, new regions and their lore, which he had managed to keenly explore. Not as a seasoned statesman but as an avid and awakened pilgrim and her partner.

Sri Krishnaprem was a Cambridge graduate and British fighter pilot Ronald Nixon turned a staunch disciple of Yashoda Mai. Having long mastered Sanskrit and Pali, taken to *sanyas* in Benaras, thereafter Almora, he had established a temple to Sri Krishna in Mirtola. Here, talking sagely of the Upanishads, singing melodious bhajans along with Sri Madhav Ashish, another Englishman turned sadhu, they were able to help, heal and awaken the Kashmiri prince to an inner sense of self as he coped with his variegated life. Happily familiar with Sanskrit, thanks to his guru Pandit Parmanand, Karan Singh felt both restored and inspired. This haven and its riveting inhabitants he had to share with his Asha – and he did.

There was something else that they would both converge on with equal zest. Wherever and whenever he discovered rare and inspired persons among women, he would strike a rapport with them along with Asha. Testimony to this is his elegant volume called *Meetings with Remarkable Women*, a book which he warns you contains nothing enticing – or salacious or scandalous or even untoward or exciting. In it you will find Durgabai Deshmukh as well as Princess Niloufer, M.S. Subbalakshmi, Queen Fabiola and Helen Keller, Gayatri Devi and Eleanor Roosevelt, Kathleen Raine and Nadine Gordimer. The very first profile is of his mother Maharani Tara Devi, very revealing of his sensitivity and his devotion to a quiet, pioneering parent.

He opens the volume with a classic medallion which encloses a stunning recent portrait of his Asha and a dedication that reads:

To my life companion Asha who was the
most remarkable woman I ever met.
May your journey towards the light be auspicious.

Reading or listening to his recurrent admiration for his mother, you knew Karan Singh was a confirmed feminist. She was not born a princess but was outstanding in that role, in her appeal and her concern for her people. With almost childish glee, the son would report that her Crown of India award from the British for her service through the War Aid Committee was ahead of his father's in the protocol of awards. He would also take genuine pride in the fact that she would include a Harijan girl in the *Navratras* dance, setting a very distinct example as the Maharani. Young Karan's inherited legacy from her was the instinctive call to prayer that he worked on with seriousness, mostly without her. Focused prayer was and is always the sage start to his day, daily meditation seeking that oneness with Brahma 'as the arrow to the target'. The Mandaka Upanishad, a text particularly sacred to him, also celebrates the national motto of his country in two abiding words from the same text: *Satyameva Jayate:* Truth Alone Triumphs.

On the other hand, his bond with his father, the Maharajah of Kashmir, was a duty-bound relationship, laced at all times with correctness. Of touching feet on greeting and bidding goodbye, of writing affectionate but formal letters every fortnight or so, of heeding his requests for holidays in Bombay each winter, of walking around the race course at Mahalakshmi where he fostered and indulged his love for horses and racing. Karan Singh could never quite change that though he chafed at this imperfection. The clasp of the father-son connection never deep, was fated to remain perfunctory.

It was Asha, no one else, who had broken the barrier and built an attachment that was real, warm and human with her father-in-law. In fact, very often, his father's many gestures made it plain that he connected with his *bahurani* more readily than with his son.

What did not necessarily restore the balance but made amends was something else. Karan Singh's mother, Maharani Tara Devi, doted unconditionally on her son – and she was distinctly less indulgent with his partner. With this Yasho coped sagely through the years and had the grace to be exemplary in her devotion to her mother-in-law when the Rani was widowed, ill and incapacitated with a stroke. She cared for the now helpless parent as if she were her own, with a tenderness that put all past tensions well behind her. It was Asha who was by his mother's bedside in her last moments, Karan Singh remembers, while he was duty-bound as Minister of Tourism in Kovalam, Kerala, unable to get away. His one consolation remained that he could not have improved on his wife's very gentle, patient attention to his mother's every need.

Time and again, Asha's love surfaced in unaccustomed ways as it trod a pilgrimage of five decades. As it did when they interrupted their third trip to Europe, hearing of his father's death, flying back from Italy to find him gone, cremated.

The Nepal princess, taught never to cry except to herself, burst into copious, uncontrollable tears. Perhaps it was the first time when Asha's grief quite overcame her. While her husband, the only son, much saddened though he was, managed every detail of the mourning, the ceremony, the reverence, the rituals – precisely and with great care.

Today, from where she is, watching him must be a special solace: sought out as always for counsel on matters parliamentary or political, religious and secular, providing more than experience – wisdom; rigorous as always in devoting himself to yoga and puja at the crack of dawn; retaining his ability to see the humour even in life's grim setbacks; being now for their children the spiritual resort he always was for her.

And she has not receded from his attention either. Dr Karan Singh has added a lead crystal *shaligram* crafted in Germany to their family temple in Jammu which has 125,000 stones, brought bathed from the clear waters of sacred streams. Here is where Karan Singh wishes placed some part of his own ashes and of his Asha's: united when gone, into an eternity they can call their own. For more years than a mere sixty.

———

A man is born into a hallowed groove, his future ordained.
Truly to the manor born, he abides by all rigours
– impeccably traditional. And then he breaks free.

Was it his father swooping him along, listening
to Bela Bartok and Ella Fitzgerald as much as to Mozart,
Bach, Beethoven? Or is it something else?

The rebel then reaches out to the world like
no other. Eighty countries he has known, sixty
he has explored, won over. He chooses none.

With nothing to clip his wings he comes home to roost.
Whatever for, you ask? Whoever for?

THE GENIUS OF A CHOICE

Shujaat & Parveen Khan

THE GENIUS OF A CHOICE

The birth of a son has long been considered a special boon almost everywhere in the world. In our country, it seems to warrant untold rejoicing, both private and public. So you can well imagine the birth of a son to the man declared widely to be a magician with the sitar, the sole inheritor of the famed Imdad Khan gharana, an ustad and a celebrity dandy. It was something else.

Four months ahead of the event, from February onwards, Vilayat Khan was trunk calling his close friends each month in great excitement to exclaim with rising gusto that the event was now 30 days closer.

19 May 1960 then arrived – and so did Shujaat Husain Khan. Vilayat Khan's longest standing *shagird* (disciple) and friend Arvind Parikh received a six-word jubilation: 'God has given me a son.'

While the famed sweets of Bengal reached all friends within the city of Calcutta, the historic feeding of the poor at Park Circus was also undertaken. The Park Circus Nursing Home did not shoo away the thronging crowd nor did the resident patients complain of noise or neglect.

The Khan and Hazra homes were on cloud nine. An heir had arrived to a revered musical dynasty and a medical family of repute who owned very nearly half of Hazra Road along with handpicked areas of Hastings, Malda and more.

A child must sense magic as attention comes with open arms, unconditional, 100 per cent. Shujaat had just that from his nani, the maternal grandmother. Although he was born to ceremony and rules and customs that were of the Khans, he learnt and lapped up from his grandmother tales of Bengal, its myths and rituals: what an *aarti* stood for, why a tulsi plant had good reason to be considered sacred – and everything in between. She catered patiently to his every curiosity; Mrs Hazra never held back in obliging her *khokha,* Shujaat. Monisha was grateful for the seasoned care her mother lavished on her first born – being a celebrated musician's wife kept her amply busy. Despite his relentless schedule, Khansahab could not wait for the toddler's hands to firmly hold a mini sitar, for his fingers to make lifelong friends with those strings.

Then comes Bombay, at six, for Shujaat. The sea amazes – he has a full view of it from his home in Stardust – one of the three buildings, alongside Symphony and Harmony in the Petit Hall grounds of Nepean Sea Road, Bombay. Playing, each afternoon, he watches the waves shimmer as the sun sets in the evening.

The teachers at the West Wind find the dimpled infant irresistible, his cheeks almost demanding to be pinched. What they do not realize is that running resolutely parallel to the molly-coddling pace at the Montessori, of spelling easy words, grasping simple ideas, numbers, tables, was the rigorous learning at home, strict and undisturbed in the room assigned by his father as his music room, the *shagird* sitting at the feet of the ustad. Little Shujaat has to practise what he learns till he perfects it and can call it his own, not before that – till it is bloodstreamed and turned to muscle-memory, as it were.

And so came young Shujaat's debut at age six in August of 1966, announcing his talent to the music lovers of Bombay at the Jehangir Art Gallery. A forty-minute solo concert exploring *Raag Des*, through all the movements, the *vilambit*, the *jod,* the *drut,* the works – with none less than Nizamuddin Khan Sahab accompanying him with due seriousness on the tabla. Vilayat Khan did always have a sense of drama, of spectacle. Bombay's famed Jehangir Art Gallery had requested him to envision and choreograph a show entitled 'Art and Music through the Ages', presenting the Imdad Khan gharana and its antecedents while launching its youngest exponent. Vilayat Khan was not one to do things by halves. The surround was just what ought to have been to proudly launch the seventh generation of the famed gharana.

The strains of Imdad Khan's sitar beckoned music lovers as they approached Kala Ghoda, the voices of Jaddan Bai and Abdul Karim Khan followed as they strolled around the gallery displaying rare historic belongings of all celebrated antecedents of the debutante Shujaat's *khaandaan*. Portraits of Imdad Khan, Wahid Khan, Inayat Khan in embroidered velvet robes of green, scarlet and gold worn on court occasions lined the gallery with their musical accessories, instruments, framed sketches and memorabilia, including father Vilayat Khan's first tiny sitar, had the curious quite enthralled. Names that Shujaat had learnt to revere, to listen to and absorb, seemed to be silently presiding as their newest exponent awaited their blessing.

The tabla maestros Ahmed Jan Thirakwa and Allah Rakha Khan walked in, bursting with pride in a young member of the musical community they knew would keep the flag soaring. The stage Vilayat Khan left pristine. It would be his young son's live show and a solo performance in every sense.

But the little hero now remembers little and is honest enough to say so. Those who were there tend to rave. All that Shujaat has to say is typical of the man. 'I was not nervous. You're not when you are six years old! Yes, the *raag* I played was Des, but I remember nothing more than that.' When it comes to himself, he lets others do the talking.

But soon enough, the Khans were to move away from Bombay and the bright lights. To a mountain retreat, to Simla. Vilayat Khan needed to be more with his music.

What prompted it was a summer holiday invitation from Maharaj Padamjit Singh of Kapurthala, a man wholly committed to Indian classical music. His own grandfather had rescued a scion of Tansen's family, Nasir Ali, from the British, and music had been an integral part of the family growing up.

The little cottage in the Strawberry Hill estate and the highly appreciative host and his *mehfil*s quite won over Khansahab. He returned to Simla the next summer. Bombay was hot and humid and his son's Montessori closed for summer vacations anyway. The second visit completed the seduction. Vilayat Khan retained his Bombay flat but moved to the hills, lock, stock, sitar and barrel. And Shujaat was moved to Bishop Cotton School in Simla – no way this celebrity's son would be refused admission. A day scholar he had to be, his father insisted. The boy had important work at home, before and after the school routine each day. He was the chosen one for a profession that could not be denied his unsullied devotion.

The schedule was choc-a-bloc. The learning of the sitar was merciless in its rigour. *Riyaaz* demanded hours that a child could find unreasonable. Growing up to be a classical musician, just one thing is central to your life, distractions are disallowed. No radio, no TV, no sports journals entered his home. Sports are for playing but not for ruling your life. News may be read or shared but they are not your concern. Pressures of the school are necessary but they do not come first.

Expending energy out of doors was a handy outlet the youngster welcomed: in his element on the football field or badminton court, especially because beating his sisters at any game in the courts at home was a given. As also in romping around with the four dogs Abba had named Jam and Jelly, Dinkey and Donkey in a typical burst of whimsy.

Early on, Shujaat had begun to sense a disquiet in his home: his parents disagreed with increasing frequency and the drinking did not help. He felt both puzzled and estranged. Also resentful that his father insisted on the strictest isolation and discipline away from the outside world only to reward him with this tormented sense of insecurity.

At such times, Shujaat found Simla's scenic landscapes a great escape. The changing light of the sun glinting over the mountains, the trees, the leaves. Also, the intense *riyaaz* preparing for *taaleem* with his father shut out all unpleasantness. It worked well.

'No *shagird* can capture that intensity of feeling latent in music like my firstborn will,' Khansahab was convinced. So technical skills came with the daily discipline where Shujaat's nimble fingers could neither err nor tire. But something else had to happen. Beauty that visually moves you must live and breathe in your music, stir the listener with the same intensity.

The clouds racing, playing hide and seek with the haughty peaks, the rain glistening playfully on inky leaves right outside your window.

The times they were together the supremo would never waste. Sitting huddled under quilts in cold rainy Simla, they would sip on the Bournville Hot Chocolate he had brought back from Britain. Transforming the thrill of visual beauty into affecting aural magic for the listener was an imperative, he would say, illustrating it in ways the boy could hardly ever forget, shaping his son into a sitar player of consequence.

But life does not sit still. Well known for that graceful turn at the waltz, the rumba, the fox trot at the club, his parents had now switched to a daily pattern of entertaining at home, no hours or holds barred. This distinctly upset Shujaat. The merriment had a way of ending in arguments, in quarrels that were audible, though not comprehensible, to a startled child. Seizing his sitar and shutting out all sound seemed a handy escape. His parents' divorce seemed inevitable.

Happy reprieves came in Shujaat's yearly visits to Calcutta over the Pujas – time spent with the person dearest in his life, his nani, Mrs Hazra. They related to each other in myriad ways, her affection for him was inordinate. The gentle, silver-haired Ratna from Nepal in her crisply starched white sari was his nanny, his Florence Nightingale, but it was Nani who made a man out of him. She encouraged him to introspect; he would need it, she felt, to face a challenging world sooner than most – and alone. Mrs Hazra taking her grandson on a trip with her to Europe made Shujaat explore and embrace life with aplomb, understand human behaviour, even forgive the frailties of his parents that would otherwise have embittered him. Nani explained gently and convincingly that good and bad have to coexist. 'Know that but do not be alarmed.' She taught him to accept that it is not a perfect world, that you cannot be undone by its imperfections.

Despite the growing distance between them, discovering a chip of the old block in Shujaat would leave his father both proud and chastened. As when at 6 o'clock one morning, Shujaat began to hum the notes of *Bilaskhani Todi* as his sitar followed his humming. The instrument resounded as the *raag* awakened and stirred. But the elders were still asleep, having revelled late into the night.

The boy was now a world unto himself as he built this *raag* with gravitas to greet the early morning. His eyes closed, his fingers deft, he did not notice a towering figure enter his room, stand still and silent by the window, watching him. That looming presence was Amir Khan, his father's sister's husband, a musician deeply revered by his father.

Before Shujaat could leap up with his '*Aadaab, phupha*', Amir Khan decided he would sing and share with this prodigy the Merukhand technique. Every bit of its seriousness, its intricacy – the melody developing gradually, deepening, varying at an almost cosmic pace. All this while seated on the young nephew's bed who followed each note of his uncle's singing to a tee, on his own sitar.

Unbeknownst to them, a live-in *shagird* had alerted Vilayat Khan Sahab. They both stole in and sat at a distance strumming their *tanpura*s to what turned out to be rare, peerless music. Several had quietly assembled in Shujaat's room by now. Legend has it that the session continued for a whole three hours undisturbed. Only the audience had swelled.

Throwing his young son to the wolves, seemed not to unnerve Vilayat Khan as father. Shujaat headed to the

Seychelles all on his own at fourteen, to the Shah of Iran's young musician's enclave – on a voyage of discovery of culture. Expectedly, Shujaat exceeded all expectations as both performer and exponent.

Let us not forget that at age eleven, he had accompanied his father on his tour of Berlin and other parts of Europe. And later New York. Vilayat Khan had no hesitation in treating his teenage son as a responsible organizer. On stage, he would signal him to play from time to time, as though he were a full-fledged grown musician. His confidence seemed inexplicable, even daring. Was it his eccentric technique of untethering his son, to let him know he could conquer the world on his own?

Travel had broadened Shujaat's outlook. Regular trips to Calcutta had stirred his interest in folk music, in Baul singing, in *doha*s. Now as an adolescent, his role in his father's life made demands that did not appeal to him in the least.

The bright, polite Khalifa-designate, he was quite the darling of his father's coterie of admirers: socialites, music lovers, students, hangers-on. But Shujaat found sycophants abhorrent. He felt they encouraged illusions; they caused a decline in his father's excellence as a musician and his nature as a human being. He felt helpless. There were all too many of them. And one of them he was not prepared to be.

Shujaat also sensed that alcohol had a lot to do with his father's inexcusable behaviour; more than indulgence, a weakness. He decided unequivocally that he would stay off the stuff. Mercifully, concerts would take him to Bombay, friends would persuade him to stay, to listen, to experiment. His independent ways seemed rebellious to his father who had tired of Simla and moved to the valley of Dehra Dun into a Clement Town home with several bedrooms where Shujaat's step-mother lived with them. His own mother Monisha had left in 1969 to set up home in Delhi's Pandara Road, thanks to Vilayat Khan's abiding admirers and contacts.

Besides their love for music, cars and long drives were a common passion between father and son, yielding many precious moments time and again. It would happen with a whimsy, predictable with Khansahab. The son would get a call in Calcutta from his father in Bombay suggesting they both drive up to Dehra Dun from Bombay! Shujaat would agree, board a train for Bombay, traversing the entire breadth of India. They would drive out the next afternoon and through the night via Baroda and Ahmedabad. With father very considerately suggesting comfort breaks so that the son may take a few puffs at his cigarette – the indulgence not yet damned as a health hazard.

On one such drive, just past dawn, Khansahab holds Shujaat's arm urging him to slow down, to stop and park. What looked like specks of bright colour were a throng of women, wending their way to the water. 'Notice their heads, shoulders, waists, arms, their carefree gait, their chatter, their giggles as they gossip. When returning their urns on their head, their pace has less sway, a different grace, a slower rhythm. Will your music lilt with this magic, Motu?' That nickname he fondly used for his firstborn yet again in their last concert together. When after stirring the hall with his resounding wizardry he turned to his son saying, 'Motu, now it is your turn.' As indeed repeatedly in their Carnegie Hall concert in New York, where they both had their audience amazed. Cementing his otherwise stormy relationship with his father were these vignettes you could call epiphanies.

School over, concert opportunities beckoned Shujaat to

other cities. Folk music had always attracted him, as had jazz. Driving around with a bunch of friends in Bombay, he decided they would stop by at the Taj Mahal Hotel in Bombay where the celebrated Sabri Brothers were in concert, holding agog the glitterati of Bombay. The listeners were now on a high that had nothing to do with alcohol. This phenomenon surprised him. That music other than the sublime ragas would wield this power, this stirring effect. This exposure he decided he would encourage, almost a landmark decision quietly made.

Shujaat had now decided to be independent of his father. To discover the world and rediscover himself all on his own. At seventeen, he came of age. Perhaps he wanted to establish to himself and to the world that his deep admiration would shun servility as much as sycophancy. That went against his grain. 'I resorted to being self-made so that my music got its just deserts.' In country after country, sixty at last count. All the way in Kiruna, near the Arctic Circle, with its renowned ice hotel, listeners were curious, impressed and very responsive. 'It adds variety and depth to your own compositions, sharing other age-old traditions.'

From villages near Nice, to music resorts in Mongolia, yes also Siberia, in seldom-explored parts of Japan, Indonesia, Iran, Lithuania, his music surprised and transported the listener to come back for more – and to plead for lessons, for ongoing connections. 'Between concerts and assignments in my teens, I picked oranges in groves and orchards to pay my way through the many cities.'

His absence left the stage free for young rival musicians. Since his presence could irk the imperious and estranged father, it discouraged organizers to approach Shujaat. But hearing of his father's indifferent health, Shujaat softened. He returned.

Back in India, Dehra Dun and the sprawling family home 'Surbahar' was his base. Here he would catch up with friends – and a father grateful that his prodigal son had returned, that their relationship was not entirely dislocated. Absence had certainly dimmed his wish to chide. Secretly the father even respected this independent streak.

Now, in his early twenties, Shujaat was beginning to enjoy the company of his young lawyer friend Iqbal Nigam in Dehra Dun. And even more, Iqbal's invitations home for dinner. The *Lakhnavi* touch too had an appeal. But the real reason was one he had not yet admitted, even to himself.

Iqbal's sister Parveen Nigam was about to finish her graduation at MKP College. Close to Iqbal in age and interests, she was included in their walks, their hours of watching Wimbledon or the recurrent cricket series across the world. The Nigam home becoming his relentless adda seemed natural. The *khorma* there had no equal. Each time he meant to suss out the recipe from the hostess, Nanhi Begum, but didn't. Her readiness in aptly quoting Urdu *shaayari* made her company you sought unlike the self-conscious socialites rivalling for his father's attention.

Shujaat discovered Mrs Nigam's unusually independent choices. She quietly, firmly refused the very eligible proposals pressed on her. She would marry only Ramakrishna Nigam, a man she respected and loved. Their children came soon after they were married, a boy and a girl. And as their relationship flourished, came another boy and girl, Iqbal and Parveen. Now Nanhi Begum worried about her children's education in Delhi with their father constantly on the move.

She chose Dehra Dun for its schools but would not abdicate her charges to boarding schools. It was decided that

Nigam Sahab would set up a home for his family in Dehra Dun, be in and out regularly himself – retaining his Delhi home to ensure work did not suffer. So home is where Parveen grew up, studying at the Convent of Jesus & Mary.

Relegated to his nani and to his Nepali nanny, Shujaat was quite unfamiliar with Nanhi Begum's way of playing multiple roles, being there for each child, finding ways to open up the world for them. Young Khan was grateful that he was not discouraged or cold-shouldered for landing up rather unfailingly at their establishment ever so frequently.

Concerts would take him away – but just for a bit. *Shagird*s too needed attention outside Dehra Dun. He needed both: an income and his independence. But getting back to Dehra Dun as often as possible became a priority.

Snatching time at the Nigams became a must – watching a new film, driving out to devour the delicacies at the local Sardarji Dhaaba, even chasing a view, a sunset, parking the car, playing pop or jazz, chatting endlessly. Being together was reason enough. At least for Shujaat and Parveen. It all seemed complete in the simplest pleasure.

The girl who had won him over was not ordinary. He had met many women and dated several, his unselfconscious confidence making him strike a chord all too easily. There was more to her than just prettiness. Parveen's eyes were not just limpid, they were hazel. A shade rare and soft. Not green or blue, but a shade even rarer – hazel. Shujaat was quite taken.

He also noticed that his father was happy to facilitate this acquaintance, encourage it.

Now Shujaat was going to take no chances. His incessant travel delayed his settling down, yet he knew he could not afford to wait. The *rishta*s for Parveen's hand in marriage were not just a few. Waiting was foolhardy, the girl he sought was very sought after, Dehra Dun's belle of the ball she was. All the more because she was not too approachable.

Vilayat Khan was only too pleased to officially represent his son, take the *paigham* or marriage proposal to the Nigams.

Nanhi Begum was in Delhi for urgent work, expecting Parveen and her grandson to join her. Ustad Vilayat Khan suggested enabling the formal proposal in Delhi from where he and Shujaat would head for Bombay. And since they were motoring down, they would bring Parveen and the nephew with them from Dehra Dun and deposit them duly in Delhi.

Expecting to leave at dawn, Parveen and nephew were invited to Surbahar, all packed and ready, the night before. The evening was full of camaraderie with games, story-telling and feasting. The next day, they were all up and packed and set to go. Vilayat Khan declared that the over-festive evening demanded a rest, that the trip be postponed by a day. Parveen was puzzled. Once again the next day, with the cars all loaded up, the maestro prevaricated with another excuse. The little nephew clapped, he was lapping up the company. Parveen fidgeted – her mother would panic, even disapprove.

While being his whimsical, contrary self, the old man was being a romantic. He wanted the kids to spend time unchaperoned. The excitement of it being unofficial was quite another joy, he knew that well. But Parveen ensured her panic prevailed and reached Delhi the same day with her nephew, Shujaat and the family entourage. All was more than well when Shujaat's father arrived in the capital the next day. He then proceeded with the chastest elegance to present his son's suit, leaving his hostess quite overcome with his immaculate fluency and regard for form. Declaring it both honour and pleasure, she assured him of the formal acceptance after consulting the family. Crucial mission accomplished, father and son proceeded to Bombay as planned, billeted to stay at a favourite *shagird*'s home.

Shujaat recalls amusedly the suspense of awaiting the Nigams' letter of acceptance in Bombay. It had not arrived. And did not for a week. Or so it seemed until the envelope addressed to Vilayat Khan was discovered lying innocently among other letters in the lobby drawer of their Bombay hosts. Shujaat was now persuaded to open it since Khansahab would be returning late at night. Only to discover it was in beautifully handwritten Urdu script, which he could not read! He then drove straight to a *maulvi sahab* to read out the gracious contents. All was forgiven, as they say. Everyone sat up waiting for Khansahab to read the fulsome message out loud for all to hear, before calling Nanhi Begum to happily confirm its contents. Typically, Vilayat Khan now insisted that the young couple be handed the phones to share their jubilation, they being the heroes of this story.

Parveen laughs heartily today at recalling how no other phone conversation could ever be as stilted or inane as the one the two of them mustered over that Bombay-Dehra Dun trunk call, silently urging the operator to declare time was up.

When they returned to Dehra Dun, Mrs Nigam came to call at Surbahar. She now wanted to know the next steps, the preparations for the marriage, the arrangements. Khansahab was very lucid. He did not see why the marriage needed to be prepared for or delayed. He requested that Nanhi Begum walk around the house with him to discover how his family planned to welcome Parveen, showing her the suite of rooms in the house intended for the couple. Any shortcomings she felt needed to be made up for, he would, he said. And left it at that.

The 29th of March of that very year was settled as the wedding date and Shujaat was requested to stay away from Parveen one whole week ahead of that date. A couple to wed should observe this sabbatical. No big deal, he is assured, just that one week. Shujaat decided to brave it one evening claiming he needed her foot size – an essential for the Khans to proceed with the outfit being readied for their nuptials. So an exception was made.

A couple of days later, he showed up to measure her for the burqas to be ordered for her. Parveen hit the roof. 'I've never seen your sisters wear a burqa, forget it.'

'But the rules for the *bahus* of the family are different,' he insisted at which point Parveen burst into tears – and everyone else into laughter. No Indian wedding is complete without the absurdly elaborate practical jokes, the teasing, the misunderstandings, the making up. And all of it did happen.

Dehra Dun had not quite seen a wedding so elaborate in detail. The guests were invited and expected to be part of it all – the *mehndi,* the *nikaah,* the *jalwa,* the *valima.* Each day had music and song of a high order. The famous qawwal, Nazeer Niyazi, sang all night the day after the wedding. Shujaat's two sisters were in their element. The *valima* or the bridegroom's big party is always the finale and the Khans did it in style. Parveen looked like a vision in the intricately embroidered gorgeous pink *sharara* (flared pants), ordered and flown in from a Bombay boutique, with a pale pink dupatta, apart from the exquisite *ghunghat,* the veil of shyness that adorns the Indian *dulhan* (bride) throughout, her face only shown for a blessing or for the clicking of camera to commemorate the event. The esteem in which these two families were held in the city of Dehra Dun, to which neither actually belonged, filled the air.

After most weddings of that scale, exhaustion sets in and demands rest. But what followed was neither planned or predicted. When Shujaat and Parveen let it be known that they were considering a short getaway to Chail, Khansahab's eyes brightened. 'Aah, good idea,' he said. 'Maharajah Patiala's palace is now quite a hotel in Chail, why don't we all go. Let's pile into our cars and be together, make a week-long picnic of it.' And that is exactly what they did.

'I was convinced the palace was haunted,' Parveen laughs. She confesses sheepishly that she insisted Shujaat keep guard when she used their grandiose bathroom, leaving the door ajar. 'After sunset, the long corridors were petrifying – with shadows like looming ancestral ghosts. Parveen and Yaman, Shujaat's sister, had their husbands drag mattresses into the bridal suite for all four of them, well-fortified against spectral visitation.

An unusual honeymoon, to say the least. Complete with them all driving up to the highest point in Chail to see all of Simla spread out before their eyes, Shujaat's practised eye picking out all the spots he knew well, having spent more than a decade of his young life there.

When they came back once again to Doon, the family settled the newly married couple in their suite at Surbahar, carefully seeing to all details. Parveen felt truly chosen. Vilayat Khan wanted at least one item at every meal to be cooked by Parveen. And at every meal, her head demurely covered, she had to be there, starting with the morning cup of tea, the *chhota haazri* and then *naashta,* she was the queen pin. Shujaat and Parveen had to be on either side of him at table at all mealtimes, the compliments, the conversation, the smiles, the anecdotes flowed best only then. But this was in some sense too good to be true.

The rest of the family felt not just neglected but also displaced, even jettisoned. What followed was decidedly, noticeably unpleasant. The general insecurity of the others in the family had prompted sneaky complaints that distinctly upset the Ustad. He distanced himself, appearing to have turned against the young couple. The attendant pettiness of it all Shujaat found unacceptable. When Parveen left for the nursing home to have her first-born, Fiza, Shujaat had decided that he would spare his wife and child all the prevailing tension. He moved out.

This was quite a juncture for the young man, a strange crossroads. Going abroad to earn through his music was one option, remaining in Bombay and wooing work was another, joining the tea plantation estates in Assam in the North East also seemed cogent. The Hazras, his maternal family, pressed him to move to 9, Chapel Road, Calcutta, cared for and cosseted in their family home while just keeping an eye on their clinics strewn over Calcutta.

A fourth alternative now presented itself. Shujaat's mother, Monisha Hazra Khan, was living in Pandara Road in a commodious government flat allotted to her ex-husband. *She* felt her firstborn should refuse all other options. 'Stay with me in Delhi and pursue your music, not become a company *boxwallah* or a landlord. Certainly not, my little granddaughter must be with me here,' she said. They stayed. It was not easy.

Shujaat was often in and out, having to make quick trips for concerts. The more he was exposed to Bombay, the less he liked the idea of settling there. The film and art world seemed hopelessly commercial, the relationships driven by money, mere appearances, often drugs, dissipation. The young sitarist decided he would visit the city to perform, but avoid settling there.

Parveen had not bargained for this. Things see-sawed, seemed always in flux. But one thing held it all together for her: the bond between them did not dither in the least despite the uncertainties. Shujaat and Parveen had a way of finding oases, of being together, making up for all the lost time. He took on a two-month assignment in Britain and basing himself in Birmingham, where he had several *shagird*s, he took her with him. And he surrounded Parveen with all the things she enjoyed.

Parveen recalls the happiest times as their rented apartment buzzed with pals and *shagird*s taking turns running chores, chatting, setting up programmes. Pauline, the English wife of a close friend of Shujaat's, would personally make for Fiza the daintiest baby dresses, even a three-tiered cake for her birthday. Parveen remembers each unexpected kindness. When it was time to head back to Delhi, saying goodbye to Pauline was quite a wrench.

When figuring out where they should locate themselves to manage students, concerts, tours, something precipitate occurred. Shujaat happened to meet Mr Varadrajan, Secretary Culture with the Central Government who was puzzled at his decision. 'Why would you settle abroad! You already have a following here, you cannot quit.' A few months later, while Shujaat was on a concert tour abroad, a set of keys was officially sent to the young Ustad's wife: to see the flat in the Asian Games Village from the quota set aside for outstanding artists in different fields. This very timely gesture was not lost on the musician. The young Khans heaved a sigh of relief. Delhi was not exactly brimming over with opportunities for young musicians at that time but based there, they would remain connected with all of India and not far from Parveen's family in Dehra Dun.

With Fiza to take care of and Shujaat committed to concerts abroad, this closeness to home was a boon. Her mother was the pillar she needed. 'I knew I could send her an SOS. It was all so new to me. I did not know whether bananas were bought in dozens or kilos, I had no clue. Nor of Delhi and its roads – what was where, its shops, its facilities. And don't forget, managing my baby was new to me!'

There was little time to pine or languish in self-pity, missing each other.

Shujaat's next trip to America was to take up a teaching assignment at the University of Washington in Seattle, entailing a focus on the theory and practice of music, quite a prized post. But it also meant months away from home and a sparkling new wife he had only recently wooed and wedded. Her setting up home alone and having to play single parent was certainly not part of his plan. Nor was it his way to negotiate advantage from either parent – or the many devoted pupils. But this *sharaafat* (decency) of neither expecting nor demanding favour made many feel drawn and committed to them as a couple.

Neil and Urmila Dongre, friends of Monisha in Delhi, found this young couple delightfully refreshing: full of grace, unspoilt by adulation. Neil promptly announced he was going to call Parveen *Chhoti Begum*. Completely amazed that Shujaat could not swing a phone for his home, unable to afford the speed money, Neil stepped in. 'I'll accept repayment only one way, just hand me the fees of your first solo concert,' he said. The next time the subject was half-jokingly, half-seriously raised again, Shujaat's fees had risen to three lakhs of rupees. And Neil Dongre promptly declared he was not going to rise to that bait, wait instead till he charged no less than Rs 5 lakhs. Best of all, the Dongres felt like local guardians for the young maestro's family, something their friend Monisha's son Shujaat, valued immensely.

The phone was an absolute necessity with Shujaat's work insisting on consistent travel. More so when Parveen discovered she was expecting her second child and would have to remain in Delhi during her pregnancy. She could not move to her mother in Dehra Dun since she had enrolled little Fiza into Mother's International School, not far from the Asiad Village and a very fine institution. She would, of course, go to her Rajpur Road home for her confinement and for the arrival of the baby. Shujaat, too, was insistent that she was en famille, especially since the date of arrival of the little one would be right in the middle of his term back at the US university.

Once post a long gap, Parveen remembers tiny Fiza actually screaming 'Who's this? *Who is* this?' panicking to see what looked like a total stranger arriving with a suitcase and heading straight for her mother's bedroom. Yes, there was something hectic and joyous in their togetherness over those sudden arrivals, but then Dad was gone for at least three months – tough luck.

But Shujaat and Parveen did manage the companionship young couples would crave for and consider their right. Like their nine-city concert tour of Japan in 1989! And that turned out an extraordinary voyage of discovery as only Japan could be. Fascinating it was for Parveen, to watch the aplomb with which Shujaat delighted and managed his many different audiences, winning eager new students, working out ways to stay in touch. This being a concert tour, they moved from city to city – Tokyo to Sendai, to Kyoto, Matsumoto, Osaka, Hiroshima, Nagasaki, Yokohama, Hokkaido, all arrangements meticulously organized. Each city and venue seemed more picturesque than the last even on that whirlwind tour. Nature as much as architecture with cafés and cuisines varying bewitchingly. Shujaat ensured that Parveen and Fiza could soak in some of the unusual nuances that engage the outsider: the quaintness of the excessively courteous, polite, caring Japanese. It was a charmed few weeks. Parveen both laughed and shuddered to herself imagining a nine-city concert schedule being organized in her home country for a star musician of Japan. *Hey Bhagwan*!

All in all, the elation of the disparate audiences to Shujaat's music made her glow. And prepared her for the months of separation that would follow when his new stint at the University of California in Los Angeles would reclaim him once again.

In a journey of ups and downs, people in love do not give up. They do not resign themselves. And so in the early 1990s, all four of them moved home to America, ending the arrivals and departures and emptiness in between. They set up home in Los Angeles, with school admissions for the kids and a generous kennel for their German Shepherd, Elsa.

The school was no challenge for the kids, the home very welcoming – with Elsa in and out of her kennel being playful and comforting and protective. This was an enormous relief. 'We felt so reassured with their comfort in the new surroundings, it was quite remarkable. This certainly had its bonuses.' When the family planned a car trip to the Grand Canyon, Fiza and Azaan were quite firm. That Mummy and

Papa should go without them and not worry. That they would stay back with Elsa and their babysitter; that they would later do the trip with their school friends. Shujaat and Parveen relented.

Recounting the trip, Parveen is particularly animated on this rare getaway. 'You know the two of us just could not stop talking right the way through!' Yes, they would have the music playing in the car and stop every now and then to gape at the views. 'But we simply could not stop talking, I noticed.' They had already been married several years. And yet it had felt like a honeymoon. Like making up for lost time.

What was most reassuring after the exhilaration of the Grand Canyon escapade was to find Fiza, Azaan and Elsa welcoming them excitedly, the kids agog to hear it all, see all the photographs. Ironically, over time, this very adaptiveness of their two children seemed worrisome. Were they going to lose entirely their sense of who they were, their Indianness – the innate sense of identity that we hold dear in ourselves, in our progeny? This began playing heavily on both their minds. Something deep and intrinsic in their lives they wanted to instil rather than dismiss from their children's lives.

The decision to bring them home and re-settle in Delhi about two years later was not sudden. And curiously, they did not regret it. The experiment and the exposure in America had seemed worth trying out at the time – it opened up the world for the two kids in a new way. Their flat in Asiad village, Delhi, was awaiting them undisturbed, the school routine resumed at Mother's International.

Between teaching the sitar at UCLA and with *shagird*s across cities, with concerts strewn across the cities of India, inclusion in more and more music conferences, Shujaat made a 'comeback'. With his energetic, fluent, comfortable stage presence, he now became the youthful face of the Imdad Khan gharana. He had something refreshing about him, minus airs of shyness or haughtiness. The young found him appealing and through him, Indian classical music most approachable.

The ustad's ease with English, Urdu, and Hindustani was a distinct asset too. Bombay films often turned to him for composition which would give the sound track of the film a flair and the credit titles a distinct sheen. Shujaat's programme every Thursday on DD Bharti, *Mausiqui Ek Khoj* covering raga after raga of Indian classical music, did very well, not neglecting the Carnatic versions of the ragas. Years representing the entire genre in the world's finest educational academies ensured he knew how to be definitive while interesting. He managed to wear his learning lightly while drawing in new viewers.

You listen to him speak or play on his sitar and sing, holding forth as he demonstrates and compares, and you realize that he has every reason to put on airs – but he does not. And few are aware of this great service to the future of classical music. By anthologizing the finest, sometimes the rarely heard, not just developing knowledge but refining taste and preserving history, as it were. His show will always remain a gem in the archives of Doordarshan. In this sharing of the *zakheera*, the treasures that he possesses, this ustad is hugely generous.

Parveen has long relished the raconteur in him for a different reason. How else can she and their children catch up with him and with the family lore that surges in his blood? She can trace all that she values in the man to emerge from these stories.

Her hazel eyes glow when he throws himself into the tale of how his father whisked him off to Saharanpur one fine day, all the way from Dehra Dun, to do the household's grocery shopping at a modest little store there. Unfathomable, it seemed to him. Having greeted the old storekeeper warmly, Vilayat Khan handed over the shopping list to his son and stepped out himself to look for his favourite samosa shop. The storekeeper took over the list, led Shujaat to the back of his shop into a puja room; right in the centre of rows of idols and statuettes of gods and goddesses towered a massive portrait of his father.

'You must be very interested in Indian classical music!' Shujaat exclaimed. To his answer, the son listened gobsmacked.

'I know nothing about music … but I'm here because of him. In the old days, I was a tea stall owner at the New Delhi Railway Station. One day, I noticed this young boy walking, not buying anything or saying anything. I offered him a samosa, he promptly said no, he was not hungry. Later, when I took out my lunch packet, he was still there. Offering him my lunch I said, "Listen, we Hindus are not allowed to eat alone, eat something, so I too can eat." He seemed happy now, he ate very well.

'And he never forgot that. Years later, he came looking for me at the New Delhi Railway Station. He was told I had gone to Saharanpur, too ill to run the shop. Saharanpur was also his mother's home. He came, he found me. *Mera poora ilaaj, ye dukaan, ye saamaan* (my entire treatment, this shop, these provisions) he bought for me. Now a big man, he has been there for me ever since. His picture should be even bigger,' his voice was tremulous as he finished hurriedly.

'*Ye merey liye jeete jaagte devta hayn beta,* sitar *ka mujhe kuchh nahin pata.* (He's like a living god for me son, I know nothing about the sitar.)' The old man now spoke in hushed tones, lest the ustad overheard him).

Shujaat may never have had a clue of this had the long-distance shopping trip not occurred.

The Khan antecedents glinted with stories like this one. Another favourite of Shujaat's is his great grandfather Imdad Khan's anecdote of his *baithak* for a Maharajah of the Central Provinces. After his concert, the Rajah presented Ustad Imdad Khan with a bag of several hundred gold coins, saying: 'Have you ever known of a Rajah as generous in your illustrious career?' He then proceeded to have the famed musician ride on his elephant around his estate before being guided to the *kothi* where he was billeted for the night. The Rajah later heard from his retinue that the musician had distributed every one of the coins to the poor as he rode through the bazaar that night.

The next morning, the Rajah insisted that the ustad have breakfast at his palace before leaving for the station. Presenting him a bejewelled necklace of precious stones which he took off his neck, he said:

'Was I ill-mannered, Khansahab? I heard that you gave my gift away in charity.'

Shujaat's great grandfather was quick to reply, 'Not at all, Raja Sahab! I too wanted to ask your people: "Have you ever seen a musician as large-hearted as this?"'

When recounting these stories, Shujaat ends by saying, 'This is in my blood, my pride in our integrity. A musician will never be a tycoon. But his integrity no one can take away from him.'

The kids and their friends brighten at these quaint anecdotes, overfed as they are on social media to which these tales eventually may or may not trickle down!

Looking at Shujaat and Parveen Khan, it seems hard to believe that their marriage is now in its fourth decade. It is not just the fact that they look younger than their years, though that too amazes. Their whole manner suggests a newness, as though they are still discovering each other. Could the many years of being sundered by several oceans account for it? After all, they had no monotony of togetherness for a good bit of their lives, no chance to be bored. At this suggestion, they laugh and protest, insisting that there was nothing romantic about their forced separation, penury, anxiety, loneliness, no! Not then, not now, whether living through it or playing it back. Catching up with all they missed doing together could account for the newness.

Parveen seems to enjoy abiding by every protocol of that world. She respects his singlemindedness when it comes to his music. For this, he gives up his routine without a thought, reaching the concert hall hours ahead, checking every detail of the sound equipment, the amplification possible, the likely snafus. Nothing is left to chance. All of this and unearthly flight timings, unending waits at studios, he spares his wife.

He arranges for her to join him later for the holiday ... now able to give her every bit of the joy, all his attention. No sponsor needs to pick up their tabs for flights or hotels or concert seat expenses. The pride, the integrity in this musician does not allow that.

In their own lives together, Shujaat has welcomed the ways that prevailed in Parveen's family home. When he was courting her, it reminded him of his nani's home and its gentle, caring ways, a natural grace of the well-bred. These are ways that have stayed, like the key aspect of self-reliance, through one's chosen way. No pressure to pursue willy-nilly the esteemed Imdad Khan gharana; the independence to choose is an imperative and independently pursuing that choice, more so. 'Society can do without pretences, without hangers on,' Shujaat is fond of saying.

And clearly he is an inspiration for his son, Azaan. For when Azaan chooses to spread his wings into the world of fusion, he succeeds in setting an example for his son: Collaborating with the Iranian musician Kalhor on the spike fiddle and the Indian tabla player Sandipan Das, he creates an album called *The Rain*. And with this Shujaat bags a Grammy Award nomination in the Best World Music Album category in 2003. Such a thrill for Azaan, a teenager at the time. Confessing to a euphoric feeling on hearing of the nomination, Shujaat's very next sentence expressed his gratitude to his Abba and to his consistent advice: give your heart and soul to music and leave the rest to destiny. Ironically *The Rain*, recorded in Switzerland, released by a German label was not made available in India!

Wearing his fame lightly, Shujaat has performed at the Carnegie Hall, the Royal Albert Hall, been the only artist to represent India at the UN Assembly in Geneva. Turning forty, he was the recipient of India's highest award for classical music – the Rashtriya Kumar Gandharva Samman in 2001. Visiting faculty he has been at the Darlington School of Music in England, the University of Washington and the University of California. Smilingly, Parveen notices how rejuvenating all his music forays are for him. And in a curious way, for her.

The Sufi albums of *Lajo Lajo*, *Sur and Saaz*, *Hawa Hawa* have broadened his appeal; he rides high with several generations. Shujaat's ability of singing along with the sitar, a line of Bulle Shah or Amir Khusro, some new, lesser known ghazal, draws wider audiences. Parveen, a great aficionado of the poets Faiz, Faraaz, Majaz and Rahat Indori takes the most joy in this side of his music.

As a stage presence, the stark black kurta and white pyjamas are his standard ensemble. He possesses at least six of those. Once in a while, he may concede to Parveen and don a bottle-green or midnight-blue kurta. No rings on the fingers, no shawl draped over the feet or slung over the shoulder. This seems like the stark opposite of his father whose made-to-order wardrobe was the envy of the connoisseur. Shujaat remembers accepting one cotton shawl from his father while on a concert circuit with him, nothing else.

'I like Parveen to enjoy varying her clothes, her bags, choose her jewellery well. She must pick what she fancies, indulge herself. That treat I enjoy.' You can see the man beam, at a casual party or formal reception, seeing people gather around Parveen, her presence aglow and graceful in warm exchange.

'His gift-giving is not punctually timed with birthdays and anniversaries. But it is such a treat because it is so thoughtful,' says Parveen. 'Once he got me the prettiest gold bangles, twenty four of them, slender, beautifully crafted, all the way from Calcutta where the jewellers do this best. He'd taken my glass bangle as a sample so that it should fit perfectly.'

After years of avoiding a solitaire, she chanced on one at her jewellers that was subtly faceted, not assertive, very much her style. But she had desisted – old habits die hard. On hearing this, Shujaat sped to buy it and surprise her with it.

'His goading moved me from my favourite pale shades of ivory, cream, buff and beige to deep reds and crimson! Now I actually like these vivid shades!'

Eventually, this very international sitarist had to come home to roost. Shujaat and Parveen explored and located a decent-sized plot in the Chhatarpur Farms area, with Parveen having a field day planning and designing the house and garden, setting up both spaces to be havens within and without, allowing comfortable access to *shagirds*, to Azaan's studio, and most importantly privacy to the ustad for his reflection and exploration of ragas, *dhuns*, compositions. There is no assertion that his is a famous musician's home. There is instead an easy, gracious, hospitable air, welcoming you to a great cup of coffee, which is Shujaat's expertise. Parveen takes over if it is tea, addicted to her morning cup as much as to the afternoon one – and more than happy to sip on one post-dinner.

'Even when we travel, Shujaat's cup of cappuccino is a constant. He would goad us not to miss an exhibit, pack us off to an unmissable museum like the Salvador Dali one in Barcelona, or the Freer Gallery in New York, or encourage hours of shopping on high streets and by-lanes while he contentedly waited sipping his cappuccino, with the extra milk on the side, watching the world go by. You don't mind his few obstinate rules, like punctuality. And the detailed arrangements his music performances entail. Otherwise he's busy thinking of amazing ways to make life fun.'

Shujaat is happy to take it easy when Parveen needs or wants to travel on her own. What he absolutely ensures is that his wife is carrying a second mobile, whenever she is not in the same city. Being in the promptest touch has to be ensured.

Goa attracts them as a home away from home now. The place has won them over quite, over the years. Its cuisine, cafés, beaches, chapels, its many undiscovered getaways beckon frequently. It is also where Fiza met the man she fell in love with – an Australian visitor whom she later married in Delhi.

In Delhi, the Khans successfully elude Page 3, stepping out happily to the odd party or a great Pan Asian meal. Avoiding the celebrity circuit, they are often a highlight at social events, but as a couple, not a coterie. 'You know, I have Shujaat now as my best friend actually, yes. There's nothing I do not share with him, nothing I keep from him at all. We talk to each other about everything'

Does Parveen realize this is a near unique compliment few marriages can claim? She must surely know that this ustad she married has quietly defied Yeats' 'The Choice' in which the poet resignedly declares:

The intellect of man is forced to choose
perfection of the life, or of the work,
And if it take the second must refuse
A heavenly mansion, raging in the dark.

Shujaat gave his all to master the music he was born to and bred by – the music his father instilled in him till it filled him quite completely. But while pursuing that perfection so committedly, he was not going to hand himself over to his ego. He broke free to find his life with Parveen – and with music.

So whether perfection exists or eludes, it is their seeking of it that matters.

There is a headlong, even reckless aspect to this monograph. Although it falls short of the promise its central character repeatedly extracted from me over our long, frequent interludes in Bombay. That I would do a book about the romances in her life, the unusual events that kept choosing her.

'I have for you enough material for a novel, a book about me you must do, no excuses.'

Her story cannot be recounted in a sequential, orderly manner. Her animated outpourings, unvanquished by interruption or inconvenience, tell her story, capture her persona. That unbounded flow formally moulded, would be anathema to her spirit.

Leila of India was unstoppable. So I present you the avalanche – she would want it this way.

This account resembles no other in this book: of a relationship between two inveterate romantics that was not 'happily ever after'. But was a life-saver. Rescuing one casting about for love – quite unnerved, undone. For love provided selflessly, almost miraculously, by a man whose passion for filmmaking would not spare him for love throughout his life.

SCHEHERAZADE HERSELF

David & Leila Lean

SCHEHERAZADE HERSELF

'Oh my God, darling don't ask me how I could have managed without your mother. Your mama has been an absolute safety valve in my life. Yes, from the very first day I saw her and met her and befriended her in school. And you know the most fantastic thing? No one could be more different than she and I, darling. Chalk and cheese! Maybe that's exactly why she's someone I cannot do without.'

Auntie Leila was Leila Matkar when I first knew her. Like a storm she would blow into our midst. She came when she was expected – and when she was not. Over our years in Hyderabad, she was in and out, any time of day. There was no pattern. Each time she came you were quite struck. You could not help but notice what she was wearing, what *batwa* (wallet) she was carrying, what perfume she was exuding, vying with the scent of the *qivaam* (perfumed sap of tobacco) folded in the betel nut casing she was chewing, in the paan she helped herself to from her little silver box. She was least aware of any of this, or of herself.

Regaling us with stories while Mama had her siesta, she

was quick to hear her stir. 'There, your mother's up now. Oh, I can't wait to tell you, Asghari …' She knew well that Mama would be lost to her once my father returned from court. 'Once his car drives in Leila is dismissed. Your Baba comes first. Hard luck.'

When we came to live in Bombay she was undeterred. But it was different. She was now of the view that I was no longer a child, I was a person now – to be addressed differently.

'I must discover why you're such a darling of your father's. If he can take you so seriously who am I to lag behind, *haan*? You will do my life story, my book, I'm thrilled. You'll not regret it either.'

Is she teasing me, I often wondered. It was all part of her unerring skill of making whoever she spoke to seem for that moment the absolute centre of her life. She had this foxing ability, there was no resisting it.

'I don't care if you're just fifteen. You're in college, even wearing saris, Your mother tells me winning over professors and scholarships, making Taki Bhai more gaga about you than ever. *Bas, bas* (enough, enough). Now you've got to make time for me.'

Auntie Leila was too spontaneous to heed her grammar. Her prattle was like those curls on her forehead – designed to prevail but allowed to be wayward. The avalanche came in the huskiest tones, directed to make you feel crucially important. You felt no wish to analyze her praise, or her affection. You just felt undeservingly lucky.

'D'you realize that all through my years in Hyderabad, in Indore, in Europe, in London, in Hollywood, in Bombay ... like a baby I've told her each and every thing. I know in every bone of my body, *jaan*, that she wishes me well no matter what I do and how I blunder along. Those lovely eyes of hers looking aghast, yes shocked … she may disapprove but she will not betray me. I don't know of anyone blessed with such a friend.'

I tried to visualize the two of them in pigtails in Mahbubia Girls' School – named so after the then sixth Nizam – quite the city's best. Evidently the Nizam's brief was that the teachers appointed from England should be the finest – indeed those the English cannot afford for their children! Hyderabad abounded with these quaint details

'Once I start on my life, telling you the weird and wonderful things that kept chasing me, you'll want to write, *manna*, I can give you more material for your book than many lives put together. Your baba won't approve, Taki Bhai is impossible – lost in his high-flown ivory tower. But you need some earthly sense in that young head of yours. Learning about life and love and hurt also makes you wiser. Not me though. I learn nothing, I'm too much of this world; thrive on making new mistakes, even the same old ones, I am a case!'

Let me picture her for you. Her hair knotted in the middle of her back but otherwise loose. Her forehead arranged with a curl or two traditionally called *kakul* – wisps of hair prettily ornamenting a forehead. Her eyes missed nothing. Though slightly hooded, they shone with a brightness. The lining of *kohl* or *surma* accentuated the enigma in them which you could not escape, not even for a second.

It would take me a while to describe her garments – all a studied carelessness unusually coordinated. A bottle green blouse of the finest net lined in the bodice but not in the sleeves, which were short and edged with small gold beads. Are they solid gold or hollow, the child in me wondered – nothing on her looked like tinsel. Her sari of the finest creamy muslin edged with narrow braids of muted gold. Then those wisps of half curls on her forehead, inviting your eyes to return.

When she addressed you, it was you and no one else. You felt you were the only person there. That you mattered to her beyond that evening like few others did. And there seemed nothing fake or self-seeking about it. That was the way she was.

She arrived with an energy that gathered in its wake whatever you were doing, deterred by nothing. If you were on the phone, she stood in front of you with her cup of tea, nodding at whatever you were saying to whoever on the phone, in a sort of happy participation.

'Your Auntie Leila will hover around even if you're talking to your sweetheart. Only because she'll find every way of helping you darling, when you fall in love.'

I would ply Auntie Leila with tea thinking that huskiness of her voice was asking for help, while making her irresistible to entirely disparate individuals.

'I'm a person who is in love all the time, I cannot help myself. I don't feel guilty,' she would say.

'I know what you mean, Auntie Leila. One gets especially struck and obsessive about something every so often – a function of being alive, isn't it? To have something uppermost in your mind: a play, melody, book, person, an essay maybe, a letter you are honing. You give it *all* you've got ...'

Auntie Leila held up her hands to stop me, shaking her head.

'So typical of you darling, for me it has only to be uppermost in the heart. Always the heart – at least for me.' Holding out her cup for more tea, she continued. 'You may be talking about some abstract, philosophical thing. Your aunt is talking of love between a man and a woman; I mean being in a relationship, yearning for it, planning for it.

'Lucky, that your mother doesn't count your cups of tea! My ma would say too much tea darkens your skin! Now I laugh. Would David be as fascinated with me if I was the colour of all the other women he knows,' she giggled a little.

'But don't start me off on David, not yet. He is the all-consuming person in my life now, but my God, you have to know and write about the many *qissas* (the stories), the *afsaanas* I went through before he entered my life with those large, liquid, tender eyes of his, smiling through all opposition. He was, and is, a kind of culmination. You can understand that *na,* you have met him.'

Yes, David Lean at the time was the most exciting story of her life. Indeed, her trip back to India with him soon after their wedding touched all our lives with a kind of celebratory glow. They would drive up in their pale blue Silver Ghost, probably one of the two or three Rolls Royces in all of Bombay. I remember she ran through our gate and minuscule garden in the Colaba flat of Heliopolis as she stepped out of the car – almost girlishly, her hand in his. His steps would follow her as would his pleased and indulgent smile. He did seem distinguished in a rare sort of way.

Auntie Leila loved recounting the first visit. 'I insisted on coming this way, dear, I love your little personal garden. Don't forget I was bringing home my English bridegroom, all very private, very emotional. I was short of sobbing with happiness that morning. *Mera kaun hai jaan, aap logon ke siva*? (Who do I have other than the few of you?) Well-wishers are so hard to find!' When more moved than usual, her tears and smiles kind of intermingled. I have to say that the blasé attitudes of my late teens did desert me watching them over those three or four days and nights when they would be over: for meals, or between interviews, appointments, shopping.

'I knew he'd fall in love with your mother's *pakvaan* (cuisine) and even more, her ways. "What a rare gentlewoman she is, your friend Asghari," were his first words as we got into our car after spending the day with your parents. Deep down he is an over-particular man, don't forget. You should see how standoffish David can be, even among the very rich and very famous – he can be scathing given half a chance.'

She promptly followed my incredulous look with: 'You're seeing another side of him altogether, he's wearing his winning side for the Bilgramis. My sisters, your family, what other *sasural* (in-laws) does he have except my friends?'

I did notice an air of pleased acceptance all around. David Lean would recline by her and as she held forth, he would stroke her open hair, his eyes indulgent, almost beatific. It was very gratifying to see her so well loved. And the ice had certainly broken among the adults when my father warned David not to waste his affection on tresses that were most likely not her own! She did wear a *chutla* (a braid of perfectly matched false hair plaited in).

In her outpourings over numerous trips, she was clear that David came as a finale to the many stories of her life that bordered on the impossible.

'It all started very early, *manna*, I was not a bad girl or anything, but I had to have love in my life, could not do without it at any stage. My father was an academic among the many the Nizam gathered around from outside his state. My mother saw a lot of herself in me and did not discourage me from friendships or romances. She could not have even if she had tried! I think in some strange way she knew it would not work. Repression, never does, don't you think?'

Before I could respond, she resumed. 'For the male species, obstacles seem to actually encourage! Makes things much more exciting, more crucial. It whips up the adrenalin as they say in the West. There was enough to discourage David in every aspect of my life: I was married, I had children, I was in a small town not easily accessible to a foreign traveller; my house was stiff, rule-bound. My husband was a ponderous host, at the best of times; my informality, my very "proper" spouse felt, was the worst possible influence on my two children, on the servants, on the colleagues' wives, certainly on visiting celebrities.

'But none of this would put David off. He was there. And he hardly ever left Indore and India, without finalising his next trip. How I blessed him for this!'

Time and again I would tear myself away, when the phone rang, or a tutorial nagged to be accomplished. But each time, Auntie Leila picked up the threads, no umbrage taken.

'Same thing with each one of my suitors. The more tricky the situation, the more eager they seemed. Darling, I'm an old woman now, at least thirty years older than you. Have you noticed I have no complex about my age? Why hide your age? I may do it in America, which is obsessed with being young. Otherwise why should I – if I'm getting more attention than I can cope with? I need my sleep, my music, my *riyaaz* (music practice). I need to talk to you. It's therapy for me.

I'm being honest now. The day all this attention starts to fade, God knows what I'll do darling. God help me. I will not survive. My God knows that, He rescues me ... I too find ways. Right now, I need a young person to talk to: it rejuvenates me. Funnily and sadly, one cannot turn to one's own children even though they are one's greatest joy. I realized soon how careful I had to be with mine, the dear, dear girl and boy I was blessed with, early in my marriage. I cannot expect them to understand. And I want them to love me as much as I love them.'

I felt strangely relieved she was sparing her children, as she continued.

'But hurdles do not discourage love between a man and a woman, never have. That's what fascinates. I mean Aala Hazrath (His Highness) himself could not stop his handsome young brother, Salabath Jah, falling in love with me, or sending me his letters, his *shayari* (poetry), his secret plans for our meetings. Even with all the spies keeping tabs on him, he found a way. I would skip the net ball sessions in school, pleading a foot sprain. His driver knew when I left school, when my last class got over; he even had my driver all on his side with some *ashrafi* or regular *bakhshish* (tip). I knew the sound of his car and I'd rush to get in before others could notice it.

'We had our hearts in our mouths. *Magar mujhey kaafi himmat thhi* (But I was pretty plucky). Love makes you quite brave, don't you think?'

'How were you able to keep it from your parents, Auntie Leila? What happened to your studies, exams?

'You should have been a professor's daughter, not I – fretting about school degrees. I managed my dear, I'm not so dumb. Your mother helped me. She'd summarize notes, make a précis so I could learn up fast. My father was a professor too, remember?

'Call it what you will, *manna,* if my heart is set on it, my mind is unafraid. *Darpok nahin hoon mayn* (Timid I'm not).' She put one of her hands to her forehead and suddenly became almost grave. Her fingers had rings vying for attention, each would have a quirky tale attached, I felt sure.

'You know so far my love has never been snatched from me by any rival, nor ever by the person himself. I've not been jilted yet. It is always an outside force. Time and time again I've been, what's that word, yes, thwarted, before I could actually call a man my own. I began to feel the world was against me, my happiness. In Hyderabad which I made my home – I learnt its ways, spoke its language; why should it reject me as its daughter?'

She continued, her unburdening unfazed: 'He sent my prince away, exiled him, *shehar badar kardiye, manna*! Just banished him far away from the city. He discovered that we managed to meet in secret and write to each other, promptly sent for my father, summoned him to King Kothhi. And said, send her away. He gave my father no choice, actually.'

Round-eyed, I felt positively indignant. 'How can you force this on someone! I hope your father put his foot down.'

She laughed at my naivete. 'Let me make you a paan, I hope you won't go away now, even if that phone is for you.' Auntie Leila did not miss a thing. She had heard the phone ring.

To cheer Auntie Leila after my call, I suggested we walk in the garden behind our house, an oval patch of lawn leading up to the Arabian Sea. A beautiful solid stone wall the sea had not swallowed up yet made it a very inviting seat.

She held my arm as we walked out of the flat, undistracted, quiet until we got to the sea. 'What a good idea to step out, darling. Imagine this place when the moon comes out. Such a boon for young people – right outside your doorstep! Your aunt refuses to grow old, can't you see? We must bring David here.'

'*You* must. And on a moonlit night,' I teased.

Spurred on, she continued her story. 'I was telling you, if the Nizam ordered you, there was no alternative. He told my father that he and I could choose where I wished to go, the expense should not concern us, nor the arrangement! This should be considered urgent – and top secret.'

'Did you manage that, Auntie Leila? You must have told your mama – and mine.'

'Gosh yes, darling, my mother had to know everything. She had her own ideas of how to cope. "His Exalted Highness may suggest the Isabella Thorburn College in Lucknow, the famous IT College for girls. But I have other plans for my daughter which he cannot refuse. He should be happy, it's farther away, disconnected from Hyderabad – it's a place I know. And my daughter has artistic talents. If she has to be deprived of her family, she must get back to her roots. Calcutta and then Shantiniketan is where he must arrange to send her. I have enough family there to handle all details." Father agreed.

'I was so shaken, I couldn't even sing the lines of poetry my prince would send to me from his lonely, miserable exile. It broke my heart to think of it. I would sob and sing it to myself. It was madness. When you're that young you're a bit *baanvra* (crazed). A little touched, as the English say. Imagine losing all your waking hours to a man who should be king but is not, who should be free to be yours but cannot be!

'*Manna,* one look at Prince Salabath Jah and you'd say he was the prince, he should have been the heir. Oh, the stories one heard right through one's childhood – from people who were not the kind to make them up. Of how the British placed in positions of power their chosen man, not the rightful heir. Making the person so beholden to them, they could treat him like a puppet. The real heir they would then place helpless, entirely in the custody of this chosen man. They would not be held responsible because now that would be reprehensible, right? This way they had both men under their control. The powerful just know how to get their way. How they manipulate!'

'Just one moment. How did you make all this out? Was it ever discussed with you?'

'My dear, don't ask. Novels are nothing. Actual life can weave such webs around you! "Fantastical", our history teacher used to say, when she explained court intrigues. Nothing could be more knotted than what was happening to someone I loved. I had to disappear before I did more harm to a helpless prisoner.'

'Did you keep in touch, were you allowed that?'

'I thought I'd never forget him as long as I lived, that I'd sing his favourite couplets, weep, pretend he was there, act as though I was Leila Chitnis or some tragedy queen, what to do? Then what do you think happened? Sometime in April, as I am settling into Shantiniketan, I get a letter from a cousin visiting Hyderabad saying that a terrible tragedy had struck two very close relations of Aala Hazrat (His Exalted Highness).'

I could not believe Auntie Leila meant the twenty-seven-year-old Salabath Jah. Surely not.

'Salabath Jah had died on the 2nd of March and his only sister on the 17th of March. It was a bald, stark bit of news.

Can you explain it, *manna*? No one could, even when it came out in the papers. I wasn't even there. And no explanation ... why, how, nothing. All it said was that Prince Salabath Jah was in Secunderabad at the time and it was a sad and mysterious fatal effect of food poisoning. *Kis se poochhoon, kya karoon?* (Who should I ask, what should I do?) I used to walk among the trees as though they were my only friends. I thought my eyes would come out of their sockets or sink into them and disappear forever, I cried so much.

'But my singing, watercolours and my brushwork at Shantiniketan became better and better. That's when the young Tagore young man, quite a bit older than me he was though, who followed me with his eyes all this while, came to my rescue. He'd sit by me with his book, his flute, his sketch pad; or he'd read to me from Bankim, from Rabindranath, but more the reflective type of verse. He did not impose himself. But, as the months passed, he changed. He gazed into my eyes, presented an exquisite sketch of me for a locket, said he cherished a lock of my hair to which he would sing. But I'd heard he was engaged to some very, very distant East Bengal cousin. I never found out. And thank God, my parents came and took me back. With Salabath Jah gone it was now deemed safe.'

Auntie Leila opened up a box of chocolates for me as though *I* needed cheer.

'Did Shantiniketan change you at all, it must have?' I ventured.

'I felt grown up, darling, and kind of sad in many, many ways. Missing your mother's wedding was such a blow. The excitement of *manjha, saanchaq, jalwa, chauthhi, valeema*, (typical ceremonies of a Hyderabadi wedding over five or six magical days). Best of all the qawwali night, guests swaying to Sufi *kalaam*, ladies in all their finery, the rousing music, its spiritual aura.'

An uncharitable thought would nag me now and again. Was David first inspired by her as a subject for his work rather than pinnacle of his love life? Was it the cinematic quality of her life, strewn with princes, poets, deaths and exiles, then a stern statesman husband – and then with himself! No, it did not seem right. How could I ascribe this calculating streak in that slender, sensitive, distinguished man I had met? How could I underestimate her effect on him, right in the midst of that arid, severe Indore home, constricted by the prim protocol of the Indian Civil Service? How could he resist that husky compulsive flow, strewn with unstinted cosseting of you, the listener?

'I seek you out like a maniac, *manna*, to tell my story. I'm glad you have no one chasing you at this moment. My God, if there is, tell me who! Heavens, I could even chaperone so you can meet more often!'

Suddenly she became earnest. 'You'll tell me won't you, jaan? Remember life is not all books, books, books. They teach you nothing about life. Incidentally, David too will want to know of the young man in your life!'

I steered her back to the series of unexpected advances and setbacks in her life – as they came, they engulfed her, as she almost revelled in each one of them.

Her secret, stormy and short-lived relationship with Salar Jung. Yes, *the* Salar Jung III, the world's famed collector whose Salar Jung Museum still towers over almost all tourist attractions of Hyderabad, was as dramatic. Just how had she lost her heart to Hyderabad's most renowned collector, valued minister, confirmed bachelor? He certainly had lost his to her. The man who died a bachelor, leaving his untold collection to no heir of his own, had once resolved to marry this rare daughter of Professor Welingkar. Deeply touched he was by her return to his city after being summarily sent away, banished by his liege.

'How did Salar Jung happen, Auntie Leila, he was nearly twenty-four years older than you, didn't that bother you?'

Auntie Leila was nibbling at one of our cooks' *gosh-e-feel* (cookies shaped like elephant ears), relishing them almost girlishly, her eyes all bright, her lips all shorn of lipstick.

'You forget counting the years, especially when a man in his forties is hopelessly in love. And so coveted he was as powerful minister, connoisseur, collector, the most valued knight on the Nizam's round table. Nawab Salar Jung was careful to keep it hush-hush, not to invite any royal wrath, my dear. So it was one morning, much before noon in fact, quietly and without fuss – in a private house in Somajiguda, not his own home, that the *nikaah* was to take place. Our *nikaah*, his and mine. I sat all decked out in jewellery that he had personally set aside for his bride, choosing the handpicked heirlooms of generation after generation, from his family vaults and from his museum collection. My hands, arms feet, my plait too was bejewelled, my head covered.'

The old girl regaled fluently the secrecy of this fairy-tale wedding. You could never guess looking at her that she felt aware of her own power – she never gave any sense of wielding it.

'I knew him to be a very good man. A fine, cautious man, despite untold wealth and power, one who loved collecting beautiful things. Nothing ostentatious or arrogant about him, with me or with any of the people he cared about. Ask your father, he was extremely fond of your father, enjoyed consulting him as much as talking endlessly over a drink with him – and not just legal matters; the man trusted him. Salar Jung called your mother *beti*, treated her like his child, constantly making her try out strings of pearls and emeralds from Basra, from Colombia, before deciding to buy them. How I'd plead with her to use her common sense, appreciate his fatherly gesture! "*Aadaab karo ma, jaldi se jhuk ke aadaab karo. Tareeqa voi hai, meri baat suno. Usskey baad vo haar tumhaara.*" (Just do the gesture of putting your hand to your forehead, say *aadaab* lowering your head respectfully and the necklace is yours. That's the custom, just listen to me).

'The very suggestion horrified your mama. So perverse! What's the *sharam* (shame), the man dotes on your husband, relies on his legal advice; he'd never let you try on jewels if he did not mean for you to keep them. Anyone else would do *aadaab* – they knew he could well afford it.'

'Maybe Salar Jung got Mama to try on the jewels only because he was sure she wouldn't swipe them with an *aadaab*!'

'Oh please *manna*, my quota of paans will finish while convincing you. If she'd listened to me, you girls would be wearing those exquisite pieces! He was an amazing collector, he could afford to be Santa Claus right through the year. Dealers, exporters, gemologists, the best jewel merchants would seek him out because he had the taste and the money.'

'But how was Salar Jung responsible for your exile to Indore?

'What happened was very sudden and very final. I knew the *nikaah* would take no more than a few minutes. The privacy of the occasion, leaves everybody out. And once the *nikaah* is over, there's no turning back. No one could then stop us from telling the world.

'Picture me sitting with my head covered, my eyes closed, my neck weighed down with the many ornaments: the *chintaag*, the *jugni,* the *satlada* (ornaments for the neck). *Sar pe jhoomar or teeka* (ornaments for the forehead) *bhi thha, manna.* That's when the Qazi came to ask whether I would accept his suit. The needed to hear my voice say "haan" three times. So what if there was no *taqreeb, asal shaadi tho ho hi rahi thhi, nikaah is the asal shaadi* (So what if there was no wedding celebration, the nikaah is the actual, legal marriage), as you know.

'But before I could lift my eyes to say yes, there was a sudden, noisy flurry from the entrance corridors. I could hear them saying, "*Yeh maamila rok diya jaaye! Shahi firmaan ke khilaaf ye naheen ho sakta! Nawab Sahab. Ruk jaaiye – pehle Sarkar ka firmaan dekh liya jaaye, padh liya jaaye.* (This proceeding must be stopped, it's against the royal fiat, the court diktat we bring must be seen, read here and now)." It was all loud and in more than one voice. Head lowered under my *ghunghat* (veil) I wasn't sure how they obstructed the religious men. *Firmaan* was the potent word, I suppose. They took Salar Jung Sahab into another room ... in those few moments it was all over. *Mayn boli na manna, ye kahaani shuroo hone ke pehle-ich khatam hagoyi!* (I told you my dear, that story ended before it even began!) If they had come after my "yes", my *haan*, the royal *firmaan* would have been null and void.

'Your Leila Auntie's destiny has much written in it – and yet not. That's why my dear, write, write – give it some meaning for me.'

I wondered how much of this was real, how much imagined, dramatized, romanticized. But by all other accounts that did the rounds over the years, all of it did occur.

As the '*nikaah*-that-never-happened' story concluded, I nearly asked Auntie Leila if she did *aadaab* to Nawab Salar Jung, appropriating the bridal load of ornaments that bedecked her. Spurned at the eleventh hour, he may have felt she had a right to it all, perhaps to more! Who knows? She would not have been offended if I had asked. But I did not. For jewels crafted to perfection were part of this Scheherazade's ensemble each time. She had dramatic stories of losing a trunk-load travelling in a boat to Europe with her Hollywood friend, Barbara Hutton. But incidents that were untouched by tinges of romance were mentioned only in passing or not at all. It kept puzzling me that her face glowed, talking of all the pain and buffeting in her life.

'Good Lord, Auntie, with all this hitting you before marriage, you must have wanted to run a mile from one!'

My companion laughed, she actually covered her face and laughed and then came back quickly with: 'That is precisely when I could not escape marriage, was led into it almost immediately. My father's family had their way. The finest, most eligible bachelor with an exemplary record in the Civil Service of the British, no less! They couldn't have asked for more or better. A most conventional alliance with a true-blue Maharashtrian, Mr Matkar, ICS. But in all fairness, I cannot blame my parents. How could they stand up against their Sovereign when he was wanting me right out of his state.

'My life in Indore was nothing like Hyderabad. That city just does not go out of its way for anybody. So insular,

I felt shut out from the very start. The sophisticates there found me naïve, I'm sure; the government officials found I knew no rules; the Maharashtrian community thought I was a half-baked, half-Bengali Maharashtrian, probably felt sorry for my husband.'

For me, this change of scene kind of refreshed the story – now picturing her life away from her home ground. Absentmindedly, Auntie Leila was making paan after paan and tucking them in the silver umbrella-like trinket with attached silver cloves.

'Was married life a change you were prepared for? You'd barely finished school, right?'

Offering me a paan she went on. 'Yes and no, *manna*. There was a stiffness in the air because of the British. Being senior in the government you take airs, you're expected to! Conforming to rules, absurdly formal, superficial, anglicized, ughh! Facing disapproval over things which were nobody's business but mine – that I really, really minded.

'One day when my husband suggested that I should cut my hair, *manna*, I burst into tears. A bob-cut like all the other wives, so absurd it looks with a sari. And then all the bother of being coiffed, hair-sets and perms. *Khuda bachaaye* (God save us)!

'It also implied something that deeply hurt me. That I was not considered good enough as I was. I spoke English well but was not anglicized enough. I was made to wear commonplace jewellery aping the West, clasps and brooches that did not suit me, blouses that made me look like a *mem*.

'The best thing about Hyderabad was that it was the *mems* and the *sahibs* who bowed if not scraped to the local aristocracy. They learnt Urdu, they even did *aadaab* in some quaint way or they left you alone respectfully. All because of the Nizam's wealth, I suppose, they knew which side their bread was buttered.

'I tease David about the "crafty" British. He accepts it readily. He laughs and says he knows this well and throws it into his films from time to time, and says "Craftiness is not just the Indian's prerogative, we give you a run for your money".'

'So let's get back to Indore,' I said, gently steering her back.

'Well, there was no overpowering presence of the Nizam. The British were all in all. Even senior government servants were expected to ape them, talk like them, be like them in public. Mimicking the British makes us look like cartoons.'

At this point Leila was an eloquent Scheherazade, her ego smarting.

'Why pretend to adore dogs *jaan*, when they barge in and wreck your hair, tousle your sari, crash the crystal, spill your juice and chew up your expensive slippers. But no, the ladies would twitter away, "Gently Rufus, my pet now, now, go away, no, no, easy!" Silly, ineffectual protests.'

Running her hands through her loosely knotted hair, she sighed. 'I'm supposed to cut my hair, look like them, talk like them, wear brocade blouses like waistcoats. Even use long fancy, jewelled cigarette holders! The paan was considered *junglee*. More, dear. The local elite would deign to say: "Let's not blame her, blame Hyderabad, where she picked up all these primitive habits."

'One tipsy officer once dared to say, "Hmmm, one hears of degenerate ways. At least, Leila doesn't snuff opium – which the royals favour in her city." Oh darling, I could have screamed out to defend Hyderabad. I was just afraid I'd burst into tears instead.'

The irony seemed immense. That Leila Matkar should rebel at the very mention of the anglicized Indian, the hoity-toity British bigwigs in Indore, her own *pukka sahib* husband – and then be swept off her feet by none other than a true-blue Brit.

'How did you cope with this Indore exile? Did relations, friends visit or help?'

'No distractions helped me, dear. But I doted on my children, spoiling them was my outlet – such lovely sensitive kids both, thank God. The more my husband feared I'd spoil them, the more I'd plead with him that loads of love never spoilt anyone. When he mentioned boarding schools for them, *manna*, I nearly died at the thought. I remember crying one whole night when my son Inder was packed off to Doon School. Another of these very "done" things, even if you hated doing them!

'Ah well, I may talk non-stop and even charm many, but I couldn't coax my husband to my way of thinking. As he got more senior and more important, things got more difficult instead of getting better. Oh, with the children away from me a lot I'd feel, so alone, so isolated. And then came David.'

The fact that David was seriously exploring possibilities of making a film on Gandhi brought him to Delhi and Indore, and had him involved in a spate of research and a mire of permissions and approvals. This, according to Leila Matkar, was 'a godsend, *meri jaan*, absolute godsend'.

'You never know how life will amaze you – I thought I'd be the last person he'd seek as company, let alone admire. But it was happening.

'Don't forget, that whole side of me had packed up. *Mayn bilkul murjha gayi thhi, bibi* (I'd shrivelled up, wilted). It was only on my trips to my sister in Geneva or the younger one in Bombay, or to Hyderabad, that I was myself, my old self. In Indore, I had no one. I broke down, nervous and depressed by turns. Unhappiness makes you so ill, so shaken, almost finished. I felt different when David was around. He drew me out. Without me knowing, he made me feel whole again.

'What David thought or sensed, I couldn't guess. I found him seeking me out in a quiet, almost shy way. And then there was his reputation – my God, it made such a hero out of him, his charisma. He fascinated me. The way David went about it, my husband actually did not notice or mind that he was always there. This foreign visitor would quietly give me all his spare time without formality. He was transforming me, yes, as well as my life. Being in love with him was a most remarkable discovery for me, *meri jaan.* I was unpeeling a completely different kind of Englishman than any of us had met or known. I'd broken through his reserve – it was beautiful knowing he was so completely conquered, it made me shed years in my middle age!'

'But surely that had happened to you many times before, that feeling of triumph.'

'This time it was a man who could not be deterred. David worked in a quiet, mystifying way. Low-key as they say. This quiet Englishman was not prepared to consider anything an obstacle. Dreading the confrontation, I broke down, my nerves packed up. It must have been the fear of losing him.

'I'd tell David, I've lost my heart to you and I've lost my mind too, unfortunately. Thank your lucky stars you never saw me through that phase, nobody did actually. But David was there. He'd come, he'd remain there with me, in that room, in that verandah where I'd be taken out; yes, from the nursing home, for long drives. Imagine what it did to his schedules, his commitments. He'd read to me, talk of his research, cajole me to talk of anything and everything that made me happy. Flowers had to fill my room. He'd come armed with journals we craved for in India. If I so much as mentioned a book, he'd order it. And was happy to read it to me, his eyes looking up, smiling every now and then. What patience! My eyes would well up and I kept explaining to him that with him, my tears were only of happiness. When it came to my husband, David was polite. He was quiet, but he was adamant that he would marry me regardless, he was very sure I would be back to being myself again ... that he could not be stopped.

'Thank God, *manna*, that David's project on Gandhi and other subjects he was researching needed repeated visits. If he'd got into shooting his film I'd have had to take second place, yes, even if sick and frantic!'

'Yes, research is one thing, actual filming quite another,' I agreed.

'Let me be very frank, I couldn't have dared to take this step if I hadn't sensed David's patience, seeing me through that time. I could not have. He was so, what is the word ... staunch, yes, staunch. As though nothing would stop him. My husband was cold in his anger. He said that he would not permit divorce until my daughter was married and properly settled. That seemed fair to me, I adored my lovely daughter.

'David was not discouraged. He was travelling, researching in different countries now, the Gandhi project had fallen through a long while ago. I knew he would be back whenever he could manage. He probably knew that my daughter was nearly engaged to a young man who was very attached to her.

'Whenever I got worked up, David smiled. The clasp of his hand tightened over mine if he sensed my hysteria. He managed my panic attacks, he managed everything. I have never known such patience. You'll be happy to know darling that he's more romantic than I am. Doesn't all this prove that?'

Auntie Leila had many, many photographs of her and David, before their marriage, after the ceremony, on holidays, literally spilling out of her bags. Picking out each one, she would hold forth on the occasion, the relationship of the people one didn't know and could not place: friend, colleague, editor, script assistant, producer, even promoter. David looked so utterly distinguished in each, without trying. Tired in some, but always looking at her, if she was in the picture. Not at the camera or in the middle distance or any place else, always at her. I don't know if he looked like a creative genius, but he did look better than most of his stars, certainly more sensitive, more distinguished.

When David moved on to the shooting of *Lawrence of Arabia*, she was to accompany him to Jordan and did. But she was back in Bombay after the first few hectic weeks to escape the gruelling schedule it turned out to be.

David was immersed, preoccupied. Coping with hectic shoots back to back, last-minute location changes. Waiting for him to be free and back in Bombay made more sense. She would renew her music lessons. Having dabbled in classical sitar and singing lessons, her ustads would be happy to resume. It would also help her pine less for David.

Her account of the Jordan shoot set-up for *Lawrence of Arabia*, of David's ambit of associates, crew, stars and superstars, whether O'Toole or Alec Guinness or Omar Sharif, was scintillating in most part, because it was so quaintly her. She peppered every description in that husky voice of hers that she never raised. She was very sure you were listening. Intense, almost graphic in her irritation with the pompous or the 'put on', and almost wittily gushing about those she cared for.

'I didn't have to be nervous about any of his fan club, darling. They were too eager to please him so they would fuss over me in all sorts of ways. I lapped it up actually, also it gave David a little respite.

'I was so sure I needed to be there, looking after him, no matter what the hours, what the crisis. His look, his touch, his head on my lap when it would all finish, my God, it seemed so worth waiting for. But schedules constantly changed while shooting near the sandy cliffs of Wadi Rum. That's when I really began to feel in the way. Not a moment of day or night would they leave him alone. Glitches needed to be solved on the spot, new possibilities discussed. David was actually not wanting to switch off; he works like that, gets totally immersed. That's him.

'I know no other way,' he said in that heartbreakingly honest, intense, quiet way of his. That's when I knew it was better my being here and thinking about him. Not being there and losing him every minute to something or someone else.

'Not easy, *manna*, to realize his work did not want me there. So, we decided I'll stay in Bombay till he finishes with the Middle East. I'll join him when they move from Jordan to Spain, Morocco, Surrey. Here, I'll ask Khansahab now to start music lessons again.

'But you just come as soon as your lectures break and get refreshed. I've requested your parents already. Your college is a few hundred yards from here. And your home even less, your friends, your French class, everything is here. That's why David and I insist on the Ritz. Otherwise, it's always the Taj.'

Through David's triumphs of *Lawrence of Arabia* and then of *Dr. Zhivago*, Leila of India was a proud and participative partner with him whenever she could be. But during his shoots, she would get out of his way and into her suite on the top floor of the Ritz Hotel. Leila Lean did have her own fan club and her evenings were spent between music recitals, dinners with my parents, their friends and her own friends. And attempts to talk and write to David.

One afternoon, punctuating tea with one snack after another, she asked me about *Dr. Zhivago*; when did I see it, who with, did I like it, would I like to see it again? I quite loved the ferreting – and obliged. And finally wound up saying, 'He tells every bit of the story with such feeling, it would startle Pasternak himself! The performances, the music, one or two sequences, it all gets etched. Just a bit mushy in parts, but the film is totally exceptional. He's actually relaunched Sharif and Christie!'

'Yes, really, *achha*? You young people, you have your own way of putting things.'

We were getting late for a sitar recital that evening, and she was keen on getting a ringside view of Vilayat Khan's fingers on the strings. So, we sped to the lift and into the waiting car.

Busy with tutorials thereafter, I had missed seeing Auntie Leila for more than a week. We agreed to meet at Rhythm House opposite my college, to head for the hotel after picking up some LPs of vocal and sitar music.

'You must choose what jewellery I wear tonight … and listen, I must show you what David wrote about your reactions, your remark.' Handing me David's letter, she added, 'He even mentioned it on the phone actually.'

I said, a little cautiously, 'What remark, Auntie Leila? I'd rattled off all kinds of praise.'

'Yes, yes, but I did add how you had found it kind of mushy.'

'Auntie Leila, how *could* you have told him that? That was between you and me,' I said *aghast.*

'Come on, David takes you seriously like your father. I had to mention it!'

I was shaking my head in disbelief, outraged.

David's postscript in the letter to her said: 'Will quiz Syeda when we meet. Right now, tell her to wait till she falls in love with a married man. And then tell me if she still finds *Dr. Zhivago* a mushy film.'

My reaction to David's comeback was instant, child-like – and entirely unrelated to the film. Why would he wish me in love with a married man?

Clearly, the eager study of literature and philosophy, characters and relationships had not taught me the language of love. How can he wish this upon me, even if my reaction to his film irks him, I chafed. And in my puerile, black is black and white is white fashion, I blurted, 'I think his remark is meaner than mine! And mine was not meant to be mean'.

'Oh darling, David wants better than the best for you, an absolute one of a kind love for you. Yes, even with a married man. David is an emphatic, incurable romantic!'

Grow up, was what she was telling me, as she defended

David. Be emotionally sophisticated, was what both of them were saying to my idiocy.

Auntie Leila too had years of growing up to do in her marriage with a man who had been married several times. Eighteen years and a lot of them glowing, triumphant.

The expression on his face as his eyes revelled in her unusual beauty, returning to her at every excuse was a charming giveaway. His unconditional and persistent care of her through years of trauma did make theirs a collaboration that was intense, intimate and quite unique. The fact that he revived her spirit to be herself, to intensely feel attachment, to care single-mindedly, was an untold reward.

But, ultimately, his first love was his own film-making. A fact she contended with regularly in her marriage: staying back, waiting for all the attention she ached for, being a celebrity all the while, but not the centre of his life.

Her years set up in a suite at Grosvenor House hotel in London, with less and less right to his time, his emotions, his immediacy, must have been third degree for Leila Lean. Maybe there was a tragic irony in her letting go without fuss. I remember I was visiting Calcutta on work when a London paper was sent to me with the write-up that she had suddenly choked over a croissant in a hotel in Paris and could not be revived, along with a picture in close-up of a drawn but still beautiful Leila Welingkar Matkar Lean. She was gone.

It was David Lean's longest standing marriage to any woman, any of his five wives. And one that awakened an intensity entirely unmatched. Leila herself had been married to her first husband for longer – in a marriage arranged to expect adjustment not fulfilment.

Regardless of all the events that overtook her, it was to romance of a headlong and intense kind that Leila was married all her life. *That* was an essential. And it culminated in the arrival of a destined pilgrim, with David. The man who held her together, resolved to save her by marrying her. Against all odds. And that David certainly did, much extending the prime of her life.

Muzaffar Ali was getting married for the third time,
Meera Saluja for the first.

Geeti Sen, his first wife, was an established art critic and editor, with whom he had a son, the talented stage and film actor, Murad Ali.

Subhashini Sahgal, a spirited and very active member of the Communist Party of India, was Muzaffar's second wife, with whom he had a son, Shaad Ali, a successful bollywood film director.

Sadly, both marriages ended. But they ended amicably.

Meera Saluja, the twenty-five-year-old US-returned architect, fell in love with Muzaffar Ali.
She had to elope to marry him. But that is not why their story features in this book.

MUCH RHYME, MORE REASON

Muzaffar & Meera Ali

MUCH RHYME, MORE REASON

It was almost customary for those born to royalty in India to boast of a quirk. Perhaps more than one, weaving itself into a legend over time.

But Raja Sajid of Kotwara did not have to resort to eccentricity. He was quite uniquely the only royal who was a communist, not lounging in any stately armchair. Geology had been his passion – he pursued it with a prized degree from Edinburgh University, Scotland. But the fascination with Marx – his Manifesto generating experiments across the world – made him join the Communist Party of Scotland, giving him a firsthand sense of the agenda before he headed home. Growing up in a position of the highest privilege in Kotwara, he had always winced uncomfortably at the plight of the underdog.

Returning to India, the young Raja Sajid declined the invitation to join the Muslim League, a party that expected his full support. He was wholly committed to sharing power with his own people instead: launching the Haljutta Party, rousing the ploughing peasant and winning election after election against the Muslim League candidate. The like-minded were moved. Vijay Lakshmi Pandit empathized, would make him sing his Haljutta anthem whenever in Lucknow. In fact, many enlightened supporters wished him the political astuteness he lacked but the local electoral sabotage was rampant. Remaining at the forefront of initiatives in his state and constituency – always putting public interest first, he realized active politics was not for him. But Raja Sajid's one expectation lingered: '*Yahan koi bhooka aur nanga na rahe.* (No one here should remain unfed and unclad.)' His championing of the less privileged remained an active pursuit all his life.

Between Kotwara, Lucknow, Mussoorie and Nainital, Raja Sajid's young son Muzaffar was growing up, learning in all the expected and some unexpected ways. There was no forced completion of the Quran at home but the aspect of Allah being compassionate and merciful to all was a reminder through every namaz. The unswerving rejection of evil tyranny was the vivid lesson through the weeks of Moharram spent recounting the martyrdom of Karbala. His mother, Rani Kaneez Hyder of Moradabad, had a strong sense of education as true enlightenment, being a descendant of Baba Farid: the Sufi famed for infusing an innate sense that the spirit should reign, not the ritual.

Between the varied instructions of the body and the mind, a story, a tale well told, was the prize. Between Ladli and Atooji, the two ladies in the *zenana,* these stories were a golden treasury. But Atooji was firm. 'Stories told after dark will make travellers lose their way,' declared the disciplinarian in her. But if neither of the ladies obliged, Muzaffar knew his last, but best resort. He would find his own father gallantly stepping in as raconteur to transfix them with tales of *Tilism e Hoshruba* (Hamza's *Dastaans* of Stunning Enchantment). Abbajan would always make it a point to stop at a nail-biting moment and say goodnight. The suspense would only be broken the next morning.

Alongside school, the home arranged a fitness routine, with the impressive Matroo, the *pehelwan* (wrestler) instructor, who was allotted a permanent room in the house. 'Thereafter the sports drill at La Martiniere College seemed a cakewalk,' laughs Muzaffar.

Another memory that recurs almost enticingly is the fleet parked in the school compound. Muzaffar gloried in admiring the gleaming vehicles in the drive – Jimmy Jehangirabad's 36 Wolsley Sedan, Sulaiman Mahmudabad's grey Ford Mercury next to his own grey Ford Super Deluxe. All these came in handy on many an occasion when the boys would cruise by the gates of the Loreto Convent for Girls, hoping to catch the eye of the comely alumni hailing their own chauffeurs.

What discovered for Muzaffar the painter in him was the view from a room of his own in the Nainital bungalow that his father had bought the family. The mountainscapes, the winding roads, the horsemen riding and leading their horses in turn. A change of scene occurred frequently. His room was littered with sketchpads and paints.

Raja Sajid felt graduating in art was a cliche to be avoided. Science it had to be and not the typical routine of getting packed off to Oxbridge. It would be Aligarh. Academic rigour and the aura of the redoubtable Hasrat Mohani, the poet who coined the rousing cry of 'Swatantra Bharat' for the country's young. A gentleman who when asked why on earth he travelled third class, would say: 'Only because there is no 4th class.'

As far as Aligarh's famous '*khichai*' or ragging was concerned, Muzaffar had managed a minor coup. By sheer instinct, not design. He attempted no flourish to register his presence or assert his personality. He remained distinctly quiet, taking it all in, making no assertions or protests, smiling whenever he could. He listened, he absorbed, he laughed – and made friends. So, it came to be that the Professor Rahi Masoom Raza who reveled in baiting him launched Muzaffar's collection of paintings while still at university, eloquently fulsome in his praise.

Muzaffar's Hercules cycle and his welcoming single room, an *adda* where *shayari* reigned, became popular symbols around the campus.

Growing up in Aligarh was happening on several fronts. News would trickle in about Manjhu Mian, Muzaffar's younger brother, which was disturbing: this lively young man was now withdrawing himself into long silences, refusing to eat and unwilling to say why. Doctors were being consulted, his father was researching the right kind of therapy, his mother did not want to leave his side trying to cheer him, reason with him, share the outside world with him. Quite undone by the anxiety and the helplessness, she began to languish physically as well. For Muzaffar, hurried trips throughout this time were both distressing and distracting – he failed an exam, lost a year.

What shook him deeply then was his mother's passing away, succumbing to Hodgkin's disease in 1964. The image of his father's car approaching the rickshaw Muzaffar had hurriedly taken on reaching Lucknow station, was agonizing. He knew at once it was carrying his mother's body home from the Medical College Hospital. To this day, the scene haunts him.

It was important that he, the eldest son, remain stalwart in bearing this loss. Abbajan was now left to manage singly

Manjhu Mian's ailment, which remained undiagnosed. The solace was that Muzaffar's youngest brother, Guddu Mian, had opted to study medicine, a line that held promise – and some certainty.

What deepened Muzaffar's grief was the potential of Ammajan that had gone unrealized. Growing up, he noticed consistently how his mother would encourage conversation and discourse without making a point of it. The campus atmosphere at Aligarh only strengthened his conviction, that she would have flowered, given the opportunity.

It pained him especially as he watched the redoubtable Zaidi Sisters in Aligarh, each one distinguished in her own right. Their intellectual stature in all aspects of culture shone, was widely recognized. Watching Zahida Apa presiding over the Art Club, masterminding its exhibits, inviting artists to orchestrate sparkling, stimulating exchange, introducing him to M.F. Husain and Ebrahim Alkazi in that charmed aura, probably knowing well their paths would cross again. Another landmark connection was with the poet Shahryar whose every outpouring touched Muzaffar's core. Its immediacy broke all barriers, sparked a rare bond. Shahryar captured young Ali's whole tenure in Aligarh in this couplet and remained a lifelong friend:

Manzar tareh tareh ke daaman mein bhar rahey hain
Ham ek naye safar ka saamaan kar rahe hayn.
(Scene after varied scene fills my encircling garment,
Arming me as I set off on my all-new journey)

Now with a degree in hand and determined to stand on his own feet, Muzaffar arrives in Calcutta in 1966. Ironically, this

Bachelor of Science chooses to work in advertising. He lands himself a job in Clarions, earlier D.J. Keymers Advertising, which had previously nurtured Satyajit Ray as illustrator, visualizer and painter. Everything about this film maker had fascinated Muzaffar, particularly his insistence on remaining in Calcutta, his focus on Bengal, his passion for the typicalities of where he belonged.

Subhas Mukhopadhya, his art director friend, enabled Muzaffar's to and fro to Ray's home where the maestro happily encouraged an *adda*, open house, when not preoccupied. Muzaffar related to Ray's staunchness about Bengal in an uncanny manner. It chimed with his own sense of oneness towards everything Awadhi. Will I ever capture my sense of place and lore like this man does for his, he'd wonder often enough.

'I made the most of it, watching Ray, comfortable in his high-ceilinged study, hardly ever alone, surrounded by young aspirants, old acquaintances and regulars.

'I was elated to see him sketching away his sequences and frames for his shots. It was so natural, I knew I'd want to do exactly that when I made my films. And the feeling Ray had for music – with that piano almost right beside his chair! I was glad to have this exposure in Calcutta.'

His painting had impressed the foreign circuit in Calcutta and got some exposure when Lady Ranu Mukherjee inaugurated his exhibition there. What Muzaffar found affected and over-anglicized was the younger fraternity, the smart set types, busily dating all the debutantes of the city. He stayed away. But this is how he met Geeti Sen, who seemed to him thoughtful – and they had interests in common. Geeti was a committed art scholar and critic, and they had much to talk about.

His initiation over in Calcutta, Muzaffar moved to Delhi, to the agency ASP (Advertising & Sales Promotion) headed by Jog Chatterji, someone known to Geeti, who was by then his wife. Next came a stimulating term of training with ASP at their Bombay office. This agency had Shyam Benegal and Saeed Mirza sparking off in him his zest for film as medium.

What caught his eye one morning, sitting over his morning tea was an advertisement of Air India seeking applicants for the role of a Deputy Publicity Manager. A man in his mid-twenties as deputy to the iconic Bobby Kooka seemed audacious. But Kooka did pick him for the assignment, said he would have him under his wing and use his talents well. Before someone could question Muzaffar's formal qualifications or experience, Kooka tweaked the title a little. The announcement of Muzaffar's appointment read the designation as Assistant Publicity Manager – not Deputy. Problem solved.

Here the field widened. Besides three quick increments, there was immense and varied international exposure. After all, Air India had both the reach and the resources for large projects. Even choosing art for Air India had Muzaffar exploring the likes of Gaitonde, Tyeb Mehta, Swaminathan and Sabavala before taking his pick. Eye-opening exposure to international art and design festivals in Europe and America were considered essential by Kooka for India's premier international airline. It was flying high.

And design was Muzaffar's forte. He proceeded with no aggression but a gentle insistence which won people over, whether writers, advertising agencies, or artists. They would feel almost honoured ... after all, the world was Air India's oyster. Relishing every moment, Muzaffar learnt while watching Zafar

Hai, the one film maker who would meticulously, repeatedly deliver that international level of aesthetic to Air India films. A perquisite Muzaffar greatly appreciated at Air India was being allowed to pursue his own artistic projects alongside his job. If this were not so, his film debut with *Gaman* would not have happened as it did.

His employer's approach made this artist blossom while securing and retaining his fealty. Muzaffar moved into an Air India flat near the airport when he separated from Geeti. Later, Air India sold to him a spacious house in Juhu, a home he still uses.

Energized by the city, the colleagues, the friends, moved by the plight of the migrant as he explored Bombay, the man was all set. Opportunities beckoned, but good counsel often advised against it. Consistently dissuading him from any arduous cinema project was friend and supremo, M.F. Husain. 'Why take on that struggle and be constantly impeded? Be the artist you are, *paint,*' he would nudge, 'the rewards will be more certain and the pain your own to manage.'

But watching the plight of vulnerable upcountry migrants in this city, where he himself flourished, kept nagging almost compellingly. The film *Gaman* had to be made. *Gaman* or 'going'. So true for so many. Each one, like Ghulam Hassan, leaving manfully to find the livelihood that eludes him where he lives. Anxious to learn, adapt, slog, compromise, prove himself and doing all of it – yet remaining anchorless.

Farooq Sheikh and Smita Patil played the fated young husband and wife, Jalal Agha and Yashodhara, the beleaguered lovers in Bombay. What made the simple story real and redolent were the words of Shahryar and Makhdoom set to music by Jaidev. They moved you and stayed with you.

Seene mein jalan, aankhon mein toofaan sa kyon hai
iss shehr mein har shakhs pareshaan sa kyon hai
(Why does my chest burn, my eyes flail in a storm
Why in this city is everyone … in a frenzy?)

Ajeeb saaneha mujh par guzar gaya yaaro
Mayn apne saaye se kal raat dar gaya yaaro
(A strange turn has overtaken me, my friends
Last night, my own shadow startled me, my friends)

Audiences across the board were moved, rapt. Muzaffar's very first film won Special Award of the Jury at the 1979 International Film Festival. But what moved the filmmaker most was Faiz Ahmed Faiz's very spontaneous hand-written remark, right after he saw the film: 'Muzaffar Ali's *Gaman* is a poem in visuals. Its tragic lyricism, its muted eloquence and deeply perceptive sensitivity and truthfully captured slice of reality around us – the beauty and the heartbreak of the human situation.'

Aagaman and *Anjuman* were two more films that followed, the first about the sugarcane producers of UP and the second about the women *chikankari* embroiderers of the region, their cause and their plight, another fine tribute to women.

Umrao Jaan was now the opus that obsessed him. The region, the context, the novel he knew well. To recreate the ways of the Nawabs of Awadh in their heyday attracted Muzaffar. The strength of a woman too was an idea that had taken a hold of him now – Umrao's persona compelled him.

The start was an anxious one. The permission to use the author Ruswa's novel was being withheld. Raja Sajid decided swiftly to go with son Muzaffar's outline of the script to see the Vice Chancellor at Benaras University, get his formal written clearance. The crisis was averted and Abbajan handed the signed paper to Muzaffar in Bombay and returned to Lucknow.

Shama Zaidi and Muzaffar took pains to cull out a well-chiselled script. It sparkled with wit, tension, pathos and the romance particular to the story, its locale, its period. Awadh was being recreated justly, Muzaffar felt.

Amiran, later Umrao, was a tough, yet beautiful challenge: her poetry as dazzling as her beauty, her full-throated singing, her sure-footed dancing, her eyes defeating all reserve in her audience. Who would deliver this? Rekha seemed right; she was asked, she agreed.

There was a stubborn belief, long rife in the film world that a hit needed a proven male lead and a hero-centric story, nothing less. Muzaffar was not sure that he could prove this wrong, but his *Umrao Jaan* did. Yes, it became the darling of the box office as much as the festivals. *Gaman* had made him the director to watch. *Umrao Jaan* now sealed and gilded that reputation.

But Bombay had still not won him over. Muzaffar's heart and attention were now captured by a cause he considered urgent – and stunningly beautiful. To explore Kashmir, understand it, to study its arts, skills and crafts – to reach out and rescue what was neglected for several inescapable reasons.

This would nag and spur him from time to time. Then came the discovery of the legend of Habba Khatoon. The girl born to eager peasants of the Chandahar village, after a long, long wait. Named Zoon – because her face had the promise and the glow of the moon – by none other than the famed Sufi Khairullah who would remain her beacon and patron saint.

Her rise then from goatherd Zooni to poet, to singer – and then to Queen Habba Khatun.

The story had an intensity because her husband Yusuf was the last of the Kashmir sovereigns to be ousted by the Moghuls who had long coveted Kashmir for their kingdom, grasping at every chance to annex it. Muzaffar was sure that a film would capture the tale beautifully, wrenchingly, giving Kashmir a story it would cherish. If made right, it would gather in its sweep the scenic splendour, the haunting poetry, the Sufi heritage that Kashmir proudly claimed was its very own.

It would be an international production. It would have two independent versions in Hindi and English, no dubbing. The writer, the director of photography, the costume and set designers would be the best in the world. After watching *Umrao Jaan*, Mary McFadden of New York had written to Ali that she be considered as designer for his next film. He knew she would not refuse this.

It is difficult for anyone to resist being moved by Kashmir. Mary began her research in right earnest on the history, the costumes, the daily living lore of that time and that particular village. Recreating seasonal wardrobes, shoes, headgear; recreating the furniture, decor, even the tableware.

The story of Zooni was intensely human, emotional, political. Not any less spiritual, with Sufi Khairullah very central to the events and to the very soul of Zooni.

Muzaffar took over a house so that his father, his sons and Subhashini, his second wife, who needed to be at the CPI headquarters with increasing regularity, could come and go as they pleased.

Work began on building a two-storeyed bungalow which would provide most of the indoor sets. The plan was to perpetuate work for the local people. Muzaffar planned it such that once filming was complete, the location would be converted to Zooni Craft Centre, preserving skills fast fading from this trouble-torn state. He had already begun mediating between craft folk, co-opting bureaucrats. But as the snow cover increased in Kashmir, protests erupted. 'Incidents' became violent and frequent, unpredictable. Safety and well-being could not be guaranteed – chancing life and limb of the foreign crew, even those who were integral to the shoot such as Mary McFadden, Ben Ingham and James Killough, seemed thoughtless. With repeated flare-ups the closing of airports was likely. Next came the last straw: the house he had built from scratch at Harwan for the shoot and thereafter for craft rehabilitation was attacked, its doors and windows smashed to the ground, the sets destroyed. *Zooni*, half-finished, had to be abandoned.

Disheartened, but not defeated, Muzaffar moved to studios in Bombay to work on the indoor sets, hoping the wait would not mean a whole new winter schedule. But things did not improve.

The crew of *Zooni* from Bombay, Lucknow, Kotwara, from England, from America retained a live tapestry of images, sounds and fragrances that now belong to them. They had to leave Kashmir, but Kashmir is unlikely to let them go.

Strangely, even Meera could not escape it.

Meera Saluja. Young, sprightly and spirited. Growing up in Delhi while schooling at Carmel Convent, one thing had become clear – her interest in design, space and structure was not a passing phase. It was a pursuit at all times, a passion that directed her choices. She was going to study design and architecture. And that she did in the Institute of Environmental

Design in Gujarat, setting her sights on doing her field training in Connecticut, USA.

On her return to Delhi, she knew that this was the one city in India that would continue to excite her passion for spaces and for designing and redesigning them – for experimenting, indulging, disciplining her aesthetic, her imagination. This is where she would be. While looking for an assignment that would expose her to practical applications of all she had learnt, she settled on an offer to work as an apprentice with Anil Laul, a well-known architect in Delhi and North India, who was very sure that he could keep her usefully occupied until he could hand over independent projects to her. Clients of different kinds, government and private, would seek him out, which meant exposure, which would enable her to set out on her own soon enough.

Meera's office in Anil Laul's Building Centre in Serai Kale Khan behind the Nizamuddin Railway Station, had her keenly scanning all likely projects, figuring out plans and drawings to have Anil Laul discuss, approve and present to clients. One morning, she had a few drawings for the low-cost housing colony project, which seemed closest to execution.

Arriving a little ahead of time, she hoped to catch him before calls and meetings converged. She found that he was yet to arrive – that the receptionist too was missing. As she headed for the telephone board, she noticed that two men had walked in and were waiting at the reception. The very tall one had picked up an Architectural Digest from the magazine spread while his companion had begun riffling through the newspapers. Unusually tall, she thought to herself, with his longish flow of hair – is he an artist or maybe an actor on stage? Noticing her, he smiled in greeting, 'Good morning, Miss – er, our appointment with Mr Laul is at 10 o'clock … we got here a bit early.'

'He should be here any minute, please make yourselves comfortable,' Meera quickly replied. 'Let me order you some tea or coffee – would you prefer something else?'

'Tea would be fine, right?' he asked, looking over at his friend. And then turning to her, 'What would you recommend?'

Right then, Anil Laul breezed in with, 'Hello, hello, Muzaffar Ali sahab, I do hope Meera has offered you our very special cup of tea, since I was not there to greet you.'

'*Neki aur poochh pooch?* (Why refuse a kindness?)' the visitor smiled, gesturing towards Meera. 'We're being looked after,' he added as she proceeded to order the refreshments.

Anil began to herd all three of them towards his room. What had foxed Meera was to see a flurry as the folk in the corridors were trying to catch a glimpse of the visitor, a couple of girls giggling a little, whispering among themselves as they watched them heading for Anil Laul's room.

Over the next couple of meetings on the Habitat scripts, Mr Ali began to describe to her at some length the series he was about to shoot on the Sufis of India for Doordarshan. He had finished *Sama*. The second in the series *Seena ba Seena* (Heart to Heart) was scheduled right away, he said. The summer in Rajasthan could be pretty punishing so sooner would be better, he explained. This documentary on Khwaja Moinuddin Chishti needed the vibrancy of Rajasthan, its people and its ways in full measure. Meera felt like a clean slate on the subject, eagerly absorbing all the unfamiliar details, riveted by every aspect of this Sufi's persona, story and the almost tumultuous following he mustered from all parts of the country. She was such a total stranger to the subject.

Meera noticed Muzaffar's quiet way of speaking that drew you in, sharing rather than informing or holding forth, or enlightening you. As though it was a journey on which you were now with him.

What gave Meera a start was when Muzaffar Ali suggested very matter-of-factly at the next meeting that he had in mind a role for her in the film, a minor but telling one. 'Me? Act in a film?' This was something she was not prepared for – she baulked. Coolly, quietly, he reassured her that this was a documentary, not an extravaganza. This young girl's cameo role fit the story and the aura of the saint very interestingly, he said, giving her a copy of the script and the shooting schedule. Meera agreed, even though she had not the slightest idea why.

Did he notice talent and potential in her, she wondered, or was it him wanting to get to know her better? Either way, she glowed. And took the pitiless teasing from family and friends in her stride – that she was launching herself on celluloid, that a move to Bombay would be imminent ... ad-libbing as they went on.

It happened very quickly. The shoot in Ajmer was on a tight schedule, the costumes had to be readied, catching the light for different critical shots was imperative as was managing the crowds. Meera reassured herself that it would also be an extended date with Muzaffar that their conspicuity in Delhi would not permit.

Ajmer Sharif is a phenomenon and has ways all its own, she realized. To this day, Meera feels that her every faculty was gob-smacked. Everything about it was extraordinary. It all comes spilling out even today.

'It was a life-changing experience for me! Who was this Gharib Nawaz, present everywhere, listening to each one, caring and calming their distraught condition? The skies looked different, the expressions in the eyes of each one praying was the softest, even though harrowed in their beseeching prayer, their *mannat* of the Khwaja. It is one thing to keep hearing about it from others. Quite another to be there, sense it all for yourself in many ways, sure that nothing like this has ever seized you before.'

The shots were taken, with Muzaffar taking care of Meera – a total novice to this world – in a gentle, unexcitable manner. 'With a patience and confidence that unstressed me like I never expected anything could.' The film, released by Doordarshan for several showings, inevitably stirred viewers as only the iconic saint could succeed in doing.

Meera adds unhesitatingly, as she recounts the time, 'I was by then madly in love with Muzaffar, frankly I was a totally different person. And I think Muzaffar was aware that something had taken a hold of him, quietly yet surely. Though neither of us admitted it then.'

Thankfully, now came their one day away from the twenty-strong crew that returned to Delhi. Muzaffar and Meera stayed back, spent a day all by themselves in Jaipur. It was time away they both deserved – to accept and rejoice in what was happening to them. While in Ajmer, Meera became surer each day that what had happened to her had also happened to him. Jaipur, an all too short reprieve, confirmed it for them.

Returning to Delhi they became as inseparable as life and work allowed. At dawn, at 6 a.m. each morning, they scheduled their date at one or another of Delhi's monuments, often the Safdar Jung tomb and Humayun's tomb and the surrounds of Nizamuddin, Tughlakabad and Mehrauli. Architecture and history being their passions – this seemed a natural resort for two people who were also seeking the rest of the day to work with each other rather than elsewhere. Meera has always had an abiding zest for spaces and structures, seen and scanned from all angles, re-cast in different ways.

As she likened a pillar here and an arch there to monuments elsewhere, he had a couplet, a *bandish*, a verse that was staggeringly apt for what they felt but could not express as well. Work was interspersed with visiting favourite haunts, discovering new ones, grabbing a bite here or an extraordinary sunset there. And something which seemed to especially delight Muzaffar: choosing for Meera a garment he felt was especially right for her, a kurta, a stunning dupatta, an unusual handloom sari with a striking *pallav*. His eye for textures, for weaves, for a svelte cut and silhouette was far keener after the Kashmir and Mary McFadden connection. He wanted to include Meera in all that excited him.

The completion of the hour-long Chishti documentary aside, there were many projects hanging fire for Muzaffar. Meera's work at Anil Laul's too was far from a standstill. But she was not easily distracted.

The people in her office knew what was afoot, which did not worry her in the least. Friends were a little bemused, perhaps worried by her lack of exposure and experience in the ways of the world, especially of cinema, even art. People spoke well of the man, but he had been married before and had two sons. Would he be able to be there for her, even with the best will in the world, like she would be in his? Why should she tie herself down to so many obligations and uncertainties? Even acquaintances turned eloquent well-wishers. They liked him immensely, but their reasons were plain common sense, they said.

Her parents too were more than aghast. They began mildly with: 'Why d'you want to take on every kind of challenge? Don't you want to strike out and be the independent, practising architect you set out to be? Make a name for yourself! Marriage can wait, we're not putting any of that pressure.'

The Salujas had vivid memories of Partition, a severe trauma for those who were hurtled out of their home onwards to a journey they would do anything to forget. They warned her, understandably so. 'The religion is different, these differences can turn bitter with the nicest of people. We want our daughter welcomed not stressed with the unknown, the unfamiliar. The man is years older than you – an invitation to trouble. Why face the ire of two sons, they would hardly welcome a stranger in their father's home?'

Their concern would jostle in her head, but no arguments could tilt the scale in its favour. Her unshakeable faith in this being her sole choice confirmed to them her naivete. They tried everything: 'Let's not blame her but let's stop her. She can work with him, be friends – but marriage is an insanity I will not permit.' Her father, a very mild, gentle parent was adamant, and decidedly so.

Muzaffar was not going to push his suit – he understood her parents' immense anxiety, their barrage of objections. Reassurances were not going to change the facts of his life. He was much older, he had been married twice before, he had two sons – his magnum opus *Zooni* needed rescue and one day soon enough, Kotwara would need to be nurtured. But yes, he would be there, committed quietly to this breath of fresh air embodied so appealingly in Meera's poise, slender yet strong. Of this, he was sure.

Meera remained unequivocal, she wanted this marriage, no other. Extraordinarily pretty, slim, young and waif-like, she was immovable. Given her father's unchanging stance, she had to move right ahead because without his nod, her mother too was unlikely to relent. Waiting would only complicate the many hurdles. It became clear that luxuriating in romance before the plunge into matrimony had to be swiftly abandoned.

Her parents would explode every now and then, their mildness notwithstanding. It did not work, except in breaking her heart. They stopped at nothing. They sought Anil Laul to reason with her against this foolhardy step. They even pleaded with Subhashini, the wife recently separated from Muzaffar, to drive sense into their little girl. Every effort to sabotage and cause misgivings got nowhere.

Muzaffar Ali of Kotwara had adopted the woes of Kashmir as keenly as its wonders – hook, line and sinker. He now faced a collapse of his all-consuming, year-long project to renew the waning craft, culture and lives of a forlorn place and its people. Every resource he had poured into the effort had been in vain. He gave up only when there was no hope anymore. A plate heaped with possibility was not just empty now, it was broken. So was his marriage.

The protective concerns about Meera's own happiness seemed petty in comparison, she brushed them aside without rancour. Delays would be plain disastrous. She had no choice but to elope. Meera surprised even herself that the commotion actually made her surer. For her, this was it.

Meera stayed over at her sister's Pamposh Enclave home, which was not unusual, on 12 May 1990. She left soon after dawn, having said she would set off early for her riding routine next morning. She headed instead for the India International Centre where Muzaffar would stay when in Delhi. The scrambled eggs breakfast duly ordered, he handed Meera the prettiest icy blue and pink *shalwar kurta* from Fabindia, so she could change and be ready to head for the Masjid in Old Delhi where the Maulvi Syed Ali Sahab awaited them to read their *nikaah*, pronounce them married, solemnizing for them a romantic, if wrenching moment. More so perhaps because it was going to be ever so private, so on their own.

Announcing her marriage with Muzaffar to her parents over the phone, Meera broke down.

She spoke to her sister in more detail, happy to find her warm and supportive – reassuring for a young bride about to board the train to Lucknow to meet with her father-in-law, Raja Sajid Husain, for the very first time. Even before that, at the Kanpur railway station where the train was scheduled to halt for a few minutes, she would meet Muzaffar's second son, Shaad. A young man who seemed happy to meet her, telling his father sagely that he must do what makes him happy. This maturity at age fourteen is impressive, thought Meera, relieved that this moment would remain a memory she would cherish.

Perhaps anticipating a fuss, a reception laced with formality, Muzaffar had not informed his father of their visit to Lucknow.

Arriving unannounced at Lucknow at midnight, they took a cycle rickshaw from the train station to Kotwara House. Having made Meera comfortable in the drawing room, Muzaffar proceeded to the library to meet his father.

As she waited, Meera had a weird sense of the surreal about the day of 13 May 1990, taking in the enormity of it all. She found Abbajan's natural graciousness warm – it made her feel welcome, even confident. She felt reassured. She was going to be all right.

Meeting many of Muzaffar's friends over the next few days was meant to be relaxing, which it was. But she realized one thing very swiftly. That her Urdu, her Hindustani was almost halting, when amid so much fluency and wit and teasing. She was going to love this challenge. It promised to be fun, though it did start off a trifle dauntingly.

She was sampling now the Lucknow environs, the language, the turn of phrase, the humour, the *sher o shayari*, the cuisine and its individual quirks. The whole aura in and around Kotwara House, Meera found effervescent, a little overwhelming.

She had not seen the half of it yet.

Starting life in Delhi was going to mean there would be plenty to do – but the thought of doing it in tandem with her husband made it seem what she always ever wanted. Their friend, Francis Wacziarg, had offered them the *barsati* type flat atop his Sunder Nagar guest house in Delhi. Two bedrooms, a living room and a kitchen with a balcony that was stunning. It overlooked a glorious, beautifully kept garden. 'With a gorgeous *gulmohar* tree shading our sit-out area. We managed to do so much in that space … including a bit of entertaining! It was a kind of "dream home" for me, couldn't ask for more,' she says in that refreshing way of hers, which has remained. Meera has not aged.

Life was turning out to be hectic for them both. The capture on film of some of the most crucial and moving sequences of *Zooni* was not easy, the magic of Kashmir insisted that every effort to complete the film was essential. The remaining sequences could be shot in Bombay.

Studios and perhaps skillful editing, the latest available technology, could do the rest. Despite trying to shoot *Zooni*'s High Court scenes in Bombay's Filmistan Studios and the scenic outdoor shots in Himachal, the perfectionist in Muzaffar felt it would tarnish the truth of the film.

They were at it, night and day, learning every trick in the book on how technology could help use footage, manage with minimum additions. Every bit of the struggle, mostly frustrating, did make them savvy on and about the Internet – which in 1990 was not in the least common among film directors.

'I can't think of anyone among them setting up his own website at that point of time,' Meera exclaims. 'We'd attend computer classes every day in Lucknow tirelessly! Our very enthusiastic teacher was bent on us mastering the most complicated computer language, enough for us to expertly write our own software!'

She muses now that *Zooni* in 1989 was perhaps India's first cross-border film project undertaken by an Indian director. Professional to the last detail: releasing every fortnight a finely written, art-directed, illustrated, printed newsletter on aspects of Kashmir's seasons, its tribes, crafts, history, poetry with updates on the progress in completing, immortalizing Habba Khatun's rare legend.

Meera realizes now that her admiration was not hero worship, her love was not infatuation. Her man was the quietest, most serious pioneer. Even in casting the much-hated Pran, the iconic villain of Indian cinema, to play the pristine, inspiring icon for a whole community – very especially for *Zooni*. The footage confirms that direction can make all the difference.

'Everyone was sure *everything* was wrong in my marrying Muzaffar. To me everything seemed right.'

She watched as Muzaffar sent hectic plans of action and proposals to complete *Zooni*, scanned every possibility of retaining the spectacular Kashmir footage, delved head first into technical advancement to enable new footage for inclusion – no effort seemed enough.

Amidst this frenzy, Muzaffar's father took ill. Treatment in Lucknow was urgently afoot and check-ups in Bombay were organized. Muzaffar, and now Meera, were a kind of emotional mainstay for him. Raja Sajid Husain had not remarried after his bereavement.

Muzaffar wanted to ensure the best medical care, Meera put all else aside. She especially valued this unusually mild and gracious elder who had shared with her the family's longstanding traditions, its idiosyncrasies, its humour. He was family. But notwithstanding all the care, he went. His heart had failed.

It was Meera's lasting regret that Abbajan was not there to bless their child. And the bereavement, the sense of being overwhelmed was acute. Grief aside, everything to do with Kotwara and the family, the Lucknow mansion in Qaisar Bagh, innumerable responsibilities and formalities were now squarely their concern. Establishing Manjhu Mian comfortably in Kotwara was an immediate necessity. Any sense of insecurity could very well unsettle his undiagnosed condition. Mercifully, the retinue of old-time retainers rallied around, they were both caring and devoted.

In all of this, they never forgot Raja Sajid's one recurring thought for his people: '*Yahan koi bhooka aur nanga kabhi na rahey.*' He had remained that staunch socialist in action.

Muzaffar and Meera took that to be his will then and thereafter. Craft in Kotwara had to create livelihoods, they decided. To develop and refine stitches, weaves and techniques well before designing, tailoring, embroidering and more. Textiles had always fascinated Muzaffar, while designing was very much Meera's gift. Starting with spaces, surfaces, drapes, she now focused on fashion and wardrobes based on *chikankari* craft, uniquely local and noticeably superior. It *had* to be expertly revived. This needed a degree of familiarity and the patience to gather and sustain both skill and enthusiasm.

Meera postponed immersing herself in the restoration of the old Kotwara Palace or the historic mansion home in Qaisar Bagh, Lucknow. Those could wait. Restoring the lives of their people to some sense of security and self-sufficiency took precedence. Reviving the local hand-stitching and embroidery turned out to be an abiding answer. This led to *Dwar Pe Rozi* (Employment at Doorstep) at Kotwara and the birth of fashion label 'Kotwara' in Delhi and later the rest of India and abroad.

Muzaffar has been quoted saying that Meera has been the 'anchor and the architect' in his life. The promise of this instinct may have been sensed in those first few days at Architect Laul's office. The curious accuracy of his words, the quiet consistency of his actions must be what makes her glow. To pursue what is distinctly arduous has become a bit of habit with the man, to dream bigger than what is easily possible has always been Muzaffar's natural impulse. 'I was hoping it would not become a habit, but in fact, it has got worse with time,' Meera adds cheekily.

She remembers well that in the midst of the screaming avalanche of 'don't you marry him!', there was one friend who coolly demurred, 'Just make sure you are indispensable to him.'

When it came to films, the feature receded as a possibility; the modalities in Mumbai continued to fox Muzaffar. Back in Delhi, the requests for television work poured in – a series of film projects almost consistently compromised on both budget and time allocation. Excellence rarely responds to imprisoning deadlines.

Before becoming enmeshed in their Kotwara duties, the Alis had not neglected another joint venture. Meera knew that Muzaffar had his heart set on a daughter that she may give him. So, *elan* at discovering the fact aside, they were able to know it was going to be one. Because at the time, there was no disapproval of determining the sex of the foetus. The excitement doubled.

Added to that came the shared thrill of proceeding to London and onward to Paris for the showing of his film *Anjuman* at Gallerie Lafayette in late May for the Festival of India. The feature told the story of the Indian artisan, centred around women and their spirit through their life and craft. It was a story, a people, a region he knew well.

In Paris, they both got the start of their lives one lovely spring morning. Muzaffar had left for the Gallerie and Meera planned to follow later. As she crossed over to the sidewalk, she stumbled and fell, eight months large with child. Mercifully it was her back that took the strain, the baby was unharmed. Hugging that comforting thought, the two days of rest in Paris did not seem such a punishment.

Back in hot and humid Delhi, they awaited the big day. When 11 July came, so did Sama. Muzaffar would not leave Meera's side right through labour at the Healing Touch Hospital. He would hold little Miss Ali unafraid and show her off to friend after friend that dropped by to congratulate the couple. Sama she had to be, a name that had lived with him through all the years that both music and Sufism engrossed him, so much so that he had even titled a short film after her. He said to himself at the shrine that when a daughter was born, she would be Sama, music of the soul. A whole eleven months later, Meera found herself reunited with Om and Shobha Saluja, her estranged parents, as though nothing had happened. In April 1991, all-forgiving smiles were the order of the day. Sama made a point at her arrival: that love and time are granted not for wasting. Meera's father soon discovered he felt far closer to his son-in-law's dreamy gentleness than to the impatient, fiery impetuosity of his daughter.

Growing up, Sama missed out on little. Muzaffar and Meera included her happily in all their weekend expeditions. 'We would regularly scan all advertisements in the Sunday papers for puppies we could rear – and horses too.'

To begin with, the couple delighted in Cassie, their first much-coddled Collie; then came Macy and Drogo the dachshunds and Saloni the boxer, later the Rampur hounds, Badli and Tara; the golden retriever Alice named so by Sama; then, Craegae, Bella, Nuriko a team of German Shepherds, Muzaffar's favourite breed. Sama also discovered a most indulgent fondness in her two brothers, teasing plentifully but never bullying. Murad and Shaad were both sports, hardly likely to have the stock, older-brother responses.

Neither Meera nor Muzaffar let up on collaborating. Each time the label *Kotwara* chose to participate in Lakmé Fashion Week, Meera's styles set the tone for haute couture over many seasons and Muzaffar's music to which the mannequins moved and glided, drew a gasp. The dreamer in one and doer in the other had each project glinting differently, making them a fairly formidable team.

Muzaffar was soon able to convince the Delhi Government to support a Sufi music and dance festival in Arab ki Serai, adjacent to Humayun's tomb in Delhi. And Jahan-e-Khusrau was launched.

Abida Parveen, now a worldwide institution herself, responded to his call with special aplomb. Year after year, she was the finale of a three-day repast. Delhi was enchanted. Meera, for her part, was the one who shaped the structures, landscaped the space to create a visual spectacle that her man had in mind. It truly was and is quite spectacularly, a joint venture.

Receiving invites for Jahan-e-Khusrau became crucial to all music lovers of Delhi. Word spread. Aficionados from Bangalore, Bombay, Kashmir arrived, many timing their visits in March, so as not to miss it. Assigning the first row to celebrities and friends, Meera and Muzaffar chose differently for themselves, seated most often on the carpeted ground right up front, as entranced as the rest of the audience. In the fifth year of this prized annual happening, Muzaffar Ali launched the Rumi Foundation, with Dr Karan Singh as Chair, which would, alongside the festival, engage in a thoughtful convergence to publish a Sufi publication titled *HU*. A spiritual feast for the aesthete, each one. And in whatever he took on, Meera's inputs became inescapable.

The ups and downs for a filmmaker can be decimating. Muzaffar's years of research and scripting for a film on Rumi caught the imagination of many but did not rustle up the renowned team he sought for the actual screenplay, the production. It remains a project. If Muzaffar had his way, if he was suitably, adequately empowered, he would present India very credibly as the Sufi capital of the world.

When the Rumi project languished, Muzaffar turned prolific. Almost compulsorily. Anyone seeking to present Indian craft, Sufi music, Oriental art, India's village traditions, sought him out. If Francis Wacziarg wanted to produce the French Opera *Fakir of Benaras*, he turned to Muzaffar Ali. For the ballet *Tajalli,* the Iranians wanted him present, confident that he could get both Indian and Iranian performers to weave magic. Even politics in one era tried to draw him into challenging no less than Atal Behari Vajpayee when he contested a seat from Lucknow! Perhaps the one area in which Ali was not embarrassed or surprised to lose. Very likely, having Meera by his side has halved his frustrations.

Despite being the couple Page 3 seeks, the Alis are most in their element when at home.

They have a way with space. In each home, they have devised over the years, the aura invites you afresh: whether the flat in Aradhana Enclave in New Delhi or a bungalow in Shakuntala farms, Mehrauli, or another such in Dera Mandi, Delhi. Or now in Kotwara Farm of Rumi Lane, Gurugram. The last is what they have built themselves.

On the wall that faces you as you enter is Meera. The likeness is startling. There is a clean confidence in the simple strokes of white, fawn, yellow, with shades of blue in the clothes. It captures the essence of Meera Ali as a kindred spirit. It is Muzaffar Ali's portrait of his wife, gifted to her on their twentieth wedding anniversary.

Nothing stiff or formal is imposed except libations you prefer and a table that serves up hospitality's finest perquisites, the subtly flavoured repast Kotwara is famous for. Served quietly by staff, long trained and well used. Each flavour you exclaim over has a quaint history softly retold. Perhaps with Sama chirping in to prompt a naughty detail or anecdote. No one is surprised that Meera has travelled the country and presented the gourmet a resplendent coffee table volume entitled the *Royal Cuisines of India* and another titled *Dining With the Nawabs*.

Their own Lucknow mansion, occasionally used for celebrations, a qawwali or concert because versions of Jahan-e-Khusrau are regularly held there, in a city they now both know well and lovingly.

An Eid or two and Moharram, the month of retreat, are dedicated to Kotwara in normal times. For the 400 families that revive techniques of weaves and embroideries, the 300 kids who school in the facilities provided through the *Dwar Pe Rozi* initiative, established in 1991. In all their remoteness and with the many restrictions of Covid, it has not been easy to ensure they smile, they flourish. But the Alis do their utmost.

Rani Kaneez Fatima of Kotwara, ensconced in the royal *maqbara*, their family cemetery, must smile in fond amazement that her son Muzaffar has given Kotwara the daughters she had not. And daughters who are pledged. Like Meera. Like Sama.

Here's a born tease unfailingly turning gravity to hilarity, swinging bat, ball, racquet to startling result, right through his growing years. The last thing you would expect is that he steep himself in a mission that gets half the world calling him the 'tea man of India'.

Then there is this tiny, stunningly pretty woman, abandoning her pursuit of art to single-mindedly hone teaching into an art. So that both learner and teacher are in a state of shared enjoyment, shared absorption. Since she teaches teachers as well, the magic perpetuates.

Mumtaz Ahmed and Uma Sondhi are these two unexpected people. Who only found their particular missions once they found each other.

Now, that story needs telling.

TEA AND EMPATHY

Uma & Mumtaz Ahmed

TEA AND EMPATHY

It stands, it sits, it lies, it sleeps by a river. Its breath often fast, excited, almost panting, could choose if it wished, which it does occasionally – to be calm, soothing, near silent. Its soil, when sought by seed or sapling, answers in full and ready and lush green measure; for it is known rarely to be parched. Every once in a while though, the air and the skies like to startle, stirring up a storm, flashing a daze of lightning, declaring there is nothing as typical, as romantic as its sweep-you-off-your-feet Nor'wester. That's Calcutta for you. Oh, Calcutta.

Where two people could very well find themselves more susceptible towards each other than they would elsewhere. Even though the two people in question came from elsewhere, but belonged here more than anywhere else.

This singular quality about Calcutta is inescapable. That if you choose to live in it, you feel you belong, often far sooner than you expected. Because it is also the one city that prefers to talk in its own language to a stranger without any offence meant. 'You are one of us now, you will learn,' they seem to assume. And they are generally right.

The two young lives that found themselves enmeshed in this city after India's independence discovered many things. The Bangla-ness of it was still very tangled in the remnants of the Raj. That it had still not escaped the colonial hangover – the veneer of *pukka* British norms that guided public life in Calcutta; they were hung on to sentimentally, not shed or resented.

This had not registered with Mumtaz Ahmed when he forayed into the city as a college-level cricketer and footballer representing Bihar. But as a young trainee at Balmer Lawrie which handpicked its young, it probably struck him that this was surely a function of history. Calcutta was where 'the Company' as the British authority was once called, had morphed itself into being the Government.

But post India's independence, the word 'Company' shed its earlier currency in India. It loomed attractively for the young Indian gentleman, almost guaranteed to provide a promising, even cushy future in business and industry.

What Calcutta pioneered in the mid-twentieth century were mercantile companies in the contemporary sense of the term: commercially proactive, profit-making entities that manufactured products of quality; priced, distributed and marketed them in order to sustain its personnel with reasonable livelihoods, giving investors and shareholders worthwhile returns. These managing agencies evolved elaborate rules and hierarchies, honing themselves into institutions.

But letting go of the past was slow. The *boxwallah* or the executive was still being honed and polished into being a near Englishman, his clothes, his manner, his habits, his accent, all vying to approximate to David Niven's if not to Lawrence Olivier's tastes and mannerisms. Independence did not demand a shedding of British ways; being anglicized was still quite the done thing.

For one such as Mumtaz, the city would be the nearest magnet and a fairly attractive one. The idea of a young boy from Patna being sent off to Doon School to grow up to be a man seemed a fitting one to a young widow of an eminent doctor. The fact that he then armed himself by graduating from St Xavier's College in Patna and a dazzling record in cricket, football and tennis at various clubs, followed almost naturally. A career in Calcutta was what he was ripe for.

Uma Sondhi too arrived into the same Calcutta – but after beginnings and journeys that were way more exciting and various than those that Mumtaz had travelled. Having known Rangoon in Burma, London in England and then Jullundur, Calcutta and Lahore, she was back in Calcutta. And Calcutta would curiously recur as a rescuing, inviting haven for Uma.

Right from the start, events and stories seemed to chase her. Jullundur is where she was born on 16 June 1931. Her very first memories date around 1934. They are of Burma where her father had been despatched to remap the entire geological map of Asia – a man driven by both adventure and ability. Aside from petrol, coal and gemstones, his unrelenting quest led him to findings, which were often exceptional.

Uma's earliest memories of Rangoon and Tonji are of vast expanses of land, clear and bright skies, often of an unusual blue as the sun would go down. Etched sharply in her mind is a memory of a prank she had no intention of playing. Their Burmese cook would send infant Uma into squeals of delight by lighting his cheroot-like beedi, and placing it on the tip of his tongue. When the chef stepped out with her parents' elaborate breakfast trolleys, Uma's dimpled little fingers managed to light the matchstick. Before she could attempt his trick, her hair, temple and eyebrow were aflame, her screams calling for a major rescue operation.

The brother-in-law of the British Resident, skin specialist and surgeon holidaying in Rangoon managed all the surgical procedures deftly. 'All scars disappeared by the time I was ready for school,' Uma recalls vividly.

Her father, Vedpal Sondhi, in the meanwhile, was learning mountain climbing when not delving the earth for its unexplored riches. This dogged pursuit yielded results dramatic enough to be kept confidential and led to larger missions. Not unrewarded, young Sondhi was honoured with an MBE in his early thirties. And a posting in London.

For a child, change is not so disconcerting perhaps. Uma wondered why her mother did not hand her a bar of chocolate for drinking all her milk like her school did. But now there was talk of Hitler, gas masks issued for each one in the house. Listening to the radio was a ritual steeped in anxiety.

'I shuddered thinking Hitler would leap in through the window, kidnap me and take me away, especially when I'd see my mother, wiping her tears as she stitched name labels on my clothes, in case I was evicted or deported to another country, or if we were separated. The crisis was averted as Chamberlain sued for peace with Germany.' The attempt failed, but did give the Sondhi family their chance at sailing home before havoc resurfaced.

Home this time was Calcutta, the headquarters of the Geological Survey of India (GSI), where there was not only no threat of war, there was an open-arms welcome into Loreto House, her new school, the nuns making safety seem much more certain. The atmosphere at home too relaxed to a comforting routine.

Uma's favourite spot when settling down to do her homework or to sketch, was her father's study. Filled with the aroma of his special pipe tobacco; his desk crammed with pens and pipes of all shapes, with papers, photos, fossil specimens, coloured quartz of odd shapes – a cozy feeling it was, with the Anglepoise lamp shining on her books and drawing pads as she sat on the carpet. Her father was very insistent that the light be just right.

A very tidy counterpart to this den was her mother's room, redolent with the fragrance of *dhoop*, placed on the shelf which she used as her prayer altar; just the essentials, powders and a little bell, a few pictures. Even her dressing table was tidy, with neatly lined rows of perfume bottles and *surma* (grey powder for lining the eyes, different to the usual kohl), a silver-backed comb and brush, an ornate little silver box for the *sindoor* and *bindi*, not one thing out of place.

Their routine had something so reassuring about it. The sound of the bell was the finale of prayers and announced by Mr Sondhi from his study with a booming: '*Ghanti baj gayi, naashta lagao!* (The bell has rung, breakfast to be served!)'

Vidyavatiji, Uma's mother, would emerge from her pooja, *dhoop* aroma filling the air. This ritual was not imposed on any one. Mrs Sondhi herself had her appointed days of the week for *kirtan* (religious singing) – as also for card games with friends. Her husband often quizzed her, 'So, is it Ram today or is it rummy?'

Several times a week, Uma would walk over to the green maidan of Calcutta where the Victoria Memorial beamed down on her. But the magical enclosure of the Calcutta sojourn was soon to be disrupted.

With talk of the Japanese bombing the eastern front, the GSI moved its headquarters from Calcutta to Lahore where the Sondhis swiftly proceeded. But Lahore and the Sacred Heart Convent had none of the gentle surroundings which had conquered Uma quite. Etched in her head was an incident setting the two cities apart sharply, almost violently.

Higher marks aside, the much cherished rewards for the girls were the prettiest little 'holy pictures': little images of the Madonna and child, pretty pastels of cherubs, Joseph and Mary and Jesus – all collected, kept and prized.

While gathering the homework one day, the class teacher chanced on a miniature image of Guru Nanak among a student's collection of prized holy pictures ... and went berserk. She tore the picture of the saint in full view of the class to their complete horror. The Sardarni student rose, tearing all of her sacred images, meticulously collected. Now the whole class was standing – each one of the girls tearing their precious images in solidarity. The teacher drove the errant child out of her class, striding behind her apace. The students waited aghast, unsure of what would befall her or them. Half an hour later, another teacher entered the class and resumed teaching. At the end of the day, Mother Superior talked kindly and amusingly to the students, mentioning nothing of the incident. The nun who had gone awry was not heard of or seen again at Sacred Heart.

Now, Uma's Nani (addressed by all as Ma-ji) in Jullundur began showing concern. '*Isey sab kuchh sirf angrezi sikha diya hai* (She has been taught everything "English"),' she objected. She insisted that Uma be left with her for a few weeks during school holidays to become familiar with the Gita, Ramayana, Mahabharata and a simple daily prayer ritual, as also some chosen kirtans. Uma surprised her maternal grandmother by enjoying the discoveries she was making – something the old lady had not expected. What would have delighted her grandmother even more was the fact that a few minutes of prayer always remained with Uma as her way to start the day.

Life in Jullundur brought curious episodes. A local wedding of Rakhi, the tailor's daughter, expected the entire family's involvement and participation. On the day of the wedding, just before the actual ceremony, the young bride started shrieking hysterically, terrified. As she was hauled back, she wailed, insisting that the bridegroom was her father in her last birth, and there was no way she could marry him. Almost in a trance, she kept gasping, choking, repeating that she would rather die. In considerable frenzy, the family proceeded to the village home and all details were verified to be exactly as she had described them.

'Ma-ji, my nani, then explained reincarnation, rebirth and past life very patiently to me – I could not question it, I felt I had seen an example of it myself, right there in that village. I held this episode to myself actually and did not share it with my sceptical convent friends. But it does revisit me, that disturbing event back in a *mohalla* of Jullundur.'

The cry for independence was getting louder and louder then. Jawaharlal Nehru was arguing in the case of General Shahnawaz, Dhillon and Sehgal who had been jailed by the British, the threesome holding the fort for Subhas Chandra Bose of the Indian National Army. The young, whether Muslim or Hindu, joined the cry '*Lal qile se aayi aawaaz, Sehgal, Dhillon, Shahnawaz!*' Little children would prick their thumbs, anointing their foreheads with red streaks of defiance.

Uma and her cousins followed every move made by her father's elder brother, a freedom fighter often underground or in prison. Thanks to him, she still cherishes having met Mohandas Karamchand Gandhi as he travelled the country. Sitting with a group of young cousins listening to the Mahatma, Uma was taken aback when the national icon suddenly asked her a question, and when her young cousin explained to Gandhiji that Uma's Hindi was weak and English much better, little Uma visibly reddened, feeling very small indeed. But before the children got up to leave, Bapu beckoned her over and handed her a *laddoo*. Lowering his head, he said quietly in her ear, 'Don't worry. Let me tell you something, my Hindi is not very good either.' That made Uma's day.

A time of uncertainty it continued to be. Half-frightened, half-rebellious, Uma's young gang would staunchly keep sitting when God Save the King played in a cinema as the movie ended. Often tensely aware of whispers of 'Get up! Stand up!' and even a couple of soldiers with guns clearing their throats in a manner quite threatening.

'All of us, including our Muslim friends, would huddle together to exchange the gruesome stories trickling in. The rioters, burning and killing were referred to as "those Baluchis"! We considered them faceless lumpen *goondas,* not as Muslim or non-Muslim miscreants.'

The last day of her final school exam shook Uma. The invigilator suddenly snatched her paper, pointing to the window where she could see swarms of ruffians jumping over the low hedge, breaking into the examination hall, carrying the crudest weapons – axes and knives and spades. Uma felt compelled to drag her neighbour who refused to move, shouting '*Chunni, meri chunni!*' running after her scarf which had flown off!

'Within minutes we all pelted out and got into cars, tongas, rickshaws and cycles and sped to our homes.'

The next day's papers announced that the building had been burnt down and the registrar stabbed to death. Partition had struck. The families were rushed across to Jullundur, amid thousands of refugees from Lahore.

'Jullundur was our home town and right then, safer than Lahore. My brother was packed off to Doon School and Mummy, my five-year-old sister Rama and I came away to my grandfather in our ancestral home.' But this was not the end of the uncertainty. There was no knowing whether Jullundur would remain with India or not.

'My mother felt that the school should teach spinning at a wheel to calm the girls. But the school had the bigger, stronger girls learning '*Gatka*' *laathhi* fighting and puny ones like me were taken aside and given small rulers smeared with red ink on one side. We would pretend that the rulers were knives, meant to cut across necks when we were attacked!'

Uma's family found itself scattered. 'Daddy was in Calcutta, but his brother and family were stuck far North in Sargoda. When my uncle arrived safely, my grandfather lost no time in herding us off to Mussourie – the hill station where we used to spend our summer every year. Here in 1947, at midnight between the 14th and 15th of August, we heard Pandit Nehru announcing India's "tryst with destiny" and our freedom. What's more, Jullundur remained with India. Finally, in September 1947, we returned to Calcutta.'

And so, they now went to live in the beautiful old house in the compound of the GSI. It had been the old court house during Warren Hastings' time with a sprawling lawn sloping gently towards a large pond.

'I'd rush past the locked iron gates to the cellars which kept prisoners in the old days – one had to pass these to enter the hallway to our home!

'When my father took me to Loreto College for admission, we were greeted so warmly by the Mother Superior, Mother Consiglio. I really felt that I'd come home at last! She remembered me at once as her "Little Punjabi" never having seen a Punjabi as tiny as me!'

Uma's hands now were full. The annual school concert had her play Shakuntala with her little sister Rama, ten years younger, playing her son Bharat. Sister Damien, the history teacher, had the girls waxing eloquent in debates over the many aspects of the Indian Constitution mooted in Parliament. Uma's batch was the first to raise India's flag on the country's first Republic Day.

While Mumtaz was settling in and making a mark as one of the brighter trainees amongst Balmer Lawrie's hand-picked executives, Uma had graduated. She was discovering her penchant for sketching and painting, she kept experimenting at special commercial art lessons at home. Beginning with objects and landscapes before she moved on to portraits. Her adored dog, the cocker spaniel Panda, who resembled one, would hardly sit still as a model. To amuse her art teacher she captioned it:

If you love me, as I love you
Give me your Bata shoe to chew!

'*Ki chamatkar! (What a miracle!)*,' her art master *moshai* exclaimed and whisked away her handiwork.

Exams now done, Uma wondered if she should aim for Shantiniketan or a local art college. Calcutta prided itself on many.

On a Saturday morning, her mother stormed into her room, asking her who the unfamiliar Englishman was at their door asking to see Uma Sondhi. Uma was as puzzled as she was.

It turned out to be Mr Watney who headed the advertising department at Bata and whose wife ran the studio of that very department. Uma's art teacher had shown him her sketch of Panda, caption and all. As it happened, his unit at Bata was looking for just the young talent that Uma had, to train and staff their advertising department. Mrs Sondhi was neither amused nor willing. She opposed Mr Watney at every stage, but he seemed curiously equipped to patiently tackle her every objection. Uma's professional training and chaperoning would be just as Mrs Sondhi would wish it to be, since his wife was their Head of Studio and would also fetch Uma and drop her back every day. Uma accepted that offer and soon moved on from Bata's to the B.N. Elias Agency which handled their account as also National Tobacco, Usha Fans and Hobby Centre, among others.

Loving her work as she learnt, Uma was making new friends, her evenings getting busier. Quite naturally, the young from all over India flocked to Calcutta because a number of head offices of companies in commerce and industry were east-based. The English companies had not abandoned ship yet.

The managing agencies set great store by golf and tennis and squash, which meant several club evenings – socializing and moving around in groups, if not dating.

Running into Mumtaz was almost inevitable, he knew

many in Uma's clique of friends. She noticed him particularly for two unusual things. He managed to make her laugh – and laugh very readily, spontaneously, not self-consciously. Even when he teased her, it seemed friendly. Despite spending more time together, he was not making a play for her, whether at the club or at a cocktail or just setting off for a drive along with friends. The other more subtle undertone was that the man was not getting familiar, which she had always found a pattern with all others she had known. It made her wonder. 'Is he simply not attracted to me in that way – or does he guess in some mysterious way that physical overtures just put my back up and spoil everything?'

Somehow it *was* that eagerness for intimacy that would instantly make her wary each time. How did Mumtaz know that? They had never talked about it. Did he guess that his ability to have her in splits of laughter totally disarmed her, worked like a wand? She found herself talking to him uninhibitedly – smiling at him as he confided in her about all kinds of things: his childhood, losing his dad young, his stints at Doon School and St Xaviers' Patna, even his past romances, minor and serious.

She found herself making sure she chose to be at the club when he was playing tennis, to tie in with the movie programmes if he was going to make a foursome, to refuse other plans if he seemed disinterested. She was also choosing what she wore with more care – playfully picking out his favourite colours. Although his teasing was unceasing, Uma and Mumtaz would tend to agree on a number of things – the places to visit, the people they liked, the books they would enjoy. She found herself talking to him about things she would keep from her friends. It took her aback a little.

Going for drives to get away from the rest of their friends aside, Mumtaz knew Uma's unfailing weakness for any and every kind of *chaat* near the Victoria Memorial, a feature the landmark revels in to this day. He teased that he *could* afford the club if not Firpo's or Prince's every now and then, knowing well that she chose *chaat* out of preference, not concern for his wallet! Unfailingly, he would buy her garlands of fresh *gajra* (flower braids) for her long hair, and she never said no.

'Mumtaz certainly told a story well, so if I'd missed something – or quizzed him about his travels – his account of it seemed more interesting to me than my being there!

'So readily put off by overtures, which we called "passes", I found myself holding this man's hand quite happily, in a movie we had gone to see. Yes, just like that, no fuss; in fact, feeling a sense of both excitement and calm. Couldn't explain it to myself then – or now, frankly!'

This young woman now had a feeling, a strong feeling that her father may not disapprove after all if she sought his blessing to marry Mumtaz. Daddy was not a man to come easily undone, he had an extraordinarily open, if not risk-taking mind. Uma remembered how, puffing at his cigar, he had put to her a question about a young Scot who dropped by frequently for a drink with him.

'Would you be averse to visiting young Bob's family in Britain along with me? He seems very eager to know whether you would consider living there with him as his wife.'

Uma was amazed at the two gents hatching this plan! She had sensed Bob's interest in her over his all too regular 'dropping in' on the Sondhis. Daddy was in earnest. Uma, however, was quite unequivocal on this particular issue. Settling down away from her country was something she was not going to entertain – it just did not attract her. Clearly, Bob was not a very compelling suitor.

But this episode made the young woman distinctly confident. The same parent would surely take her relationship with Mumtaz in his stride. Its fructifying into marriage would also seem to him a perfectly plausible suggestion. And she was right. Vedpal Sondhi, in fact, liked Mumtaz Ahmed. The young gent did not strike him as the usual courteous but superficial, anglicized *boxwallah*. He had a straight-off-the-bat quality that appealed to the older man.

Neither father nor daughter realized that her mother, Mrs Vidyavati Sondhi, all of four foot ten, would be of quite another view. Apart from the religious difference, how could their girl belong for all her life in a home that may not welcome her? No, she said quite simply, adding that this would also hurt Ma-ji immeasurably. In fact, the feisty, old Ma-ji arrived on the scene threateningly, with her '*Merey pakke baalon ki qasam*' (vowing on her grey hair) that this could not happen.

A decision was made that Uma and Mumtaz will not see each other for a while – several months at least. The elders believed this would sort the matter out almost painlessly. Out of her social circuit altogether, Uma would feel helpless and isolated, her feelings would blow over. Distractions would be fittingly arranged, other proposals seriously entertained.

Uma, on her part, refused to see any other suitor more than once politely, would not entertain the idea beyond this, no matter how rosy the future painted, how 'suitable' the match, how persistent the proposals. Monosyllabic, listless and paler by the day, she caused concern among all the adults in the family. They began to feel responsible – rightly so.

Mr Sondhi would try to distract Uma with official GSI parties and lively international visitors to shake her out of her exile. And very thoughtfully, when travelling away, would request his deputy to step out with her for lunch or tea to the Bengal Club for the girl was starving herself, nothing could cheer her.

Mrs Sondhi, praying abjectly, would also visit Belur Math every Thursday seeking the guidance of her guru, Bharat Maharaj. In him she confided her fears. 'Find out about the family, stop this pointless worrying,' he advised her sensibly. He wanted to know everything – who Mumtaz talked about, who he was close to, who influenced him in his family. Would they accept her daughter if she married into the family?

Mumtaz had often spoken of his older brother, very much the family hero, Colonel Mahboob Ahmed. How the Japanese had captured him and held him prisoner in Malaysia when he served in the British Indian Army. How for three whole years, the family had no idea whether he was alive or dead. How a chance radio message was received by his mother after a harrowing silence of three years. How he had refused the Japanese packing him home safe, insisted on not deserting his regiment. How he had met Subhas Chandra Bose and joined the Indian National Army and finally upon his return to India, was imprisoned in the Red Fort along with Saigal, Dhillon, and Shahnawaz. The story did glisten.

As Mrs Sondhi repeated this to Bharat Maharaj, his eyes kept widening. Nearly dropping the half-finished teacup in his hand, he exclaimed 'Bubie? What! You're talking about Bubie? Col. Mahboob Ahmed of the INA? Ma, without worry, give your daughter to that family. I know them – she will never find better in-laws!'

Her guru now insisted on meeting Mumtaz. Later, he began to expect the young couple whichever Thursday they could manage to drop by at Belur Math, with or without Uma's mother.

Mumtaz had achieved his own not-so-minor coup. Having dug his heels in that he sought no family approval, or risk Uma being disrespected in any way, he invited his brother-in-law Justice Naqi Imam for a drink with Mr Sondhi and his daughter. No one could decide who enjoyed the evening better. The judge got on famously with Uma and her father, heartily agreed that the Ahmeds of Patna be prevailed upon to celebrate this liaison. His own approval was vociferous. This cheered the Sondhis.

But Mrs Sondhi was not entirely mollified. 'The family *zenana* (women folk) will *not* have any of this towering gentleman's English breeding or broad-mindedness. Their role is to preserve their *gharana*, its eminence, set an example for their community.'

She had witnessed the dark side of India's partition first-hand. In Lahore and Jullundur both, up close and personal, as an adult, not as a child. She had seen the worst side of a brutal severance with all its terrifying uncertainties.

But the real victory came in winning over Ma-ji who had dramatically staked her every grey hair on stopping this alliance. The Belur Math Maharaj's applause for the Ahmed family was certainly a reassurance. But what swayed the old lady quite was watching her darling girl wane to a reed but not succumb – eyes sunken, voice lifeless, frame almost skeletal. No threat seemed to move her or her will. Responding to these signals, she sent a message from Jullundur – her trusted family astrologer had studied her *janampatri* and declared that this was a *janam janam ka rishta* (a relationship transcending lifetimes). Ma-ji declared she would not stand in the way. The astrologer's words and her nani's reaction took Uma right back to her Ma-ji's lecture on reincarnation in Jullundur, prompted by Rakhi, the tailor's daughter, screaming as bride to stall her marriage.

A highly amused but relieved Mr Sondhi chuckled, saluting the old lady for this brilliant face-saver. His daughter had been saved. It seemed appropriate for him to now proceed with Mumtaz and Uma to the Registrar's office to set the date. July the 3rd it was going to be, in the year 1955. The wedding was engaging in its simplicity and the reception thereafter at the Calcutta Club heart-warming and spontaneous, not ceremonious or overly formal. The menu was lavishly chosen. Their relieved circle of friends and colleagues, Mumtaz's bosses and their wives attended – intent on jubilation.

'Quaintly enough, me in my bridal finery and the other ladies all dressed up to the hilt had to be led through the back gate of the Calcutta Club, since at that time, ladies were only allowed in on Wednesdays and only through the back gate! Bizarre, when you think of it now.'

What can be more picturesque and romantic than a honeymoon on a houseboat in Srinagar, which was all arranged. What they had not accounted for was that the whole Sondhi clan of cousins, young and old, had an earlier plan for their summer holiday in Kashmir. Voila, the honeymoon morphed into a glorious extended picnic with nieces and nephews thronging around the couple; two sons-in-law whisking Mumtaz off to the club bar; even a concert being rustled up with the locals for flood refugees – with Uma participating full-scale in rehearsals!

When the couple proceeded on their own to Gulmarg, it turned into the glorious escape a honeymoon is meant to be.

'Actually, the very first time I realized what carefree meant was when we boarded the plane for Srinagar after our marriage. I felt nothing could come between him and me ever, no one could spoil it for us. I trusted him. I just did. It did not seem daft to do so.'

Her mother continued to be Uma's very persistent counsellor, insisting that she must melt Mumtaz's disdain for his family's approval. Mrs Sondhi insisted that Uma had to initiate the approval that he refused to seek.

'He's doing it out of pique, this breakdown of bonds will not do,' she said. 'In the end, the blame will be yours. As a daughter-in-law, you have to mix and meld with them all. You're now "theirs" without question, change your religion if you must, don't cause a distance, Uma. You'll regret your children not growing up with cousins, fond aunts and uncles, the warmth and security of an extended family.'

From seeming oddly conservative, it began to sound far-sighted, even wise, to Uma.

'I felt prompted to write a straightforward, pleading letter to Mumtaz's mother, that I'd do all I could to belong to and cherish Mumtaz's family. That I wished to be fully accepted and would be happy to change my religion, allowing no rifts whatsoever.

'I believe my letters caused quite a stir back home. They were circulated and debated over among the elders, especially Lady Imam, Mumtaz's maternal aunt who tended to preside over the family. The latter announced that she was in favour of welcoming Mumtaz's choice with open arms. Not once was there a mention of the desirability of conversion.'

Mumtaz had no idea that Uma was in correspondence with his mother. He was puzzled when she kept quizzing him about names and ages of the family he cared about and shopping for gifts for each one of them on their honeymoon!

'When a letter from Lady Imam arrived, inviting us to Patna, I had to confess to Mumtaz that I'd listened to my mother's anxieties and taken the plunge without consulting him. Mumtaz was not furious. Perhaps it made him reflect on his own impetuosity – it certainly softened his stance.' He sat down to write a letter of invitation suggesting that his Amma and Bari Amma visit the couple first in Calcutta to bestow their blessing.

Uma gave into the frenzy of planning every little detail over the three days of their visit to ensure that they would not feel let down. Mother and doughty aunt discovered how Uma had created a home for Mumtaz with a natural grace that touched them. She also seemed to know how they liked their tea, what drives they would enjoy and who to invite for lunch. Their three days sped by – they were in no hurry to return.

But over one thing, both Uma and Mumtaz stuck to their guns. They would not accept largesse from either family (Uma had returned to her mother the jewellery adorning her as a bride). Mumtaz did not discuss inheritance. They earned the wealth they possessed, and gradually Uma got from Mumtaz all the pearls and daintily crafted diamonds she could wish for. In any event, Uma had never had a voracious appetite for glitter.

The first two years of their marriage were close to being a carefree lark. Of being able to laugh even when things went horribly wrong. Mumtaz retained his unflustered air, his quaint sense of fun and yet, underneath the flippancy, his care was staunch.

Nainital had lured their group when Uma was expecting their first-born, Anjum. Setting out on charming walks with friends in and around the Nainital hills, Mumtaz seemed unflappable. But his teasing care surfaced as he walked ahead of her, picking tiny twigs and leaves out of her path. When questioned on this absurd behaviour he declared, deadpan, '*Meri bibi zameen par chith ho jaati hai* (My wife keeps falling down flat, you see).' And everyone dissolved in laughter.

Anjum arrived with the full fanfare of a firstborn. Ayesha and Adil followed with gaps of about two years between them. Each quite distinct from the other, sparking an abundance of fond ties with the larger clans on both sides.

With traces of the Ahmed and Sondhi in each of them, all three can claim distinction in what they have chosen to do. Anjum sings, writes, curates and publishes; Ayesha teaches and sings; and Adil is an international marketing honcho. None of them have airs but yes, several graces.

Romance quaintly dotted the busy lives of Uma and Mumtaz. On a train trip to Nainital in 1958, they had rather interesting company. Mumtaz was a great aficionado of Indian classical music and travelling in a neighbouring compartment was none other than Vilayat Khan, the sitar maestro, along with Monisha, the woman he had singled out for himself among his countless admirers. Cloistered in the limbo of a long train journey, acquaintance tends to intensify, and soon the foursome began to feel like long-lost friends.

Well before reaching the journey's end in Calcutta, the sitar genius made of Mumtaz and Uma a very earnest request. Knitting his English and Hindustani deftly together, he urged: 'We've touched so many common chords, Mumtaz bhai … I'm going to now ask you a favour you'll please not refuse. I'll put it simply: we would like to get married in your house. I will take Monisha home from *your* house. The fact that you've done what we are about to do so fearlessly, made such a success of it, assures me *yeh bohat mubarak hoga. Ye maslehat hai ke iss safar ne hamen juda diya hai aap se.* (This will be auspicious for us. This journey was ordained to unite the four of us.)'

Monisha echoed his sentiment – all other arrangement options presented to her had only daunted her. The cementing of the friendship among the foursome was inevitable as the wedding, elegantly arranged at the Tollygunge bungalow, the Ahmed home, made for gracious, very memorable hospitality. Whenever guests thanked Mumtaz profusely for such an evening, he would nod graciously while murmuring under his breath, 'The kudos goes to my Pocket Venus.' As the years went by, he tweaked his quip to, 'I've spoilt her, she's now my Pocket Battleship.'

'The funniest was him standing with hand on a banister and looking up at me wherever he found a grand staircase with, "Uma, do I remind you of someone?" Clearly some silly girl had told him he looked like Clark Gable in *Gone With The Wind*! I obviously teased him mercilessly on this illusion of his. You won't believe it, years later at a Tea Association banquet, a foreign delegate's wife kept staring, yes blatantly staring, at Mumtaz throughout dinner. She apologized profusely for being so ill-mannered but my husband did so remind her of Clark Gable. "Has nobody told you that, Mrs Aamed?" she asked in surprise. Mumtaz dined out on that forever!'

The marriage retained its genuineness because Mumtaz, as he rose higher in the official echelon, changed not a bit. He had not the time nor patience for any affected, supercilious airs rife among most *burra sahibs*. The Ahmed home, always open, hospitable, and vigilantly maintained, was never ostentatious. Yes, there was art and there was crystal; and there were some rare rugs. Maybe an antique or two as well, but finding their natural place, not exhibited, whether in their colonial bungalow at Tollygunge, or the Tivoli Court flat, or in the sprawling 20 Lee Road and 52/5 Ballygunge Park Road house, their last shared home.

At work, Mumtaz was so level-headed, thinking big sagely, being that stickler for detail in his no-nonsense fashion. But if he was poured a sob-story, his chances of being diddled into generosity were strong. Staying out of it mostly, Uma would chide just once in a while, 'Half the time you *dullo* (fall for it), Mumtaz, it's not always the needy, it's the parasites taking you for a ride.'

'But what about the *other* half?' he would counter perfectly cheerfully, and that was that.

'No one quite escaped Mumtaz' teasing. Even the poor nuns were not spared when they dropped in for tea or brought work home. Once he suddenly told one of them, "Someone must explain this to me, Sister. Just *how* were you allowed to take the veil, with those eyes of yours. Tsk, tsk tssk." You can imagine her blushing confusion.

'But I didn't exactly spare him the teasing either. When I was large with my third child, Adil, and found it difficult to move around much, I kept hearing from friends that a very glamorous woman had been partnering with Mumtaz regularly on the mixed-doubles tennis courts. I decided to land up at the club to watch Mumtaz play with a bunch of friends' kids, instructed to rush up to Mumtaz yelling "Hello Papa, hi Papa!" before we settled down ostensibly to watch the game. The kids were convincing – a clearly embarrassed Mumtaz introduced me to the players and proceeded to finish the set. It makes me laugh even now.

'He admitted that I'd succeeded in making my point, albeit quite unnecessarily!'

In an almost inadvertent fashion, Uma began to discover her niche. She would stay back each day at her daughter Anjum's Model School Nursery on Rowland Road, which adopted the latest teaching techniques. Watching this, Sister Patricia took charge and had Uma acquire a Bachelor of Education degree. The Teacher Training Course came next – Uma's career was more than afoot. It seemed the most natural thing for this mission to consume Uma, almost unavoidably. Mumtaz was hardly one to meddle. 'He probably felt it was a profession that would keep me closer to the kids, not neglect them! In any case he was not the kind to control.'

He himself was working at Balmer Lawrie's Tea Department, immersed in pushing forward Indian teas abroad. Spending the first three months of each year travelling to the West unfailingly: matching taste and demand in country after country, arranging exports, developing trust in relationships, promoting leaf and dust from Assam and Darjeeling.

But life often stops you unexpectedly. While taking class in school, Uma suddenly received a call. From London where Mumtaz often had meetings. His colleague alerted her that Mumtaz *must* be operated on for his thyroid the day after tomorrow as they spoke, no later. It was an emergency. The urgency was to avoid his thyroid bursting, which could result in him losing his voice. 'Do not worry,' they said, 'a handpicked specialist from Harley Street will be on the job.'

With tears in her eyes Uma was rushed by Sister Caroline to the Mother Superior and the Carmelite nuns who would pray ceaselessly that she get to be by his side, which she did.

'I just could not bear the idea that Mumtaz would lose his voice – it was especially dear to me. Quite girlishly, I'd say to myself often how "deeply attractive" it was. Sleep had eluded me completely. Oh, it was many hours of waiting before he was wheeled out of the theatre on a stretcher.

'Before I neared him, I heard him say "Uma!" in that voice of his and promptly fainted. I just fell in a heap, just too relieved, I suppose, to discover that he had not lost his voice after all. And also perhaps because I had not eaten or slept at all post landing in London.

'Heavens, how happy I was to discover a Catholic Church, a quite beautiful Church of the Lady of Fatima, just a walk away from the Oriental Club where I went in thankfulness. And to say that I'd revisit whenever in London.'

Back home in Calcutta, they tried slowing down. Both eager for books, Mumtaz would read critiques ordered regularly from his book club and order particular titles that fascinated him while Uma was in and out of the club library. 'We talked constantly about what we were reading, so it was a kind of sharing anyway!

'The movie going was also pretty regular. Mumtaz had a chance to see the latest foreign releases and was happy to recount them in detail if they were not going to hit Indian theatres. But off we did go to Lighthouse and New Empire theatres every now and then. Oh, the amount of Westerns I suffered!

'He was a great one for reading reviews of films, rattling off the background of the cameraman, the music director. And how much the film unexpectedly managed at the box office or otherwise. We watched Hindi and Bengali films pretty regularly too.'

Over the 1970s business and industry 'Indianized' effectively, and pros such as Mumtaz were highly sought after. He knew the plantations of all the regions, the labour, the product, the factories, the tea tasters, equally the preferences worldwide. This informed championing of the product enabled Indian tea to stand out and be recognized in country after country.

At a visceral level, Mumtaz had an easy unaffected charm and candour that worked. With the plantation worker's mother, as much as the bargain-driven *bania* wholesaler, the fastidious Calcutta tea-taster, the conservative Marwari plantation owner or the titled knights and hoity toity Earls in and around the many London Boards. He had also dealt with shrewd tea exporters all over Europe.

Mumtaz now felt he had to move on from Balmer Lawrie. Setting out on his own was a sea change after twenty-three years. Uma was by his side unquestioningly, nervous, but unafraid. The Ahmeds moved into a transit flat in Wood Street. He had plunged into the setting up of the new Makum Namdang Tea Company. But Mumtaz Ahmed was just the asset B.M. Khaitan wanted to snap up and did. Steeped professionally in the tea business, his having no vested financial interest in the company, was the icing on the cake. The family of five then moved to a house in 52/5 Ballygunge Circular Road, with a home and garden much envied and admired but superbly devoid of artifice or pretence, thanks to the Ahmeds.

Expectedly, the two girls, Anjum and Ayesha, were settled in Loreto House and Adil sent to board at his father's alma mater, Doon School in Dehra Dun. Spending less and less time on tennis courts and golf courses, Mumtaz now tended to follow the games on television and in sports journals instead, hoping for glimpses at Lords and Wimbledon if travel coincided and permitted.

The fallow hours when Mumtaz travelled, Uma immersed herself in the side of her she had long neglected, her gift with the brush. She began painting on fabric, whether on a sari or a swirling skirt or a scarf or a cushion or a tablecloth.

'It made gift giving more thoughtful somehow. And it certainly kept me from missing him too much and moping!'

Stuffed and embroidered toys for every festival were another handy outlet – Uma could be delightfully prolific with those, and still is.

'It kept all the Loreto sisters gratefully supplied for their charity sales on festival after festival through the year.'

But when back from his frequent foreign trips, it was family time for Mumtaz: recounting incident and crisis and triumph with both verve and good humour. His sense of the droll allowed teasing but no airs and affectations.

The Ahmed household let religion live and let live in a natural, unforced way. Uma would hear Mumtaz apologize quietly if he entered the room to find her praying, not meaning to disturb. She found Mumtaz saying his namaz at home once in a while, or stepping out with Ali Hassan, their bearer, to the mosque for Eid prayers, perhaps. She had a shelf in her closet dedicated to all the deities she prayed to – including Mother Mary. And he had his prayer rug rolled and neatly stored in a corner of his room for when he felt the need to pray.

What they would do with some aplomb was celebrate every festival. Gathering friends and lighting *diyas* in their home and garden for Diwali, treating orphan girls from Loreto

Entally so that they got a taste of Diwali festivities, keeping open house for one and all during Eid. Uma's very prized Loreto connection made Christmas time particularly hectic with cakes, candles, stockings for gift-giving, with stars dressing up the living room and Uma rustling up hand-made Santas for all the kids that dropped in.

Professionally, Mumtaz Ahmed had settled in at Williamson Magor, now a corporation, respected as a key person in the tea industry. His reputation for fair play and integrity moved him up the helm to chair the Tea Board of India, Indian Tea Association and Bengal Chamber of Commerce alongside others. For the Reserve Bank of India, Mumtaz was their man for a key industry they wanted buoyant. At Doon School, this old boy had to be Chairman of the Governing Board, no escape.

'He did give me another fright health-wise,' Uma recounts the trauma of discovering that he had to have one kidney removed. This was not an emergency and the doctors were very reassuring that the remaining kidney would not be undone, his life would not be too slowed down. The procedure was in London again but this time Anjum from Calcutta and Adil from America had arrived and she was not alone.

Back home, she was relentless in upgrading her teacher training, enabling lessons that were enjoyed and absorbed not dictated or dreaded. Her book *Festivals* invited every Indian kid to explore the myriad ways in which each of our festivals are celebrated across the country, capturing India superbly.

The marriages of the three children, one by one, the birth of their grandchild Diya, each family landmark seemed to rejuvenate them.

'And when our son presented us with two sons, there was a fullness to our lives.'

Though very proud of their garden, Mumtaz would often get the flower names mixed up, calling a sunflower a dahlia – and worse. But when it came to Uma, he was undeterred, reminding the gardener to ready 'Memshaib's flower'. That one fresh-off-the-shrub gardenia in her hair was Uma's signature style, replacing the *gajra* he sought for her at the Victoria Memorial nearly every evening all those years ago.

Uma now was being stretched thin in all directions, turning into a quiet celebrity. She was invited to serve as chairperson of the Indian Institute of Cerebral Palsy and later appointed the only lady member of the Human Rights Commission, West Bengal. Being a never-say-die type, she was well known to use the Commission's own very slender police force to track down victim after victim, most of whom were defenceless children and women. While teasing her soundly, Mumtaz was distinctly proud to hear Uma being addressed as 'Your Honour' at her workplace. 'She's beaten us all – she isn't Pocket Battleship for nothing.'

'When Mummy needed her heart bypass in 1997, it was the first time Papa was not himself. He wouldn't leave her side, literally spending day and night at the nursing home till she recovered fully. The next year, he insisted on proceeding to London to have the latest tests conducted. He was a nervous wreck until the doc gave her all the okays,' Anjum recounts, shaking her head fondly at the intensities her parents retained until the very end in their more-than-forty-five-years of marriage.

Mumtaz died before Uma finished her five-year term at the Commission and while he himself was in the thick of his directorships. His heart took him on 9 January 2000. Like the sportsman he was, he did not linger. Uma felt hollow, undone. 'How can I possibly cope with life – life without him?'

Pouring in came the messages, the announcements, the calls, the letters, the obituaries from all over the world. Prestigious institution after institution published notices pointing out significant things Mr Mumtaz Ahmed had done but not talked about, eloquently mourning a man remarkable for his amused self-deprecation; more grieved and missed because he made himself out to be so ordinary.

Now, in Queens Park, across the lane from her beloved older home in Ballygunge, Uma is ready to welcome her kids whenever their lives allow them to visit. As also friends from across the world, nuns, teachers, students and ex-colleagues in Kolkata. The fabric painting and toy-making remain therapeutic delights for her. Something she is deft at even while drawn to the TV by Judi Dench or de Niro or Cumberbatch. Or Wimbledon and the US Open, for Mumtaz's sake.

Photographs of Mumtaz, smiling, thoughtful, mischievous, dot the walls and rooms.

'Most things around me, big and little, remind me of him and his teasing ways.'

He must wonder if Uma still wears that pale cream gardenia in her hair. She does.

All those who know about Lord Ganesha also know the story of how this elephant deity became the ruler of the universe. How did he vanquish the other chief contender, the indomitable Kartikeya who was as set on the goal? A goal over which they would continue to war if they had their way.

A fitting way had to be found to settle this crucial issue – and Narada did find one. Narada proposed that whoever circumambulated the universe thrice would be crowned Lord.

Kartikeya was pleased for he was confdent of beating the portly Ganesha. He proceeded apace. Ganesha was nonetheless pleased. For he went to his parents and took three circumambulations and said, 'This is my universe.' The heavens wept for joy. And that was that.

This legend somehow applies to the story I am about to tell. For it is of couples born together who stayed together bound by love, a love so encircling that only life could take it away. It is of a romance so unusual, so larger than life in so many ways that it could hardly go unrecorded.

DOUBLE OR QUITS

The Chandra Twins

DOUBLE OR QUITS

You are in Delhi, and you roll back a little to before the time the Carpet Cellar reigned over Delhi as the last word on the pile and thickness the cognoscenti tread on, ever so softly. Yes, before the Carpet Cellar invited the aesthetically inclined, as also the plain affluent, to become connoisseurs of weaves and textures – of carpets and rugs, of shawls and stoles, of wall hangings that the world would envy.

This story dates back to the time before this legend began to lure the aesthetes and homemakers of style from all across the world, often making one wonder who one would run into – diplomats were dropping in for coffee, bringing their visiting friends or academics with a home in upcountry New York or Vienna. It could be a boutique hotel owner from Portugal or a designer looking to feast her eyes; a Bombay industrialist wishing his flat was more generous with space to a couple holding hands and asking questions on sizes, prices, figuring how to surprise their equally devoted parents on their thirtieth wedding anniversary. It felt as though Delhi's tourism wing and all the five-star hotels had put the Carpet Cellar on their must-see list.

Yes, before people who had read up on carpets of the world realized that India could give them the region's best: Iranian, Afghani, Uzbeki and Kazakhi, or even the choicest from their own hubs of Amritsar, Badohi and Mirzapur.

Step back from this arena of the 1990s, another couple of decades. To glimpse the lives of two young men, who grow up in Simla. Not as boarders but as day scholars in Simla's Harcourt Butler School. With great spirit and adventure, perhaps just a shade flamboyantly, as inseparable identical twins. Meet Sheel and Akhil Chandra of Simla, later to be of Delhi.

At sport, they team up; as fliers, they are uniquely daring together; as guides and hosts, they collaborate; and at trying out careers too they insist upon going hand in hand.

Their childhoods unfold between Simla and Delhi during the school years and then the DAV College at Jullundur means that the boys gather friends from practically everywhere. The backdrop is not an isolated hill resort of the Himalayas. In the 1940s and '50s Simla was still the summer capital. The influx from the cities was immense. And the hospitality of the Indian Governor at the Viceregal Lodge was no less splendid than that of the Viceroy's colonial 'at homes' earlier. The hotels competed to invite, encouraging occasions and events, celebrations, any excuse to have a throng of visitors, old and new.

Their father had made Simla his base. He was from Himachal – he belonged there. There were few who Sheel and Akhil's parents did not know. Visitors tended to gravitate to their open, hospitable home away from their own, whether local or pan-Indian or foreign. The schedule the family managed seemed hectic because the Chandras were not summer visitors, they belonged. They were all too often the hosts.

Gorging on their mother's reputed meals did not deter the boys from competing to find the best dhaba with its very own speciality; a college canteen that served a fantastic six-egg omelette, dripping hot *jalebis* that were safe even for foreigners … the list went on. Both Sheel and Akhil remained almost inordinately interested in the menus at the dinner table for each day of their lives.

Rustling up drama and theatre too, the Chandra twins were adept at – but always together. Often enough, their Bombay film producer friends would tap them for locations in and around the hills of Simla. When foreign travel was restricted, far from free and easy, hill stations tended to add filmy glamour of exotic flora, mountain-scape, even snow peaks. Good friends with Shashi Kapoor, the acclaimed film and stage actor, Sheel and Akhil often sat around genially at the odd film shoot, watching whole sequences being completed. A story fondly recalled is how once, when one was approached for a bit role in the film *Rajnigandha*, which went on to become a blockbuster, the refusal was firm. 'It's either both of us – or neither' was their instant stance with no offence meant or taken on either side. It seemed to them perfectly reasonable, while it amazed the director and the crew.

Just what would be the fun of one struggling or shining without the other in cahoots? 'Halving the trouble and doubling the triumphs works best for us,' they were fond of saying. And that was that. Naïve, eccentric, child-like – call it what you will – it certainly ensured that no one ever forgot the Chandra brethren if they had met with them even once.

Their father had long run a thriving real estate concern in Simla and its very promising surrounds. Growing up, Sheel and Akhil could take prosperity for granted. It allowed for choices and very decidedly for their indomitable spirit of enterprise. It also sowed in them a natural generosity towards those deprived or in trouble. As they studied government policies and trade practices in India – and in country after country that showed potential at the time – their confidence mounted. Together, they could make it big. They felt this in their bones.

But soon enough, the property business began to dwindle. Practised sharks broke all rules of the business, proceeded ruthlessly and caught Senior Chandra by surprise. He was not one to succumb to wheeling and dealing to retain his supremacy. It was no arena for the scrupulous anymore. The Chandras opted to be comfortable rather than prosperous. Senior Chandra decided to move residence to Delhi. During this time, his wife was drawn more and more to Rishikesh and its ashrams, their house in Simla had ceased to be the homestead it had always been. Watching the rules of the game turn ghastly, the young Chandra twins were ready to explore cleaner, clearer waters, wider fields.

Yes, they needed to head to Delhi and make new beginnings. Coming down from Simla was surely a coming down to earth – and of finding their feet. Although decidedly cut out for business, they needed to set up anew. A steady income was the first essential for survival – they needed jobs.

As far as hotel management was concerned, neither of the boys had any formal training. And yet two of Delhi's handpicked hotels realized that all the orientation could follow and brought them on board. The Chandra brothers were inherently talented at hospitality, public relations, food and beverage excellence and for their unabashed initiative with clientele of different tastes and multiple business ambitions and plans.

Claridge's in Central Delhi settled on Sheel. Ashoka, the premier government hotel near Diplomatic Enclave, offered Akhil just the challenges he would excel at – and almost straightaway. Let us not forget that they had both been readied by a childhood of working hard, playing hard, learning how to fly, helping host dignitaries, filmmakers, the farthest flung travellers – and perhaps most effectively by seeing a thriving business dwindle.

Both hotels had a very loyal and regular clientele, yet with different needs and expectations. The government circles, diplomats and the more formal foreign visitors frequented the Ashoka. The business and travel celebrities found Claridge's very stylish. Both hotels had gained unexpected assets in these two new entrants. They could be relied on to make an impression and to follow through dependably on most needs, anxieties and wish lists of their guests.

Being unfamiliar and discouraging for the business prospector at the time, India could be daunting. The Chandras' hands-on approach to hospitality had a special edge with foreign and Indian seekers of business. Every individual client received attention pertinent to their particular ambition, task or worry. And they enjoyed it all. The clients began to feel preferred and tended to become both staunch and vocal in their loyalty. And as the boys learnt the ropes of negotiations stage after stage, they gained experience far beyond the hotel trade.

Their familiarity with the local processes and approvals, their mediation became crucial for the German, Belgian, Turkish, or Japanese traders. Trust became their unique and abiding quality and reputation. Soon the pressure to move beyond the hospitality function became insistent.

The Chandras took that plunge. Sheel's zest and interest in carpets, local and foreign, had always been keen – he could never resist looking at local craft, visiting showrooms, dropping into museums, noticing them at hotels and the homes of his parents' many friends. He would typically, easily enthuse Akhil with this passion of his. He began sourcing publications old and new, reading up, holding forth. Akhil did not need any goading. Given their breadth of contacts, creating a business of trade in wool and silk began apace. The two young men did not sit still. They studied the markets, they travelled widely, choosing the less frequented but very yielding markets of the 1960s and '70s. Places where many Indians didn't travel readily for general or particular reconnaissance – Kenya, Australia, New Zealand, Japan. Together, they were unstoppable, one meshing in with the other, working rigorously and always in tandem. They developed trade lines, signed agreements, faced setbacks, charmed clients, spread their wings, acquired reputations and left no commodity unexplored.

The brothers also proceeded to make very clear to their elders that they could not see themselves making lives and families except together. And in all seriousness, as grown men of the world, not excited teenagers, they requested their parents that marriage should not be mentioned to them without the prospect of a life together. Their weddings must not create any distance between them.

In any event, there was no hurry to settle down. Having seen a very flourishing real estate business collapse, they were intent on moving slowly albeit energetically, resolutely. In the uncertain world of buying and selling and undercutting, what worked was trust built on an unfailing spirit of 'yes-can-do'. Indeed, also the human quality of forging relationships with manufacturers, traders, customers and very significantly with the government, which at the time was very insistently in the picture. Appointments given to the Chandras were rarely postponed.

The import scene was not dull either. With its appetite for 'foreign' goods, India welcomed the merchandise the twins chose to bring, with an infectious elation. Word spread like wildfire, and customers began to recognize the sure eyes of the brothers.

To men so full of heart, romance is inescapable. But it is yet to happen – the two travel incessantly, work relentlessly. What occurs, then, is far from commonplace.

On the evening of 4 June 1973, Sheel is persuaded to accompany a friend to the birthday party of Sunil Pardesi, a friend of a friend, on the assurance that it would be a casual celebration with a fun crowd and great food. The gregarious Sheel is sipping his drink, admiring a painting, greeting a common friend and then – he finds himself riveted. Among the photographs on a carved wooden cabinet, there is one that frames a face which stops him in his tracks. Who could this girl be? He moves towards the frame encircling her face, looks closer. Sheel begins to feel quite certain now that there can be no girl more beautiful than the one in the picture before his eyes. He looks around to ask who she may be as casually as he can muster, to discover that the face belongs to Nandini Pardesi, the sister of their host, Sunil. Where is she now, he wonders.

The man is quite convinced that this is the beauty he is looking for in a woman, in his wife. That she and she alone surely, should be the mother of his children. Having discovered who she is, Sheel is even more emboldened. Would Sunil brush off his brand-new guest, a good friend of a very good friend?

He follows up with the brother, pressing him to reach to the Pardesis his formal letter of proposal, arrange a meeting. 'This is a very earnest and urgent request,' he says to Sunil.

Pleased and slightly amazed by the eloquent written proposal, the Pardesis of Pune, originally of Ahmadnagar in Maharashtra, are willing to entertain the young man and have him meet with their daughter. Sunil's friend and his keen approach certainly seemed to merit a once-over being arranged. A date in early August is duly confirmed.

Astonished to discover that his dream girl was one of twins, Sheel is now even more set on this project. Since Akhil is immersed in sizing up markets in countries remote and nearby, Sheel plans to undertake the first formal round on his own. If the subject of the twin sister is raised, he intends suggesting Akhil or cousin Binny – both equally eligible. Sheel was not going to be deterred from making this happen. Nandini Pardesi's face keeps returning to him.

It is now the thick of the Bombay monsoon in August – there has been a torrential downpour all morning. Sheel arrives at the station to discover that the Bombay-Poona train is going to be at least two hours late. He proceeds anyway, brooking no delay in hiring not one but two tourist cabs (why risk a breakdown?) to ensure certainty. Filling both vehicles with bouquets of the choicest blooms from the best florists en route – one at Flora Fountain and one at Churchgate – he proceeds. He would rather smother Nandini with flowers than with a lament about the Indian Railways and his bad luck. That is how he arrives at the Pardesi home, two and a half hours later than expected.

Nandini and Sunanda, their parents and their home had awaited the eager suitor Sheel Chandra at half past seven in the evening with every gastronomical delight that a summer high tea could warrant: from fresh bhelpuri, to tandoori legs of chicken, to the Swiss chocolate gateaux that Poona was famous for and more. From being eager, to puzzled, to worried, they had finally assumed that some misunderstanding over date or time may have occurred.

The high tea is kept away, dinner is done, and they all retire. In fact, when Sheel's rather insistent doorbell resounds in the house at half past ten, it is Sunanda who rushes out in her nightgown to open the door. Only to rush right back instantly for her housecoat in order to let in the visitor who announced himself as Sushil Chandra from Bombay, amid the resplendence of many bouquets, which he mentions are for Nandini. Having now ushered him into the living room, Sunanda proceeds to rouse Nandini and her parents.

What begins as irritation mixed with relief turns steadily into a pleasant, engaging surprise. The delay, the long drive, the late hour had not fazed the visitor in the least. The Pardesi clan is disarmed by the gust of cheer, the *joie di vivre* that has taken over all personae present. Sheel seems to enjoy whatever is served to him. He has all members of the household stirred and entertained by his most recent business trip to Japan, the many escapades, one story leading to another, on to a joke and yet another story. Everyone is floored, even a little carried away. Nandini too is fascinated. Feeling quite won over, they part with Sheel on the note that they would most certainly be in touch.

The next day is saner though the family has not quite recovered from the drama and the exuberance of the whole encounter. Nandini, however, is not on cloud nine.

'No, I am not being unreasonable, I expected him to be much younger.' As they champion him, she protests: 'He is eight whole years older! Did no one notice his hair is thinning, okay not *chandla*, but balding.' Nandini is shaking her head, unable to see why things have to be so rushed.

The general high of being charmed off their feet recedes. The parents are a little deflated, relaying the news to Sheel on the phone, their partiality to him quite apparent even in their refusal.

Sheel is unfazed, does not argue or persist or plead his case. But with an innate, uncanny confidence, he says very articulately that this refusal is a great pity. Especially because on his return from Pune he had mentioned Sunanda, Nandini's twin sister, to his twin brother, Akhil. And Akhil's response was elated and immediate and indeed very insistent that they both formally propose to Nandini and Sunanda, respectively. Sheel adds that they had always been set on doing everything together, each step of the way. Live, work, laugh, explore, travel – always in unison. Akhil would turn up within the month, Sheel announces, so that Sunanda can see for herself and decide.

The Pardesis had listened intently, taking it all in. Now the actual possibility of the 'twin' marriage and ensuing togetherness started to win over Nandini. It seemed almost too good to be true – or to be missed. Clearly this inherent 'twin syndrome', this twinship began to steer, becoming a deciding factor for the girls as much as for Sheel and Akhil. Nandini felt a minor miracle was being arranged, and she had no business to demur. She felt strangely confident that it surely was meant to be, almost ordained, like a signal. The parents felt this change of heart was a godsend. Sheel got a response from the Pune family in the clear affirmative.

So it comes to be that Sheel with Nandini and Akhil with Sunanda take their vows and turn their *pheras* under the very same *mandap* in a gracious Friends Colony hotel on 30 January 1974. They are surrounded by family and friends from all over. Most wedding guests that Sheel and Akhil dealt with abroad wanted very much to discover the India of the two brothers, much beyond the India they knew thus far.

Sheel and Akhil had always won friends wherever they went, exploring markets, trading wool and silk; discovering importers and sizing up India's growing appetite for artefacts, carpets, rugs from all corners of the world, the less familiar the better. Their unaffected curiosity and charm always won hearts unfailingly. And once the girls set up home, the Young Turks were rather more in their element.

The four of them seemed to create a world around themselves. It was not a joint family, it was one family. That is how it started in January 1975 – and that is how it remained naturally and automatically. Being together and being a very integrated foursome saw them smiling even through the years of the Emergency which had shaken many. And even thereafter when the Licence Raj deterred most except the unputdownable. 'We also exploded our first nuclear device, after all. We may have nationalized the banks but then expanded them enormously,' Sheel would quip, refusing to be dispirited.

Gradually, their trade of wools and silks sailed and flew and flourished in countries of Africa, Europe, the Middle East, and very actively in the Far East. Dealing with the Chandras gave the business prospectors a confidence they did not otherwise feel when they forayed into India. For one thing, the brothers had the implicit trust of the locals right from weavers and mill owners to textile manufacturers – the modest and the stellar both. For another, the Chandras were simply not interested in gaining at the expense of trust. It had to be not just public relations but strong personal bonding.

Visiting the Chandra hearth, the buyers would find the hosts in their element. Watching Sheel with Nandini too was a delight. His attentiveness, his teasing, his picking her a gift at every turn, caught even the stranger's eye.

Quite a phenomenon they were, he being 'Shahji' to her and she his 'Nanni' to him, as she reigned in their home. Sheel would choose her every ornament, value even her every passing opinion. She was not just a casual mascot. She would have to be seated next to him when he gambled – when he played *Teen Patti* at Diwali, he always played blind, because his 'lucky charm' was beside him.

'Once I had won her over, I knew she'd win me everything else. *Har baar* (each time). And if she moves away so does my luck.'

Sheel was convinced that he had, ruling his heart and his home, a woman to be treasured. Her name had to be on his every bank account, his home, his shares, his every owned bit of real estate, his antiques, all his insured belongings. She would only be chauffeured around in a Toyota at a time when importing cars into India was riddled with obstacles. Sheel himself would happily drive or get driven in his hardy, homegrown Ambassador engineered at Birla's Hindustan Motors factory.

Friends would touch wood watching these two couples. Seeing Sheel dote on his Nanni, they were not surprised that he was Shahji to her.

'He's solving each of my problems with his "Is that so? Why couldn't you tell me earlier?" He's explaining everything with, "*Samajh gaye na?* Got my point?" Always helping every deserving person he meets with his "I'll keep at it always, as long as I can." I don't want to stop him.'

Akhil and Sunanda were not dissimilar in their devotion to each other, but they were shyer, far less dramatic. They would unfailingly be there at all the gatherings at the 'Durbar' that Sheel and Sunanda's home was fondly called. But often Akhil and Sunanda would be ensconced at one or the other of the city's hand-picked restaurants. Being gourmets and long-standing friends of all of Delhi's hotel honchos, they were both regulars at the *Frontier* in Hotel Ashoka, where Akhil would reject Sunanda's favourite *burrah kebab* until it was just the way she wanted it. Other haunts were Oberoi's *Tabela* and Ashoka's *Supper Club*, where the band, on seeing the couple enter would almost immediately strike the chords of the then favourite melody *In the Mood*, inviting them to the dance floor. Akhil and Sunanda were only too happy to oblige, sometimes even before getting to the menu to order dinner.

On one such date, Akhil needed to attend to an international work call he could not defer or cut short. He moved to a quieter corner. All the while the dance music played on and a highly presentable gentleman, with a beard as elegant as his tuxedo, danced up to the Chandra table, requesting Sunanda, very politely but insistently, to step on the floor with him despite her equally polite refusal. Call over, Akhil returned to his table and alerted the man firmly that the lady was not unescorted. The rather cocky gentleman was now quick to make himself scarce. Once again, the Chandra couple were on the floor, with the band playing the numbers the couple often requested. The evening proceeded as if nothing had happened.

This spontaneous panache in handling a situation deftly was a quality the Chandra twins had in common.

Incidentally, Sunanda who everyone else in the family called Su, remained Sunanda for Akhil. To him that name was pristinely hers. 'Su' did not reflect the esteem he felt for his Sunanda. *Tea House of the August Moon* was their other pet haunt. Where Akhil insisted that the Talumein soup arrive piping hot for Sunanda before dinner. Akhil and all other guests would perhaps choose to skip the soup, but Sunanda had to have what he knew she wanted.

On the subject of atypical cravings, the couple's drive back from their Simla retreat cannot but be recounted. Akhil and Sunanda were driving down from Simla to Delhi. Their two children Dhruv and Divya were ensconced in the backseat of the car. Sunanda was expecting their third child. The entire clan, young and old, and particularly Akhil, were eagerly anticipating the event, with preparations afoot and elaborate to welcome this new addition to the family.

Now it is not unusual for an expectant mother to have a special craving of this kind, she is almost expected to do so. Sunanda, at that moment, was yearning for the melon called *kharbooza*, a fruit that arrives like a refreshing saviour each summer. She was not inclined to wait till the next morning once they were home safely. It had to be right then. Though she was being far from petulant, Akhil was determined that she got what she wished for. He knew no shop, no restaurant would be open post-midnight. He decided to take a detour into Sarojini Market as soon as they neared Delhi. Given the late hour, all the fruit stalls were shut. No *kharbooza* or the possibility of one was in sight. He kept driving ever so slowly, hoping to see a light, a half-opened shop, an owner not quite in deep sleep. The white Ambassador HPS 3211 wound its way ever so slowly, almost mysteriously, to wake a fruit seller quietly, so as not to alert a cop or disturb anyone else.

The kids, now up and puzzled, wondered why the basket of fresh cherries, peaches or strawberries, being carried back from Simla, could not be opened up for Ma instead. 'Give these to Ma now Daddy, *whichever* one she likes, don't wait to get home,' little Dhruv sleepily suggested, trying to be helpful.

But Sunanda only wanted the *kharbooza*, nothing else. There was no resort. Akhil alighted from his car and in the gentlest but firmest manner, ruffled the sleeve of a fruit-seller lying peacefully next to his shop. The man appeared to be dozing, not fast asleep. Akhil then quietly pleaded with the amazed, half-awake man that he should just let him have the *kharboozas* in his shop. That he was prepared to buy his entire stock of the fruit as long as he could cut a slice right away. Preferably with a clean fruit knife. Dhruv and Divya, watching from their rear window, were getting more and more alarmed at their mother's unexpected behaviour – they had always thought of her as more sensible than anyone else they knew.

As children came to the Chandra couples, the bonds between them did not scatter or diminish. They seemed to deepen – it was as remarkable as the love of their sets of parents. Even if the kids were scrapping as kids do, they were kissing and making up with as much gusto. Sheel's Nishant, Nandita, Pranav and Lado were one with Akhil's Dhruv, Divya and Mudita. Each one had to accept that they would be treated equally by all involved. They had been shown no other way.

'The *most frustrating* thing was that it seemed impossible to come between our parents, let alone pit one against the other

– no matter how we tried! No chance. They told each other everything, *every* darned big or little thing, for God's sake. So, you could get nowhere trying to make any trouble,' recounts Nandita now. It bothered all the little Chandras.

Whenever Akhil would return from a trip abroad, especially if it was Singapore where the shopping was a fiesta for tourists and especially Indians with the then severe limits and duties on imports, the excitement would be sizzling. The suitcase was like a gift hamper. But always first shared with Sunanda. And then the two would sit, with all seven Chandra children gathered in their 25 Anand Lok home. Only then would this Mr and Mrs Santa Claus preside over the allocation of the gifts. There was always a little more than expected, so that comparing was fun and squabbling not necessary.

Akhil would get for his Sunanda cardigans, slacks and tracksuits, all that could persuade her to start playing golf, more than just accompanying him to the club which she often would, impeccably dressed. He had always been an avid golfer but almost as determined to not have her languish at home.

With restricted entry of foreign brands in India at the time, Akhil needed no prodding. Her favourite perfume, brand of handbag he would ensure, looking out for more. She remembers jumping in excitement when she got her just-launched vacuum cleaner. 'Perhaps before any other housewife that I certainly knew!' laughs Sunanda, also knowing well that he would get one for Nandini on his very next trip, if Sunanda was happy with her purchase.

Their concept of siblings as one was unique: even when married, they would be inseparable in public, private and official lives, a much remarked-upon phenomenon. They had this ability to turn each friend into a specific and cherished connection. For instance, the pact with Tiger Pataudi was that he gets a bottle of his rare brand of rum each time either twin made a trip abroad; and the deal was that his bat should be theirs if he crossed a century in any match – they would be in the pavilion to claim it anyway.

D Block Defence Colony it was, over the early days of bringing up their children and building their business to flourish into an institution. Later, both the Gulmohar Park and Anand Lok homes were open houses. Friends, colleagues and bureaucrats, whether in Delhi or anywhere in the world, were welcome to treat these like their second home.

Nandini had an unswerving rule in the house. One extra place, with every piece of cutlery required and a fresh napkin, would be placed on the table for lunch and dinner. Whoever would drop in was made to feel that they were expected to stay. She may have known too well that her Himachali food was requested for unabashedly, certainly her prawn pulao was to die for.

No one needed to wait for festivals and occasions. The unexpected celebration, the charmed evening of music on the terrace presented itself at least three or four times a year, for no special reason. Friends arrived readily to their expansive Anand Lok terrace, prepared to be there till the wee hours of the morning. Indranil Mukherji was a repeated favourite – he just expected to sing the night away on all the special days of the year. Every member of their warm and varied circle could be certain to receive their exact preference of whisky, their choice of wine, right down to the temperature, expect a toast of champagne at dinner and hours of semi-classical music –

even the newest *ghazal* jostled with the oldest film song as the evening proceeded. '*Farmaish hojaye* (name your choice),' the Chandras would prod their guests, to name the melody they wished sung or played. Their hospitality was legendary in the city of Delhi.

Even the musicians knew that the long wait for them to dine when the music was done, was well worth it. Nandini took special care to ensure that a hefty wok of prawn pulao was kept aside for them along with the rest of her lavish menu.

When selecting musicians, Sheel would encourage Indranil and the other ustads to bring with them eager, undiscovered pupils, committed but unrecognized. Hard work excited Sheel like nothing else did. He felt strongly that it must not go without reward, some reward if not due reward. You would not see the man handing out alms ever. But the sweeper, the garbage collector, the half-starved coolie or construction site worker he would look out for and give regularly, almost systematically, each weekend. 'He needs what you give much more than the one who asks,' he would say.

On Sunday mornings in winter, Sheel would set off with the car loaded with neatly packed sweaters, socks, blankets and mufflers to personally hand over to the needy. 'If the cold won't stop them from working, shouldn't someone be protecting them – that's the least we can do.'

Among the first to support the NGO Par Dada Par Dadi for education of girls in the neglected district of Anupshahr, Ghaziabad, were the Chandras. They knew Sam Singh, the founder, had both the character and the genius to mastermind the project into an admired institution. The lives of the community in the surrounding villages changed. '*Dard mitaaney ki khushi bohat khaas hai, hai na?* (nothing equals the joy of leavening pain, right?)' Sheel's characteristic push of his chin as he said this, insistently sought your agreement.

'Experience is the best teacher, but the fees are very high,' was something he would sagely repeat. Experience had certainly extracted its toll, the Chandra and Pardesi twins had not escaped shock or pain or misfortune.

As young men, Sheel and Akhil had to hold it all together when their adored younger brother, heading to receive from the Defence Minister of India his NCC award of honour, did not make it back. Shiva died in a car crash as he headed to the Republic Day event. To recover from this blow was tougher than any other challenge the family had faced.

Both the Pardesi girls, too, felt orphaned in irreparable grief, even while their parents lived. Their brother Charu, much admired for choosing the Armed Forces as his career, had to undergo a simple nose surgery correcting a deviated septum before joining the coveted service. The routine procedure ought to have been no more than fifteen minutes. The surgery was duly performed but Charu did not emerge from his anaesthesia. Even the doctors were mystified. The girls would wake up morning after morning, feeling utterly bereaved.

Perhaps these painful events were preparation for the foursome. Within a week of giving Sheel their first-born son, Nishant, the glowing mother, Nandini, lost her father. Sheel had to be by her side like a rock and by her widowed mother's, just as much. Mrs Pardesi now had to take on the role of anchor to the entire Pardesi *parivaar*.

Then again, when senior Mr Chandra fell to the ground while trimming the roses in his Simla garden, Sheel was there in a heartbeat and able to hasten the diagnosis of the brain tumour and enable its prolonged treatment. Their mother, happiest now in her Rishikesh Ashram for steadily longer stints could be persuaded to come back to Delhi or Simla only if her favourite, Akhil, drove up to fetch her. The shock of her husband's collapse and surgery may have caused the onset of dementia, through which both Akhil and Sheel patiently nursed her over many years. Her going took an emotional toll on each of them. The kids were so used to feeling that their granny would always be there.

Each of these setbacks for Sheel was easier to bear because Akhil was there – and vice versa. And because Nandini and Sunanda were by their side. But they certainly ensured that both families, ever working as one, did not disappear for holidays together or left for too long a spell. One of the two couples stayed behind. Their elders they took to Simla yes, but never too far away from medical care.

In 1989, holidaying in Christchurch, New Zealand, Sheel and Nandini trooped back to their service apartment, happily exhausted after a hectic tour of the picturesque South Island. The manager stopped them at the door. A call from Delhi brought bad news, he said. Mr Chandra's brother had died in Delhi, he should get in touch. Sheel assumed in great distress that it was his elder brother. But the phone was answered by Sunanda who said it was Akhil who had gone. Gone, gone where, why? Sheel took a while to accept that Akhil had so suddenly left him, left the world. He had collapsed to a cardiac arrest in his sleep. The blow took a special toll.

With this pillar gone, the family was more resolved than ever to be one. Sunanda and Nandini became even more inseparable, their children closer. It was not like them to wilt under pressure.

The Chandras were no longer the inseparable foursome, but the three who remained were more close-knit than ever. The children too were in and out of each other's homes. Akhil and Sunanda's togetherness, their romance was as marvelled upon as that of Sheel and Nandini's, though they were not in the public eye as much. And their foursome often had people guessing who was who, though Akhil was decidedly the more understated one.

When the 1990s arrived, the Iran-Iraq war occasioned a flux in the region as indeed did the US retreat from Afghanistan. Much shaken, all business refugees, knew that their prospects back home in Europe, Russia, West Asia were uncertain. Opting for a sojourn in neighbouring India, seemed a welcome refuge, an opportunity. India's lenient refugee policy made it easier for them to find ways to set up base, devise linkages, if prepared to trade all their moveable assets, whether objects d'art, carpets, wall hangings, precious heirlooms, jewellery or furniture. Thus weighing anchor, rearranging their lives for the next step.

Watching a plight of this kind would bring out the best in a man like Sheel Chandra – and it did. He became counsellor, promoter, buyer, client and benefactor to families fleeing from war-torn areas – he seemed a godsend. In helping them rehabilitate, he examined their artefacts, rugs and carpets with the practised keenness of a connoisseur. The different histories of the many wools and silks, the different properties of their fibres, their yarns were grist to his mill.

The decade or more had honed him into an expert, almost an authority on the floor coverings of different periods of history, in different parts of the world. Sheel was never a junk collector. Now even less so, with such a varied array before him. His every option he would scan discerningly; each piece would have a history, a story, a reason to be his.

Soon, the pile of museum pieces began to accumulate as a casual not-for-sale collection. It gradually overtook all the living space available and began to need a whole floor of their home. Nandini protested. 'But it is all for you to feast your eyes,' said her doting spouse, undeterred. Until one day, she resorted to a firm ultimatum, 'It's either me or your collector's zeal. Today is the day you decide whether I remain here or the museum upstairs. It's exquisite but it has to be *elsewhere*. I want to look at it, not live with it.'

Shahji relented. It was becoming amply clear to him that his appetite for the unusual, the tasteful, the historically significant, did not need curbing, it needed space. An extension and a sharing which could turn 1, Anand Lok, into an outlet for his passion, seeking involvement and participation beyond the ken. And so, the Carpet Cellar opened its portals and Sheel got the world to come – treading carefully but feasting its eyes. He also saw it as a medium to the world that all the Chandras would inhabit. That it would be a convergence of the zest, the drive, the ambition of each one of them, in whichever role they chose.

Akhil's son Dhruv and daughter Mudita were brought into the business along with Sheel's own sons Nishant and Pranav. Pitching in expertly as Head of Production & Content Management but also teacher/demonstrator of yoga on TV, was Sheel's daughter, Lado, formally Saudamini. Nandita and husband Jesse were thriving in New York. Sheel did not lure them back to Carpet Cellar on account of Jesse's solar technology venture, Soltage LLC. Having come to know Jesse well, he would almost gloat: 'Have you detected any fault, even a single fault in this young New Yorker, no matter how hard you look?'

The Carpet Cellar continues to be where rugs of many weaves, textures, skills abound. Nishant, Sheel's eldest son is the chief honcho, the sounding board for all family decisions, called and considered Godfather. Akhil's son, Dhruv, is his closest partner, his mainstay. They can answer your every question, explain a process, show you a weaver's manuscript, a demo film, an old history book, a Moghul miniature – and sip with you very fine Turkish coffee.

Sheel's younger son Pranav heads operations, but having founded the travel company, the Great Indian Adventure, flits from Rome to New York to Delhi. When in Delhi, he urges sister Lado to accompany his guitar, show off her piano skills.

Sheel departed 25 years after his inseparable twin Akhil, at peace that the younger generation abide in that oneness, cherish their twin mothers. When you hear Nandita speak, that aura returns. She, a very successful theatre artist in New York, and Jesse, heading up Soltage LLC, are inseparable.

'We carry their generosity, their love for people and animals, desire to live life king size, to go on adventures but always come home, serve our community, spread light, love, joy, when it's hard to do so. We've all inherited their love for music, art and beauty. We've all ended up with supportive, intelligent partners who love us unconditionally – because our parents set such a good example.

'My first-born is named NanniSheel in their honour, fusing their wonder and oneness. Sheel means tranquillity with a nuance: the feeling that washes over you when you see the full moon reflected on still water. Our second girl is Niyamat, the blessing that followed four years later, in 2021.'

Listening to Nandita, the inimitable Chandra twins are surely smiling, somewhere up there. And here, all friends of the Chandras are revelling in the memories they so generously left behind.

When you dismiss 'happily ever after' as that total absurdity you grew up with, this story taps on your shoulder – the wedded partnership of Aruna and Viswanathan Anand, the chess grandmaster.

One touches wood, seeing this couple together. They seem to have a halo around them that keeps them unspoilt by the glare of attention, of competition, of worldwide buzz and acclaim – and the price of these things. Even as he moves on to being considered world authority on the game in very lively, vibrant ways. With her by his side.

THE ONE UNCHECKED MOVE

Vishy & Aruna Anand

THE ONE UNCHECKED MOVE

Many Indians have won many world honours in many fields. They will continue to do so, no doubt. But there is one who has a planet of the universe named after him. Quietly, many years ago and without undue fuss. Immortalized as *4538 Vishyanand* in our galaxy, the down-to-earth Vishy wears his wry smile and dismisses it with – 'Ah, these things happen.' As he would, each one of his several victories starting at age six and crowding in on him unfailingly as the years went by.

Their beginnings as individuals may not have been dissimilar.

Both Aruna and Anand were growing up in Madras, born into families not vastly different from each other. She was being groomed like all good South Indian girls are, with a decent education and training in Bharatanatyam, so as to make a very suitable match. But about chess she had not a clue. The boy would have to be a bright young man brought up to excel hopefully at a hi-tech skill, in order to land a secure, coveted job. He did not have to be rich or famous. Whatever for? Those kind of spouses entailed all manner of fuss, were often self-centred, even negligent. And, in any event, Aruna was in no hurry. Life was fun, it was busy and there seemed to be a lot to learn. There was a delightfully spirited, carefree side to her growing up.

'Just *how* will you explain your shaky handwriting to your teacher,' her mother would chide, horrified to find her finishing her homework in the car going to school!

Aruna's blithe reply would be, 'I will say sorry to her, Amma, it will be all right.'

She tended to take whatever came in her stride, her eyes twinkling. Her mother was often exasperated but not overly worried.

After having graduated, Aruna completed a training stint at an advertising agency and was beginning to enjoy the assignments; they were varied, demanding. Finding her bright, promising and keenly interested in all she did, the agency valued her.

Anand too had excelled at school and in every subject – but with him there was a rub. He was constantly outdoing his mother at her favourite game, chess. To a degree that there was no question of his missing a single chess championship for the young in the state and country. His mother would ensure it. His triumphs would egg her on.

The Don Bosco School in Madras raised no objections, his results in school were outstanding, his reputation as a young chess genius kept them in the news in a way that was flattering and unexpected and frequent. The Lightning Kid was what he was soon called. From age fourteen, Viswanathan Anand would win award after award to also earn the sobriquet: Tiger of Madras. He had now hit the national scene with the international arena to follow anon.

Was the early exposure in and to the Philippines the reason for his calm in taking on the world – or was it just him? It could be the quiet but insistent persistence which made him return from school and participate in the television chess sessions that his mother would copy out for him at home because the TV programmes were at a time during which he was still attending classes. Yes, day after day. Neither person was of a kind that would leave a stone unturned. So, the most was made of the Manila posting and the Philippines government's focus on chess as a national game.

Back in India, he would enter every available championship and he would shine. The tensions of playing and the triumphs of winning, the boy took in his stride. In those early days, the angst of losing hardly ever happened, perhaps. Chess was not India's favoured sport, cricket was. Even football and tennis took precedence.

Soon came Loyola College and international championships for Vishy. This was a different ball game. And soon there were eight of them, these high-level tournaments. They would come in a flurry over the first six months of the year across different countries of Europe. So, it seemed to make eminent sense for young Anand to base himself in Spain rather than scurry back and forth, taking on travel hassles. It meant, quite conveniently, that the second half of the year would remain freer to spend at home, back in Madras, managing all the India engagements and whatever else cropped up elsewhere in the world.

Even as an international champ, Viswanathan Anand had now matured more than considerably, moving up the scale of player after player to take on Kasparov, no mean opponent. Indeed, Vishy had already shone in two contests with that star, winning in rapid chess as well. He was now in his element.

Marriage as a prospect was not in discussion at this point, it would be an unnecessary distraction. There were fans and admirers galore, they seemed to multiply. But they barely lingered in his mind beyond the autographed signature or perhaps a cheering, warm message if he was not in a mad rush. The months and years seemed to fly between preparation and travel; tournaments needed him one hundred per cent, the focus had to be single-minded. But now at twenty-five, it seemed essential to his parents. Meeting a 'suitable' girl had to be arranged.

This loomed urgent – they had to facilitate, not force the issue, but they had to do it soon.

How could he possibly choose right, zipping back and forth between tournaments, surrounded by fans, photographers, media, and now based in a foreign country? Where did he have the time for any such pursuit?

He needed to come home after a championship to someone he could share with all that was important to him: his unusual life, his ambitions, his pressures, his triumphs. And there was a distinct danger too perhaps, which may have worried the parents more than a little. That left to his ceaseless schedule, he may plump for a gushing fan or an infatuated chess enthusiast, living all by himself in a country far away which was not even an English-speaking one!

Parents in India consider it their duty to choose right for their offspring. And friends and family abound with suggestions, matchmaking with an energy that rivals all the mothers and aunts in Jane Austen's novels. Clearly Anand's parents had honed in on his meeting Aruna after much scouting, checking out, mulling over, perhaps undue diligence! They would not take just any plunge, it would have to be a thoughtful, considered choice. The girl's life would not follow any familiar pattern or be too predictable. She would be taking on some rather unusual pressures; in some way taking on the world too, as it were.

Vishy Anand's parents kept it simple and private. The meeting was arranged at Aruna's home as is the custom. Quiet and not too formal it was meant to be.

Well before the evening was done her parents were more than taken. They found the young man's humility so elegant – and so unbelievable!

'My mother sped me to the kitchen saying that I simply had to agree. "If I had another daughter, I would not insist, so it has to be you, *make sure* you agree!" she simply did insist.'

Anand's parents were clearly as impressed. Aruna seemed bright-eyed, well-spoken, poised. Despite the smiling shyness, there was an openness in her countenance. She was not coy or aggressive, she seemed so right for their son who was already all set to take on the world, wherever it beckoned him. Aruna's parents were reasonably sure that their spirited young daughter would be equal to what she would be taking on, she was always one to brighten at the prospect of something new, even challenging.

Looking back, Vishy and Aruna are now amazed at the readiness with which they both said 'yes' to each other after 'literally five or ten minutes of FaceTime'! After all the scrutinizing accomplished by the parents, the boy and girl just moved, decided. Almost headlong.

The two or three dinner dates that then followed once they had agreed were also not unchaperoned! A courtship, an engagement, discussions, announcements, the usual preliminary fuss was dispensed with entirely – and quite happily. Neither side had protested. Both Vishy and Aruna knew that it was only when they were away and on their own and getting their breath back that they could take it all in: discover each other, allow each other to be who they really were.

It must have so astonished Vishy's fans worldwide that this star performer had settled for his life partner in this one fell swoop. They were in for more surprises.

Just three days after 27 June 1996, the day the nuptials were sanctified, the couple flew to Dormund, Germany for a crucial tournament in which Vishy was to take on Kramnik.

Imagine the scenario right then. While congratulating the young Anands, the chess world teases Vishy roundly that he should expect to lose at least 70 Elo points – perhaps more. Both rating and performance seem at risk. Losing that undiluted focus, that cut-throat keenness is more than half-expected. Happiness can turn out to be just the distraction that sets a champion back. Chess needs a single mindedness from its rated players and Kramnik is formidable to say the least. Hard luck.

Aruna dreads the blame – however well concealed, she would not escape it. Surely she did not deserve this setback right at the outset. Both matches turn out to be nail-biting finishes but Vishy is in good though tense form. He holds out well.

He is not defeated. He draws even though the title on points goes to Kramnik. His Elo points are intact, his performance right through, undistracted. Every well-wisher is amazed and relieved at once, that this young champ has the nerve to take a whole bunch of varied pressures in his stride. An Indian wedding, an international flight and the distractions of a once in a lifetime event ... the honeymoon. The world salutes and Aruna is spared.

Dormund done and behind him, the good sense of this landmark event in his life, his marriage, was becoming evident. Moving to a shared stage of his personal life, having all his life responsibilities halved, was giving him time to gauge not just his game, but more: of his journey as a champ he begins to take stock, reassessing his competition and his strategy to become more fierce, more formidable. He now finds the time to ponder, re-examine, even discuss it threadbare – he has a companion. And she is bright, observant, brings a different perspective, is not shy to express it.

Always strong on his competitive streak, Vishy wonders now if he needs to be less detached, move away from the gentlemanly game. In short, sharpen his killer instinct. This seems imperative to him now – and certainly in the long haul.

On the personal front, the whirlwind *en famille* stint in Chennai and thereafter Dormund had been absurd. Aruna is now in a home of her own, no longer a stranger to Vishy's life. She warms to it. The newness of it is an intrigue and the sharing of it all, including tense situations, is a very special sense of bonding. They feel entrusted to each other.

Perhaps saying 'yes' at their first meeting is more sacred as a pledge of faith than all the ceremonies that tied the knot, certainly more personal, more one to one.

The reprieve in their Collado Mediano home in a quiet Madrid suburb is calming. Allowing for time to be spent together, companionably, in reading, swimming, listening to music, when he is not delving into intricacies that ready him for the next chess tussle. The Anands are on their own and loving it. Their aversion for publicity – and flattery – is serving them in good stead. His game is far from neglected and his young bride less and less homesick – he is there for her.

And because life outside India has no surround of domestic presence, of family overtures, if not intervention – it is more focused.

With each passing day, one realization is now acute for the young Anands. Temperamentally and by training, Aruna seems the best candidate to pick up the details of chess protocol, format, courtesies thoroughly – *and* become the Grandmaster's manager, to arrange, to mastermind. The foursome of her own family – she, her parents, her brother, were well-known and much teased for their over-meticulous planning of every holiday they considered, every trip, every project. Whether they eventually undertook it or not, they most certainly revelled in the flawless detailing of every phase and aspect of it! 'This was a family joke, not unfamiliar to all our acquaintances, this tendency to overdo the micro-management, without fail, each time!'

Vishy had neither the taste nor the head for this. All arrangements in his mind for all his years were for the black and white moves and patterns on the chess board. This 'managing' burden he was delighted and relieved to shed. Her ease and expertise was striking, it seemed to be too good to be true. He could sense it day to day and most certainly when they were seized by a crisis.

Toying with the idea of becoming his manager transformed into a serious decision when Aruna realized over the 1997 Groningen/Lausanne championship how myriad arrangements regarding negotiation of dates and time and travel commitments were intrinsic to his profession. That he should be spared these distractions seemed imperative. She did not wait, and Anand did not object.

Perhaps she warmed to her assignment as his manager

because she had put away her own career pursuits without chafing. What she took on now seemed so much more significant per se, in her personal life and his – and especially at important junctures. There were times when she could anticipate, plan, perfect, once she got to know his responses well. The challenge may have seemed new and daunting at the outset but also kind of delicious, she had always been sparky.

Watching Anand become steadily exhausted by a series of matches as he approached the crucial 1997 Championship Final to play Adams and Kramnik, Aruna had sensed something. She knew in her bones that Vishy would welcome having his staunch friend alongside him at this juncture, and she had alerted Pablo Carullo in Madrid to stand-by and take a flight to Lausanne if need be. She had also taken the precaution of sending him an open ticket.

Combining the instinct of a wife and the efficiency of a manager, she got a special kick out of arranging the right thing at the right time and saving the day. Anand moved to the World No 2 position the very next year after the spectacular finals at Linares and back home, *Sportstar* declared him the 'Sportsman of the Millennium'.

Things were picking up, the pressure was mounting. While being on a high over the first two years of the twenty-first century when he shone across the chess world, there came the five-year bonanza of the man reigning in splendour as world champion, starting 2008 right up to 2013, exciting years that just sped. They were on a high.

Vishy also received the Padma Vibhushan, the highest Indian honour, not granted to any other sportsman. It almost seems blandishment but other than championship awards, his national and international honours seemed vying to be awarded, amongst them the Arjuna Award, the Padma Shri, yes, even the Padma Bhushan. Nothing seemed to turn his head or distract him, mercifully.

The couple were now in tandem, needless to say, working in the dovetailed way which had become their trademark. Sometimes with untoward drama. Like when they were stranded in Frankfurt, along with their team, just ahead of the crucial 2010 finals. There had been a volcanic eruption in Eyjafallajokull and all flights were cancelled until further notice. This was not a minor matter of schedule adjustments. Just how would they make it in time? Any serious attempt seemed an invitation to disaster. The prospect of dashing across many countries of Europe to reach Sofia within five days seemed near impossible. In any event, it was cutting it very fine because even the one-day postponement had been granted to them very reluctantly. Listening to Aruna urging, negotiating, arguing – in call after call to the championship organizers, the airlines, the car hire agencies, the hotels – Anand cautioned her.

Would withdrawing not be the best option given all the uncertainties, he suggested? Why take on the near impossible? Was the harrowing tension, the dealing with the unpredictable elements, the unfamiliar terrain, the nail-biting urgency of it all, worth it? And all just before a gruelling championship?

But noticing his wife's clear and confident energy take over, Anand relented. Promising that he would not contest Aruna's decision once taken, not resort to blame even if things went awry at the other end! This was it – it was a deal.

He had watched his gutsy, resolute manager: she was hardly off the international call circuit and equally meshed in how to equip the car that would brave this perilous journey.

Their life at such moments could read like a suspense thriller in progress. World contests do have a way of building tensions and urgencies, punishing the nerves with a vengeance until it is all over.

'The world is watching' is an awareness that hounds the champs and each member of their teams inescapably, like a warning. Needless to say, the manager is right at the centre of this entire crazy spin. But Aruna is determined to take it on. For a reason only she was sure of, she does not want to waver.

So the large black Mercedes van, piled with the luggage and all eight passengers – the Anands, the five team members and the driver – weaves through Austria, Hungary, and Serbia over a 40-hour journey filled with uncertainties to reach Frankfurt, just in time. Whhew! Even they are amazed, though exhausted.

Topalov at the other end remains more than usually cool. He awaits the team on his home ground, unexposed to any of this tension, the excitement, the exhaustion. Also, he plans to use his Super Computer for the very first time in this match. Something his opponent, Vishy Anand, has no idea about, he only just finds out! It all seems almost tantamount to a jinx. Something one would not wish on any champion.

As it happens then, Anand loses the first match. And as promised, he blames no one, he keeps the promise he made to Aruna. And very reassuringly, he then gradually proceeds to gain ground and finally, excitingly, triumphs in the World Chess Championship 2010.

As it happens, Queen's Gambit Declined is deployed by Anand among the many master strokes he played, making that match more memorable than most.

You can well imagine the public applause and the private enjoyment of those elating moments and how each detail of those would provide an anecdotal feast. But, you would have to ferret it out of this smiling, straight-faced duo – they prefer to leave it to your imagination, rather than wax eloquent.

These instances of the life-partner meshing with the chess manager abound, they no longer amaze. And they make for a mutual respect and a rare partnership. Best of all, they manage to stave off the cliche that most couples begin to sense and admit to as the years go by: the gradual but inevitable 'taking for granted' that creeps into a marriage, all too often. Neither Anand's work nor his temperament allow for this.

Perhaps another quirk keeps them from falling into a predictable groove or a boring pattern. Despite their backgrounds having much in common, their tastes in music, books and cinema are refreshingly different. Astronomy seriously fascinates Anand, perhaps his way of being star-struck. While most others are happier swooning over the ever-changing terrestrial variety, his are in the firmament, enjoyed best hiding quietly behind his sport.

'He spends hours poring over books on astronomy and training his telescope to the skies. I would rather have my nose in a novel if I can manage any leisure. Though once in a while taking a peek, sharing his excitement is fun,' Aruna says.

Different styles of prose and poetry draw her immensely when time allows, but as his manager, leisure is rare. Music of the '80s and '90s is Aruna's usual predilection, although she is open to some of the new, more melodious groups. What she finds quaint is Anand's fondness for the old Tamil songs he grew up with as he was honing his chess. It amuses and endears her that despite all his years away and the exposure to music across the world, nothing else moves him quite as much.

Her own serious pursuit of Bharatanatyam she gave up after the first few recitals in Spain (the Indian Embassy would also frequently request her to perform at their functions which she accepted since it pleased both of them, far away from home). Time did not allow for any serious schedules of practice that classical dance demanded and gradually, she began to feel uneasy about public recitals. Her pottery too Aruna tended to neglect over the years, it could not be helped. Managing a star chess champion's many tournaments, the correspondence, the agreements, the contracts and their details, the travel schedules, was not an easy nine-to-five routine anyway, whether abroad or back in India.

'I wonder how we would have managed if we were the socializing, club-going types!' she laughs, knowing well that there was never any risk of that.

Aruna and Anand had to be very, very patient before becoming parents. You may say it was a prolonged extension of a honeymoon, spent savouring unusual and very welcoming parts of the world, working hard, taking breaks. And the world outside may have thought they were doing just that. But no, it was more than that. It was a long wait that certainly was neither intended or planned. For the wait seemed interminable and was dotted by the unexpected mishap, the miscarriage that would recur and dash the cherished expectation of the couple and of all those close and dear to them. The excited anticipation of a pregnancy would create a shared closeness in things big and little for the Anands, whatever the work pressures. And then the wrench of a miscarriage would intensify their one-to-one support, cementing the 'I am there for you' pledge each time. Sorrow and loss too have a way of adding to this many-sided prism. They deepen a facet, not subtract from a relationship.

Waiting for fifteen whole years before Akhil could be born was also a great deprivation for the two sets of grandparents, avidly awaiting a bright little person they could call their own, lighting up their quiet, more retired lives. Akhil arrived on 9 April 2011, and the very busy lives of the Anands they now had to adapt, which they did delightedly.

A side to her husband now surfaced, that had Aruna glowing. She found him fascinated with the infant, later zestfully playful with the toddler, and then carefree, almost rowdy with the little boy. Vishy she found in his element, which to her is his 'best *avatar*'!

Akhil cannot get enough of his appa. And Appa can never forgive himself for missing Akhil's very first gurgle of laughter, claimed by tournaments as he would constantly be. Infants have a way of fascinating you with quirks which are very much their own – and switching to new ones before you have revelled enough in them.

Vishy would catch all the time he could with mother and child, while contending with his many hectic returns to glory and fame which were all too consistent after his World Champion triumph in 2008, even more so thereafter, year on year. Chiselling away at the killer instinct now, he was even more sharply focused on strategy. On the publicity scene, he was neither flamboyant nor reclusive – remaining his usual quick-witted self. With the media he was unpretentious, direct, sparse.

To everyone's surprise, in his own country, Anand was unassuming to a fault. Very matter-of-fact about himself. As was often pointed out to him, his fame shines in over 150 countries where chess is a popular and celebrated game, while high-profile heroes like Gavaskar and Tendulkar can reach and excite precisely twelve countries (Afghanistan has been included recently) of the world which know and play cricket. As it happens, chess turned vibrant in India only decades ago, from being a languid, if favourite, pastime of the disappearing princely class.

Indeed, Anand represents India's new, scintillating breed of *Shatranj ke Khilari.* On chessboards and at championships in the many continents across the world, restoring its status in its own birthplace. And, who knows, he may fill with verve the generation that waits to shine. Because his life and career do demonstrate that a champion can be a superb instructor, not just a star. Today his coaching of the young brigade, readying them for the Asian Games Championships is a stalwart effort to have India triumph again. His book *Mind Master,* his cool, unassuming nudges and guidance and tips and pointed suggestions are live grooming methods that will prepare the Indian team to face the finest of international competitors.

Vishy Anand's remaining stubbornly low-key continues to be a matter of amusement, not just amazement. As you discover, when he relates the story of how a venerable companion en flight in India opened a conversation with him – and having chatted a while asked about Anand's occupation, his work. On learning that it was playing chess, the man insisted on knowing how he actually supported himself. When Anand persisted with his response that he played chess, the gent becomes genuinely concerned and placing his hand very paternally on Vishy's forearm, he admonishes him gently but firmly, 'You *have* to get yourself a job, a proper job of some kind.' You can't possibly bank on earning a decent living, young man, by playing a great game of chess, for heaven's sake. *Nobody* can ... unless you are Viswanathan Anand.'

And the co-passenger then moves away, patting his arm, shaking his head, tut-tutting under his breath. And Vishy, being who he is, listens, nods in agreement, gives nothing away.

How joyously his mother must have approved of and repeated this story! She has always rated humility very high, Vishy has always known that. And she had firmly disallowed all temptation to hurt, to harm – under any circumstances. This firm prod had clearly become second nature to him. She had taught him a great deal more than chess.

The bonus for all who meet Vishy is his unexpected sense of humour. It never deserts him. When teasingly questioned about how he manages the insistent adulation of doting female fans, he would come back with, 'Well, my wife does not accompany me on all my championship tours, as you must know,' shrugging his shoulders, not batting an eyelid. Knowing well that his Aruna would giggle and dismiss these quips.

Vishy is quick to give her every credit for the matchless role she plays when he needs it most. When she is by him, which they both try to enable for every championship, it is a warm, involved companionability. And long distance too, she surprises by the unexpected strength she communicates, shares vividly enough to empower him, as it were.

One instance certainly is the beginning of the year 2018. He had just finished a very disappointing season, which is a punishment not easy to weather for a superstar that he is and has been at his game. But then no one can win each and every time. And over the winter season of 2017, it had been a wearying set of tournaments, with Anand losing out, beginning to get not just dashed, but dispirited. Defeat plays horrid games on the nerves, it unsettles, the doom seems insoluble. And

Vishy could not escape experiencing that low which begins to pervade.

The couple had decided to recover from the pressure, revive the spirit, take a holiday in Chennai with a friend from Spain. It was just at this point of time that the Fide president requested the worn out champ to enter the Rapid Chess Championship. Anand was hesitant. He felt too badgered by the last harrowing setback, which had been all too recent. His morale was low. But when he sought Aruna's advice, she was persuasive. Focus single-mindedly now, say yes, she said. The confidence she has in him and in restoring his spirits, is immense.

She convinces him to go ahead. He agrees to accept.

As it happens, he is the first to finish his last round, which is both a relief and a triumph. Because Vishy is stunningly rapid at Rapid Chess, you see him stride across gracefully and swiftly, you wonder how he knows which move to make on board after board: the tension is dramatic even for the viewer, but this wizard of ours seems to escape it. 'I may have finished first but I could face three opponents involved in the tie break. Magnus' face kept reappearing though …' he smiles. Yes, even as he faced and won the challenge, his earlier defeat would resurface.

But the call he made to Aruna held him strong – and focused. He won.

When lauded for all she does, Aruna glows but she is quick to suggest that it is some quality in Vishy that inspires the devotion of others. And she warmly mentions Maurice and Nieves, the neighbouring couple who were near-parents – guardians to him in his first years in Madrid. And in more recent times, Hans Walter has been an unequalled ally. 'He will take a bullet for Anand,' she says.

Almost predictably, at every other turn, there is a milestone reached. The year 2019 and his fiftieth birthday saw Anand spelling out his uniquely varied chess experience in the book *Mind Master*, detailing lessons, explaining each cogitated move, garnering from the hectic experience of over four decades, a book every young chess aficionado across the globe will surely own and devour. 'Mind Champion' has long been his title as the brand icon for India's prime academy for computer education.

When it comes to competing as chef extraordinaire prior to the Norway Championships, Vishy has triumphed two years running. In 2018, turning out hollandaise sauce with Dan Ringer and in 2019 with MVL, presenting Salmon a la Chef Anand. Vishy's daintily presented gourmet serving was flashed worldwide, with glimpses of the maestro in what he considers his wife's domain. Pleased to see him so applauded, Aruna is yet to be convinced of his expertise in the kitchen.

'He may not be able to distinguish all the ingredients stacked up in the kitchen, but yes, he has learnt to open a box of cereals quite niftily,' she remarks.

What did create a stir was his adopting another formal and new incarnation: Vishy's formal acceptance to partner with the West Coast Chess Academy bodes well for the next generation of wizards. So far he has always insisted on the urge to 'Enjoy the challenge'. Now it will be more.

Knowing only too well the decimating effect of an unexpected defeat, a rogue turn of events, this approach also coaches on how to survive, bounce back. Here, he readies to show the new brigade how, going into every possible detail. His focused approach probably finds ways in which they can suss out his mystique. Having Aruna team up here probably rounds it all off and ensures the latter.

'Fifty per cent of the world's best under-eighteen players are Indian. That will obviously give India a status of clear super power for years to come,' says Emil Sutovsky, the Director General of Fide and Grandmaster. Vishy and Aruna must surely glow listening to him – they could very well take some of the credit. Very sagely all the while, they expose Akhil fully to all they are doing for chess but spare him the pressure. Who knows which way this youngster will surprise as the years go by.

When their chief minister, Shri M.K. Stalin announced that in July-August 2022, the 44th Chess Olympiad would be hosted not in Ukraine but in Chennai, the chess capital of India, Vishy was quick to thank in his singular way: 'Thanks for making Chennai all about chess. Chennai Chess always had a good ring to it.'

And the Tiger of Madras is delighted to have the new young wizard R. Praggnanandhaa of Chennai in touch with him every now and then. The game runs in both their veins.

All along and very reassuringly, that directness, that delightful simplicity survives, permits no affectations. And the wit the Anands possess surfaces when least expected. Whether in their previous home in Spain where they lived for years or in Chennai where they belong, or in any of the many championship arenas of the entire world, Vishy and Aruna present a natural, unaffected togetherness. Having reigned so long as world No.1, some drama, some impatience, some sensationalism, some temperament would be half-expected, even justified. But they disappoint. You may want to check on this with their domestic help – or indeed their head of state, in either geography. You would get the same answer.

How do you explain today a totally unspoilt celebrity – or this unflaunted, unselfconscious partnership? It all seems a contradiction in terms. The mystery deepens because their background had given them zero preparation.

Consider a sheltered young girl seeking to be a professional turns housewife overnight. Born of very traditional, if not conservative mores, she is thrown into a country where the language is quite alien, where Indians do not congregate, where customs and etiquette are unfamiliar – and where the glare of publicity is unrelenting, unforgiving. And how much could he have held her hand, while under the gruelling strain of being *numero uno* at chess. How does he make the time, lavish the attention that a romance generally wilts without? How has she coped, why has her smile not faded? How does Vishy share the kudos, the flattery, the applause, the attention that he garners, while she remains in the penumbra? Clearly the man is grand master yet again.

Despite all their unpretentiousness, their reserve, it does seem that his ease with himself in his tensest moments is to do with her being there for him: as he zips down a large hall playing rapid chess and beating each player on table after table in a vast room, the camera following him and his every move as he strides from one table to the next, barely stopping to make his move. Or indeed as he sits, deep in thought, with one of the unnervingly sharp opponents, looking for that one slip from him, to displace him as champ.

Aruna enjoys telling you that Vishy's mother is the chess genius who lit the flame in her son and kept it aglow till there was no looking back. It is an arena in which she is careful not to elbow herself in. She leaves that special link alone, intact.

Aruna herself has always been liveliness of the most infectious kind and even though she sits still, her eyes dance and smile, meet yours directly, readily. With the vermilion *bindi* on her forehead as vivid as her deftly draped *kanjeeevaram* silk sari, she reminds the world where they come from, there is no mistaking it. Especially if the occasion is formal. And having seen the world now more than most, Aruna does not avoid interviews. She has come a long way, baby, as the oft-repeated line goes. Indeed, in 2018 Chess Base India presented her the title of Tigress of Madras.

By her side, Vishy does his customary number. By being quietly unassertive yet making sure his wit catches you totally unawares and not infrequently. Wearing his fame lightly, the genius is always to be seen dressed casually. But when required to be formal the same man ensures he is sprucely, flawlessly well-tailored. Or maybe she makes sure of that.

One thing hits you as you see them together: boarding planes; being feted by celebrities; mobbed by autograph-seekers; reminiscing about Spain's villages, hilarious coincidences, champion tantrums, misunderstandings; or suspenseful moments in the chess capitals of the world; or just quietly sipping coffee at home or abroad: that one without the other would be eerie. The Anands just must, and do coincide.

'I still have to figure out one thing though,' muses Aruna. 'What is that one magic sentence, gesture, sop, suggestion to lift a champ's gloom post a botched-up game? I've not cracked that one yet.'

GRATITUDE

All those who enabled this book have been remarkable. First, for who they are and second, for their immeasurable patience.

For a working person with a demanding schedule, I had managed a spontaneously commissioned monograph about two rare and much celebrated persons. Enlarging this into a book of many more such stories – aglow with other extraordinary couples – needed time and nurture. It had to wait.

I submit deep gratitude to Pramod Kapoor for pioneering the idea, for championing it. Equally to Priya Kapoor, very much at the helm as publisher now and shining as she combines ability and elan with patience, with grace. For this unusual mix, for being enabler, I salute her ... and thank my luck.

The 'couples' featured here sparkle for reason after reason. They are unexpected as individuals, intriguing in their bond as their lives unfold. Their enthusiasm and grace in being part of the book, their readiness in delving into detail was both reward and treat. Especially, given their hectic time commitments. Discovering their amazing attractiveness as human beings and trust in sharing their surprising relationships has been elating for me. One felt proud and rewarded for having chosen them, each of their stories has a reason to be here.

With much warmth, I thank Isha Maniar, my editor at Roli Books, for her acute observation and sensitivity to both author and reader. Her sense of language has the inspiration of an artist and the precision of a lawyer ... which she happens to be! I loved the experience. And will miss it.

For the cover design, I turned to Nitin Srivastava whose aesthetic sense and spark I have relied on confidently, consistently ... it is rare. I thank him zestfully as usual.

Both my sons, Sajjad and Mustafa Imam, have my gratitude for being the discerning readers they are and for being patiently responsive throughout, as I turned to them for comment and criticism.

My gratitude indeed to each member of the team at Roli Books who ensured *Like Fine Wine* reaches the reader, each one in their own special way.

If there is anyone I have omitted to mention here, I seek their indulgence, their forgiveness.